"This book is well-described by Gretta Vosper herself as a 'confrontation.' It's articulate and hard-hitting in its analysis of the urgent problems facing the church today. While the author's description of her personal faith differs significantly from my own, many, including those who feel they 'have no need of God,' will applaud her efforts to create an inclusive model for reshaping the church." —Tom Harpur, author of *The Pagan Christ*

"Vosper's book exemplifies her own criteria for a good church: open-mindedness, passion, creativity and intellectual rigour." —Joanna Manning, author of *Is the Pope Catholic?* and *The Magdalene Moment*

# AMEN

# AMEN

## WHAT PRAYER CAN MEAN IN A WORLD BEYOND BELIEF

## GRETTA VOSPER

*To Caroline!*
*Enjoy!*
*Gretta*
*AHFA 2015*

HarperCollins Publishers Ltd

*Amen*
Copyright © 2012 by Gretta Vosper.
All rights reserved.

Published by HarperCollins Publishers Ltd

Originally published by HarperCollins Publishers Ltd in a hardcover edition: 2012
This trade paperback edition: 2013

HarperCollins books may be purchased for educational, business,
or sales promotional use through our Special Markets Department.

HarperCollins Publishers Ltd
2 Bloor Street East, 20th Floor
Toronto, Ontario, Canada
M4W 1A8

*www.harpercollins.ca*

Library and Archives Canada Cataloguing in Publication
Vosper, Gretta
Amen : what prayer can mean in a world beyond belief /
Gretta Vosper.

ISBN 978-1-55468-648-3

1. Prayer—Christianity. I. Title.
BV210.3.V68 2013          248.3'2          C2012-905993-5

Printed and bound in the United States
RRD 9 8 7 6 5 4 3 2 1

*To Hazel and Izaak,*
*you are the light of the world.*

# Contents

# Introduction

## What about Prayer?

Military drills are precise. They need to be, working as they do to create a camaraderie that will bind members of a unit together so strongly that in situations of the most desperate conflict and stress, the bond will hold. If something is out of place in a military drill—someone out of step, turning the wrong way, dressed incorrectly—it stands out.

That's how the soldier off to the side of the platoon looked: he stood out. He didn't move, remaining perfectly still while everyone else went through their complex motions. Although he'd obviously walked onto the square at one point, as onlookers watched, he did not join in, he did not march, he did not move from one side of the square to another as the others did. He simply remained at attention—close to, but not a part of, the team.

Most paid him no heed beyond a quick glance, his lack of movement an aberration but no cause for interest. Their attention was tuned to the manoeuvres the rest of the unit was making. But after a time, one of the more curious among the crowd raised the question: "What is that man doing? Why is he just standing there?" The answer was simple: "He's holding the goat."

Except. There. Was. No. Goat.

Apparently, years before, a regimental mascot—a goat—had joined the soldiers in their ceremonial parades. Although the custom of keeping a goat as a mascot had since fallen out of use, one soldier continued to practice, day after day, the precise art of holding a place in the ranks as keeper of the mascot.

I heard this story at a leadership-training event and was familiar with the scenario because I grew up in Kingston, Ontario, home to Old Fort Henry, a limestone fortress built in the 1800s to stand guard over the Rideau Canal. The Fort Henry Guard, who are active only in the summer for tourist purposes, still have a goat, and it still takes part as the soldiers make impressive marches across the parade square. Many times, in the summers of my childhood, I visited the fort, stopping at the special pen where the goat lived when it wasn't fulfilling its ceremonial role. I wonder if it ever got used to the cannons blasting as the sun went down.

The story was used to illustrate the lesson that doing things the way you've always done them just because you've always done them that way may be neither productive nor an efficient use of resources. But that's not how I'm using the story. I'm using it not because we're like the soldiers, but because prayer is like that goat. To some, it is present in a meaningful day-to-day, inspirational way; to others, it is mostly out of sight, present only for occasional ceremonial purposes. Sometimes it is entirely absent, its empty place, if noticed at all, only a curiosity.

For those who keep prayer an active part of their lives, it remains significant. Throughout the day—perhaps at regular times or when it's needed for a special situation—they make use of it. Its presence in their lives focuses them, strengthens them, reminds them of those things that are important. Like the mascot, it encourages them not only because of its presence but also because it has been a significant part of the history of their people; it is tied to their lives, to their stories, to the sagas of generations, both in good times and in bad. When the world spun out of control, their forebears took every step accompanied by the power of their confidence in prayer. When the world settled into a rhythm of beauty and harmony, prayer was part of the picture—always significant, always present. And in the cycle of birth, life, and death, everyone knew it was close at hand, knew its value, knew it could bring them peace and joy and, yes, even luck, if you dared call it that. As long as prayer is a regular part of their lives—as long as they stay close to it—they can convince themselves that things will be all right.

For some of these people, prayer is a positive element in their lives. It connects them with God (or something they might identify as a benevolent force) or the universe and through that connection assures them aid, assistance, courage, protection. When they use it there is a presence they can almost feel, a resonance with something completely transcendent yet utterly immanent. It comes to them, surrounds them, wells up within them, flows out from them. Prayer makes their lives more meaningful, more purposeful, and in the meaning they derive from it, their world makes sense. They cannot imagine living without such an important facet of their lives.

Yet for others who still hold on to it, prayer has often been a source of frustration, confusion, and despair. They have followed the teachings on prayer found in their scriptures and have claimed its promises; they have repeatedly asked God for help, for healing, for change; they have believed and trusted and tried to be patient; they have surrendered their will to God; they have humbled themselves before the Almighty. And nothing happened. Nothing. Things stayed the same or got worse. They had long been told that God was loving, powerful, wise, and willing to help them, but the promises of prayer only mocked them. They try to figure it out. If other people have prayers answered, why not them? Is it their faith? Their method of praying? Their unworthiness? Their sin? They want to know, but if they pick one of these reasons, things get even more complicated. They have to see themselves as unworthy of God's love—or worse yet, see God as uncaring and unloving. For these people, prayer has not been a blessing.

For still others, prayer serves a purely ceremonial function. They pray, but only when they are at church or on special occasions—maybe when they sit down to Thanksgiving dinner. It's a tradition that has meaning only because it's what civilized people are supposed to do—a practice revered more because of its place in the lives of their forebears than because it has any significance for theirs. It has become part of the nostalgia, the Norman Rockwell illustration of what those simpler times were like—the times of their parents or their parents before them. Despite what it may have meant to those previous generations, prayer now holds only a symbolic place in their busy lives, and most of the time, it is off duty, resting in a pen somewhere.

The ability of prayer to function as a spiritual tool has diminished for these people, despite their awareness that it seems to make a difference in the lives of others. Perhaps for those among them who are avid churchgoers, participating in the ritual that is prayer brings about significant feelings of belonging and acceptance, but they dismiss out of hand any idea that God or the universe is conspiring to make their lives any better than the next guy's. Feeling good about themselves may be the chief characteristic of their relationship with prayer. When it *feels* good to pray, they pray.

Still others are like the onlookers who knew nothing about the goat and are oblivious to the oddity of the man standing to one side. They know little, if anything, about prayer. Oh, they might be aware that there are those who use prayer, but they have no reason to seek out its meaning, to find out what it is about or what its purpose is. Occasionally, they might find themselves in a wedding service or at a funeral, where they see people engaged in prayer, but they are really only ever observers. Most of the time, there is not even an empty space in their lives where prayer might have been. They have lived long and well without it. Even the soldier who held the goat has left the parade square.

God, for these people, is a concept that doesn't have any bearing on their lives. As far as they are concerned, other people made the concept up, and those are the people who have to live with the consequences. To them, the universe is a physical reality that doesn't have any overtly or covertly spiritual properties. Appeals sent out to it are pointless. Anything that has a whiff of the supernatural is simply of no significance to them.

Some experience incredible benefits from prayer, while some experience great disappointments; some experience prayer as a significant ritual in which they engage to honour their heritage and the importance of tradition; some live full, meaningful, caring lives without giving it a second thought. Those who are strengthened, edified, comforted, challenged, centred, and grounded by prayer argue that without it, life would be shallow, bleak, or even unbearable. Those who don't give it a thought can't imagine being so dependent upon a concept they can neither justify nor comprehend. Such extremes challenge us with their deep contradictions: because people live and thrive with prayer; it may have something very worthwhile to offer. Because people live and thrive without prayer, it cannot be necessary.

## WITH OR WITHOUT PRAYER

My personal prayer life would not impress many people. I don't have a discipline I follow. I don't spend intentional prayer time in any particular place of worship. I don't use a specific tool or have a practice that guides me. I don't have a set time when I pray. Because I don't turn to an interventionist deity, I don't feel the need to humble myself before it or to make a petition framed in any particular language using specific prayerful words. I don't equate the aesthetic enjoyments in my life with prayer, or the time I spend advocating justice, and so I don't identify my life as one long, rapturous undertaking. There isn't a mantra I have repeated so incessantly that it now hums beneath my every thought. And I don't feel guilty about any of that. But I do "connect."

To explain what I mean by that, I need to tell you about my experiences of living in different "spaces." It is almost impossible for me to talk about the different ways in which I interact with or experience the world—the variety of ways in which I function or relate, the assorted methods of connectivity (or lack thereof)—without using spatial imagery. I "need my space" in ways that go far beyond the generic "leave me alone" meaning of that simple phrase. Spatial concepts are crucial to my ability to assess and work through difficult situations. The blank facial response I display while I'm moving from one "space" to another can be frustrating for those waiting for me to reply, but the energy it takes to move my "self" to react to a changing set of circumstances or access different resources within me is sometimes enormous.

I move into one particular "space" when I connect with—or perhaps more accurately, get riveted to—my understanding of deep reality, the truths that undergird the why and the what of everything we know. It is the place where I visit the why of my existence, of our world, of the suffering so many experience in it. For me, it holds that understanding of what really is that can destroy everything I thought really was. It can scatter all my ideas of who I am to the wind, leaving me bereft of the familiar constraints and easy assumptions by which I identify my place in the world. It is a place from which the more carefully constructed, vehemently protected, and discretely experienced categories in which I function—mother, wife, minister, writer, daughter, friend, etc.—have been barred. Here, I can't pretend the comfort of my white, middle-class, educated, suburban lifestyle is enjoyed by everyone. I am irritated by reality, rubbed raw by truth.

This is the place that most resembles what others refer to when they use the word "prayer." It is the place into which I pour my despair and out of which I drag my often elusive, often reluctant hope; it is the space into which I spiral, as well as the connection that rescues me there; it is the transformative work in which I am compelled to engage; it is the loss of everything I have ever relied upon and the gift of everything I need to continue my pursuit of truth. The connection I find in this place is essential to my being, but what it is to/with/by which I connect, I am not able to say.

In most of my experience of communal prayer in mainline denominational church, I get nowhere near that place. In traditional, mainline church services, there's neither opportunity nor permission for me, or anyone else who finds prayer a time of vulnerability, to get very close to such a place, to this depth of transformative experience. Goodness knows what might happen if we opened the portal to each heart and let its contents spill into the crowd, seeping into other hearts, intermingling everyone's sadnesses and triumphs—tears, laughter, hysteria.

Most common descriptions of personal prayer don't come close to what I might define as prayer, either. Like conversations about the concept of god,\* those about prayer require definitions and clarification of

---

\* Not capitalizing the word "god" is a contentious issue in many circles. For the purposes of this book, "god"—with the little *g*—can mean a concept, as in the idea of god (which needs no capitalization and can be referred to as "it"), or a supernatural being in the general sense of one. The latter has no name because it has not been domesticated into relationship with us, and so does not need capitalization either. "God"—with the big *G*—refers to a supernatural god we happen to have named "God." It is something like calling your dog "Dog" or referring to a god by its proper name ("Zeus," for instance).

terms before any meaning can be discerned. If someone asks me if I pray, the answer is not a simple one.

Nor is my answer to the "What about prayer?" question, or to the "To whom can I pray now that I don't believe in an interventionist god?" question. I want those answers to be informed by the learning and reflection worked out by so many through the centuries, especially those brave thinkers we in the church have not been eager to listen to. I want the answers to freely leave behind anything that has been unhelpful or obstructive, including the terms "god" and "prayer," if need be. I want the answer to be filled with all the wisdom we can gather—sound, practical wisdom for living in this world in a loving way, here and now. And I want it to offer fresh options.

If you presently believe in something called "god"—whatever your idea of it might be—I'm not going to try to wrestle you out of it. You might, however, be challenged to think carefully about it. You might be challenged to say what you mean by it, and be clear about why.

If you pray, you will be asked to think about what you're doing, or trying to do—what it is you experience. You'll be asked to struggle with me as we seek new ways of accomplishing those things without a construct of god that may make us passive or otherwise diminish our accountability for the situations the world currently faces.

If you neither pray nor believe in something you'd call "god," you won't be urged to adopt a pseudo-religious, pseudo-secular, quasi-supernatural, metaphorical, popular, or any other kind of concept others might deem necessary for the discussion of these topics. There are countless books available for that. No, the theme here is still that the way we live is more important than what we believe doctrinally; compassion trumps doctrine every time.

I do think it's fruitful, though, to ask what makes prayer such a significant support for some. Are those benefits available elsewhere or in another form? Indeed, are they things that may make the future better for all? And if so, can we extract them from the detrimental elements of the practice of prayer and make the benefits available to everyone? As we separate out from the tradition the very human aspects that are going on in the average prayer—the needs, motives, expectations, and explanations involved—I think we can make some important discoveries about what is helpful and what is not, what is essential and what is optional for living lives of justice and compassion.

In this book, I'm inviting you on an exploration of the concept and practice of prayer—with or without god—to see what we'd like to put into a model for living and growing together—with or without prayer. We will examine what it is that prayer has offered and might offer the world into the future. If all prayer can mean in a world beyond belief is distraction and disappointment at best and strife, segregation, and discontent at worst, then we must get up from our knees, unclench our hands, and let it go. If we find that prayer is an essential ingredient to well-being, then we will have to find ways to preserve it and make it as practically accessible as possible. If there is even one beneficial aspect to prayer that we can extract and bring with us, we will. The model we create of it or put in its place could unite us—*all* of us—because it would be devoid of any particular doctrine, dogma, ritual, or formula. It would exclude no one. It would move us beyond the beliefs that divide into vital, dynamic community.

## DISCOVERING WHAT PRAYER CAN MEAN

Here's the plan. In Part One, we'll examine the story at the core of prayer and note some of the big problems there, including the reluctance of the keepers of the core narrative to share more of what they know about it. We'll consider what it would take for us to stretch beyond the received tradition and look at prayer from a new perspective. We'll zone in on the assumptions underlying traditional prayer to see where they lead in terms of expectations and interpretations of experience. And we'll identify the framework we'll be using to both take apart and build.

In Part Two, we're off to church to see those assumptions in action in the average service. We'll find awe, guilt, gratitude, and need, each expressed in keeping with the traditional core narrative.

Part Three is a confrontation. It's not meant for those who fully accept and believe in the core narrative behind traditional prayer; it's aimed at those who do not, or at least don't fully, yet sound like they do, at least publicly. And it's a challenge to move—crawl, limp, walk, or run—out of our comfort zone and commit to saying what we mean, naturally, at least in public.

Part Four urges that whatever label we put on it, we need to continue expressing awe, gratitude, and need, and deal with guilt. And so here we consider some non-supernatural ways of expressing those important experiences. We'll find that some of what we thought could come to us only through supernatural means, or at least ones that sounded supernatural, is accessible to us naturally. We'll also reckon with the fact that some of it isn't, and actually never really was.

In Part Five, I want to end with what I believe is absolutely essential for the way forward, that which we cannot leave behind. And I suggest that we can develop this most necessary quality even more deliberately and effectively in a world beyond belief.

While we are together, I'm going to ask you to consider points of view from both the comfortable and familiar inside and the disconcerting and exposed outside. I'm inviting you to approach with an open mind, to open yourself to new ways of thinking and new thoughts, and to handle the initial discomfort newness often brings long enough to sense the worth in the ideas and the suggestions. I'm inviting you to come with passion. You wouldn't be holding this book if prayer weren't an important topic to you—either because it's part of your life or because you have strong opinions about it. I'm inviting you to explore the intellectual terrain, toughen up your feet on it for a bit, and let your ideas grow.

PART ONE

# In a World of Beliefs

# I

# PRAYER:
# RELIGION'S MAIN EVENT

They reach for strings of beads. They spin colourful wheels. They light candles. They raise their arms. They hold one another's hands. They wave smoke toward their faces and over their bodies. They bow their heads. They hang flags on string and leave them to fade into the wind. They stand before a community and open their hearts. They dance. They set lights afloat on murky waters.

People of faith the world over assume such positions, enter into such actions, begin such rituals, and without a word of explanation, any who see them know that they are moving into what is for them a sacred moment. Despite the variety of postures, the task is the same: to engage in the ancient practice of prayer, which encircles the globe in many difference guises. Within what are often termed the "Abrahamic traditions," it is characterized by a desire to be in communion with the god, God, or Allah, an otherworldly being that Jews, Christians, Muslims, Baha'is, and Unitarians recognize. Followers of Eastern traditions base their practice on theistic beliefs similar to those of the above-noted Abrahamic ones, with a particular god or gods as their focus; on temporal virtues such as non-violence; or on spiritual practices that lead to detachment or enlightenment. Aboriginal spiritual practices are predominantly pantheistic, with followers seeking guidance from gods

they believe infuse the whole of the natural world. New Age devotees pray to "spirit" or the universe and seek connection with these
or with otherwise latent residual powers within natural objects. Over
the millennia, prayer has evolved in much the same way as birds, fish,
and mammals—whatever led to greater stability, harmony, or victory
in each particular context won out over other forms. So it is that we see
different kinds of prayer practised in different sects, cults, religions,
and geographic areas.

Whenever individuals engage in prayer, regardless of what other
things they are attempting to achieve, they are identified as religious
people within a particular religious tradition. Prayer is often recognized as the practice that defines whether someone is religious or not.
Ludwig Feuerbach, a nineteenth-century German theologian who
revealed an atheistic perspective in his later writings, wrote in his
essay "The Mystery of Prayer" that "the ultimate essence of religion
is revealed by the simplest act of religion—prayer."[1] Friedrich Heiler,
also a German theologian as well as a historian, used the opening
paragraph of his book *Prayer: A Study in the History and Psychology
of Prayer*, published in the early twentieth century, to emphasize that
many theologians argue prayer is the defining element of religion.
He quotes several to undergird his positioning of prayer as "the central phenomenon of religion, the very hearthstone of all piety."[2] And
in the opening section to his mid-twentieth-century collection, *The
Prayers of Man*, the Italian anthropologist and religious historian
Alfonso DiNola goes so far as to state that "the history of prayer is
the history of the religious development of mankind. . . . Prayer is the
heart, the centermost point of religion. It is not in dogmas, institutions,
rites or in moral ideas that we are permitted to perceive the substance
of religious life, but in prayer. Prayer is the individual and collective
reaction of the religious soul when confronted with the cosmos."[3]

## So What Is Going On?

Okay. So it's big. But have all the words on the subject managed to get at what is going on? It's doubtful. While perspectives on what prayer is and does can be gleaned from the words uttered and the stance taken on the subject over the course of history, there is great discrepancy among its practitioners. Indeed, an individual might use prayer at one time to seek shelter in their god but may rail against the same deity at another time. The Psalms, that great poetic centre section of the Bible, offer us glimpses into the prayer lives of the ancient forebears of the Judaic, Christian, and Muslim faiths.

> While I kept silence, my body wasted away
> through my groaning all day long.
> For day and night your hand was heavy upon me;
> my strength was dried up as by the heat of summer.
> Selah
>
> Then I acknowledged my sin to you,
> and I did not hide my iniquity;
> I said, "I will confess my transgressions to the Lord,"
> and you forgave the guilt of my sin.
> Selah
>
> Therefore let all who are faithful
> offer prayer to you;
> at a time of distress, the rush of mighty waters
> shall not reach them.
> You are a hiding-place for me;
> you preserve me from trouble;
> you surround me with glad cries of deliverance.
> Selah

Prayer, for this particular psalmist (there were several of them), was a way of lamenting the distance he'd kept from God and reaffirming his allegiance to him. God, three thousand years ago, is described as a hiding place, the shelter into which the psalmist can curl and take respite from the world. Prayer was an act of reconciliation and healing, of reclaiming that shelter.

In the seventh century CE, St. John Climacus, known as St. John of the Ladder, described the reconciliation forged through prayer less as a blessing and more as a spiritual responsibility. In Step 28 of his Ladder of Divine Ascent, he refers to prayer as "a dialogue and a union with God. Its effect is to hold the world together and to achieve a reconciliation with God."[4]

Reformer Martin Luther, who wrote an extended letter on prayer to a barber friend, agreed. Using the Lord's Prayer, the Ten Commandments, the creeds, and the Psalter to pray, he describes a four-stranded discipline: instruction, thanksgiving, confession, prayer.[5] Prayers of eighteenth-century French writer and philosopher Voltaire reflect the humanitarian ideals of the Enlightenment: "Thou hast not given us a heart that we may hate one another, nor hands that we may strangle one another, but that we may help each other to bear the burden of a wearisome and transitory life."[6]

Mid-twentieth-century theologian Paul Tillich examined prayer in the context of providence (what God brings about in the world), calling it "God's directing creativity."[7]

Australian author Michael Morwood, silenced by the Catholic Archbishop of Melbourne in 1998 following the banning of his book *Tomorrow's Catholic*, worked with Australian Christians for over thirty years and speaks about prayer as no longer to an elsewhere God but to an everywhere God. Morwood remains focused on the traditional teaching that "prayer [is] concerned with raising the mind and heart to

God," but the "raising" is to that idea of God being everywhere—an awareness of the sacred in the midst of the ordinary.[8]

Episcopal pastor and best-selling author Timothy Jones writes, in *The Art of Prayer*, of a friend who refers to prayer as "our ache for cosmic specialness."[9]

Prayer, in each of these pursuits, connects humanity to the god, God. In each, it is a central element of life.

2

# Stretching Beyond
# the Core Narrative

Lying just beneath the surface of everything humans do, choose, eat, wear, and believe are stories or narratives that, when we need them, supply the answers to our "why" questions. They identify us and help us identify one another.

We sometimes refer to these stories as myths. Myth, in this sense, is something far beyond a simple story concocted to explain a particular quirk of human behaviour or experience.[1] Instead, it's something that carries what we believe are the foundational truths supporting our understanding of reality. For most of us, myths are stories handed to us, created by our ancestors and cultures, reinforced or tarnished by experience, tuned to or made dissonant with circumstance.

The stories that define us—the ones through which we view the world—are our core, or root, the belief systems that order not only our personal behaviour but also what we do as a group. They are a way for us to represent the ideals for which mundane words are inadequate, and in both nuanced and straightforward manner, they inform the way we live, our habitual behaviours, the reasons behind our relationships. Our stories keep us in line by laying out for us what is acceptable and what is not, positively reinforcing behaviours and norms that strengthen society and condemning those that do not.

Think about that for a moment: a core narrative moulds systems that mould human behaviour in response to them. In other words, control the core narrative and you control the people. Those who control the core narrative have the greatest power within the system. For significant portions of human history, in all parts of the world, that responsibility has been held by religious groups.

Our religious traditions have served in the past as custodians of our culture, vehicles that have carried our understanding of the universe, life, and the way we should live—our core narrative, in other words. Religion helped us make sense of the world and set our moral standards—based on the core narrative—to carefully protect us by guiding how we should behave. The core narrative that underlies a religious system helps individuals make choices by offering a lens through which to view reality. Often, those individuals are unaware of the imperceptible distortions the lens makes, and so they are unaware of the impact their core narrative has on their lives.

A religious tradition offers a lens through which believers not only see the world but also view themselves as actors in the root narrative. If their role in the narrative is as individuals who are inherently good, they will act and pray very differently than if they see themselves as inherently bad. It matters if we see ourselves as blessed or cursed, as perfect or flawed, as isolated and alone, or as connected to everything in the universe that has gone before or ever will be. Religion has over millennia laid out a root narrative that has helped us make our moral choices, find our place in community, and recognize those who share that narrative with us.

## CORE DIFFERENCES

Of course, we all know that considerable variety has developed within the overall religious root narrative. For instance, we may believe that there is a benevolent being who set the world in order but no longer alters that world or engages us. If so, we may move through our lives recognizing the wonder around us, appreciating its beauty, and praising its maker, while also cursing the laws of entropy, gravity, Gumperson,* and any others that seem to drag us down at every turn. But we will neither wait for nor expect things to be changed by some supernatural force.

On the other hand, if our core narrative had that deity able to intervene in the world on a grand scale, sending us signs of his or her intentions from time to time, we might live with a higher confidence that, were things to get really bad, our god, God, would care enough about us to pluck us from the jaws of destruction. We'd live our lives lulled by the sense of our ultimate security.

Include in God's repertoire of powers the ability to intervene not just in cosmic events but in our personal affairs, and you'll find that we spend a lot of time trying to figure out which things really get her or his attention as we seek to gain favour or avoid disaster. Now tack on to our narrative a little afterword about the afterlife. Include in it the concept of a judgment day, at which time we're going to have to account for the choices we made throughout our lives. Or build into it the concept of karma or reincarnation, either of which will make sure we get repaid in a manner appropriate to the choices we make while alive. What's important, then, is figuring out which choices are good and which are bad. If we can't distinguish what we should do from what we shouldn't, how will we ever prepare ourselves for the coming of that day?

Every great religious tradition has argued that special docu-

---

* Gumperson's Law states that the likelihood of any event happening is inversely proportional to how much you want it to happen. In other words, whatever you really, really, really want to happen won't. Whatever you're not so hot on is what's coming your way.

ments, available for use down through the millennia, are able to clear up that little problem by identifying just what is true and what is false, what is right and what is wrong. When the issues become complex or when clarity within the sacred documents obscures, those same traditions have had trained and able religious officials willing to interpret the intentions of the deity for us. The staggering discrepancies between what one religious official and the next has said, rather than causing us to pause and question the validity of the perspective, have only reinforced the strength of our choices, our preferences, our prejudices. We rarely question, though we always choose.

## CORE MELTDOWN

Now, of course, this raises the question "If our religious documents told us that murder was okay, would we raise it up as a virtue rather than a sin?" You might think no comes as a natural answer, but it doesn't. The answer is sometimes yes and sometimes no.

Think about it for a minute. Almost all of us have seen smeared across our TV screens the scattered remains of vehicles, restaurants, and communities hit by suicide bombers. You may have even seen footage of the bombers' farewell videos, in which they have spoken about how excited they are to be doing the will of their god. That's an example of upholding the divine command as a virtue, even when that command is to murder.

It's easy to point fingers at "other" religious systems and identify in *their* texts dangerous images, outrageous commands, and shameful conditions espoused by *their* gods and prophets. Indeed, it was just that distrust of the writings of Mohammed, sacred to the people of Islam, that sent Terry Jones over the edge in the summer of 2010. The pastor of a tiny church in Gainesville, Florida, Jones caught international attention when his plan to burn the Koran on the anniversary of the terrorist attacks on the World Trade Center was publicized by an Islamophobia watchdog.

A few days before September 11 of that year, I began writing an article addressing the issues raised by the congregation in Florida. I hoped, at the time, that nothing would come of Jones' threat, that he would decide against going ahead with his plan to "honour" the 9/11 victims by putting the sacred writings of Islam's prophet to the torch. The day passed. The fire was not lit. But demonstrations around the world ended in deaths and injuries, and brought to the fore the destructive force of vitriolic religious debate.

As members of the Florida congregation gathered tinder for their incendiary gesture, religious and spiritual progressives, such as those in the Network of Spiritual Progressives, of which I am a member, decided upon their own gesture—agreeing to gather together to read from one another's holy books. The action was intended to symbolize what the three Abrahamic faiths—Judaism, Christianity, and Islam—have in common, to highlight respect and tolerance, and to expose Pastor Jones' threats as the intolerant rant of a dangerous fundamentalist religious mind—something most, I think, already knew.

But let's take a look at some of what *could* have been read from those same books at the Saturday gatherings of such interfaith heroes as Michael Lerner of the Network of Spiritual Progressives. If the following passages had been read, people gathered to hear what Judaism, Christianity, and Islam have in common might have been quite shocked.

From the Tanakh:

> If you hear it said about one of the towns the Lord your God
> is giving you to live in that troublemakers have arisen among
> you and have led the people of their town astray, saying, "Let
> us go and worship other gods" (gods you have not known),

then you must inquire, probe and investigate it thoroughly. And if it is true and it has been proved that this detestable thing has been done among you, you must certainly put to the sword all who live in that town. You must destroy it completely, both its people and its livestock. You are to gather all the plunder of the town into the middle of the public square and completely burn the town and all its plunder as a whole burnt offering to the Lord your God. That town is to remain a ruin forever, never to be rebuilt, and none of the condemned things are to be found in your hands. (Deut. 13:12-17a)

From the Christian Bible:

Then the righteous will answer him, "Lord, when did we see you hungry and feed you, or thirsty and give you something to drink? When did we see you a stranger and invite you in, or needing clothes and clothe you? When did we see you sick or in prison and go to visit you?"

The King will reply, "Truly I tell you, whatever you did for one of the least of these brothers and sisters of mine, you did for me."

Then he will say to those on his left, "Depart from me, you who are cursed, into the eternal fire prepared for the devil and his angels. For I was hungry and you gave me nothing to eat, I was thirsty and you gave me nothing to drink, I was a stranger and you did not invite me in, I needed clothes and you did not clothe me, I was sick and in prison and you did not look after me."

Then they will go away to eternal punishment, but the righteous to eternal life. (Matthew 25:37-43, 46)

From the Koran:

> I will cast terror into the hearts of those who disbelieve.
> Therefore strike off their heads and strike off every finger-
> tip of them. This is because they acted adversely to Allah
> and His Messenger; and whoever acts adversely to Allah
> and His Messenger—then surely Allah is severe in requiting
> (evil). This—taste it, and (know) that for the unbelievers is
> the torment of the fire. (Sura 8.0012–8.0014)

It is clear from these readings, and dozens more like them, that
the pastor of the little church in Florida wasn't that far off the mark.
Nor would the members of a mosque be far off the mark if they
chose to burn the Torah, Judaism's sacred scripts. And if a synagogue's congregants lit a brazier for the purposes of torching the
Gospel . . . well, it appears their choice would be well within the
commands attributed to the god, God, to whom members of all
three faiths bow in adoration.

The truth of the matter is that the scriptures of Judaism,
Christianity, and Islam are filled with violence, divisiveness, and
condemnation, much of which is *directed* by God.[2] So, too, are they
filled with passages that condone the destruction of property and
the annihilation of persons of other belief systems and nationali-
ties. It is also true that such content can, as Pastor Jones and suicide bombers remind us, be used for appalling purposes. The good
pastor, like the hapless victim of fundamentalist Islam, was only
doing what he believed his god expected him to do. And if we think
that we were persuasive in getting him to call his plan to a halt, we
need to think again. Jones wouldn't deny his god for anyone. Not for
his president, Barack Obama, who pleaded with him on behalf of
Americans around the world. Not for his evangelical brother in the

faith, Rick Warren, who called it a "cowardly act." Not for any "progressive," like Christian historian Diana Butler Bass, who drives a car with a "Coexist" bumper sticker, each of the letters formed from the symbol of a different religion. And he would certainly not deny his god, God, for a progressive Jew like Michael Lerner, who brought together Jews and Christians and Muslims to participate in an act that Jones could only ever think was against God's plan.

In the end, the pastor's plan was not cancelled because of any arguments against it. God's plans are never cancelled—they are simply changed. And so the book burning didn't take place because Jones felt "God was telling [him] to stop." God's plan is God's plan, as far as Jones is concerned, and he won't deny God—even if it means changing his mind on network news. The frightening reality we must acknowledge is that he has come to know that capricious god, God, through the Bible, a text most Christians would argue has the right to be called sacred. Unfortunately, those who point to horrific passages in the Bible as reason to condemn its use as the authoritative word of God for all time (TAWOGFAT) are usually met with the dismissive accusation that they are taking the passages out of context. Their accusers are happy to point to passages that depict an image of God that supports their prejudices, rarely—if ever—acknowledging that these are also being taken out of context. Indeed, the biblical context is so foreign to the realities we face that, as is made abundantly clear in this chilling episode in the life of a fundamentalist congregation, it is no longer relevant to our moral consideration of anything.

## CORE CRITICAL

*We* choose when we want to uphold a divine command and when we don't. Divinely mandated orders to kill children who disobey their parents; stone those who eat shellfish; cut off the fingertips of unbelievers; cast people into the outer darkness if they do not believe as we do; go in and take land belonging to others, raping and pillaging as we do so—these commands have, for the most part (I wish I didn't have to say "for the most part"), been disregarded as we have scraped and stumbled our way toward a moral understanding that rises above tribal perspectives reinforced by ancient documents purported to be divinely inspired. We choose where we want to go with the moral obligations outlined in our religious documents.

It is no surprise that religious conservatives argue most fiercely against abortion and homosexuality, since almost every other prohibition in the Bible is now acceptable practice. Our context has changed sufficiently that even most conservatives embrace what the biblical text disallows. For three years, I have faced Christian fundamentalist Charles McVety weekly on the "Culture Wars" segment of a Toronto talk-radio show. McVety is a star in conservative Christian circles in Canada. Educated at his father's Bible college, of which he is now president, McVety is the go-to guy when the media want the drama of a fundamentalist perspective. When we debate abortion and homosexuality, he is in his element, claiming divine guidance for the finer points of his discriminating agenda. But when it comes to questions about the place of women in the family or in the church, he'll quickly shift to a non-biblical perspective and raise the image of his grandmother, a suffragette who fought for women's rights. Despite claiming to follow the Bible in its entirety, he ignores passages that say men should have authority over women (1 Cor. 11:3), or that assert it is disgraceful for women to speak in church (1 Cor. 14:35). And he doesn't show any of the exhaustion journalist A. J. Jacobs experienced trying to balance the finer points of irksome biblical demands as he tested his ability to live biblically for one full year.[3] Like the rest of us, McVety cuts and pastes in whatever way suits him best.

When we cut and paste scriptural texts, as all Christians do, we undermine the moral authority of the *whole* document, not just those parts of it we can no longer stomach. This is a critically important point. *We* have become the authority, using our own moral discernment to decide right and wrong. We do it the same way the original writers did. But we are not stuck with the task of applying this discernment exclusively to religious documents, even ones our tradition has honoured as the main source of truth and the guide for moral choices. We need to take our discernment, nurtured and developed within community, and apply it to everything.

## CORE GRADIENTS

Several years ago, I helped lead a program that, over the course of two years, engaged members of my denomination in congregational workshops about core values and core beliefs. I can credit that program for much of the work in which I've subsequently been involved. Some of the workshops sought to get at the beliefs individuals hold. Which core beliefs (conscious or not) buried within their Christian tradition informed their choices and their ideas about what was sacred? Out of the process, my co-facilitator and I came to recognize a huge discrepancy between what we, as theologically trained church leaders, understood about Christianity, and what those we engaged in conversations seemed to understand. In uncanny numbers—unless participants had some theological training or had spent time working closely with others who did—they had what I would call an "elementary" understanding of Christianity. In itself, my label offends many. Understanding what I have meant by it has offended more.

People generally react badly when presented with a developmental chart that places them at some distance from what they'd consider the "top." Oh, you can lay it on its side and call it a continuum if you want, but you're not fooling anyone. James Fowler, a developmental psychologist whose Stages of Faith theory has been around for several decades,[4] places most people at Stage Three, the Synthetic-

Conventional stage, with a literal understanding of the beliefs that authorities have presented to them as true. A much smaller segment of the population will go on to the subsequent stages: individuals who have achieved the Individuative-Reflective faith of Stage Four struggle through the aftermath of learning that much of what they thought was true is not; in the Conjunctive faith of Stage Five, people become capable of embracing their former beliefs as myths or stories that help interpret life; in the Universalizing faith of the sixth and final stage, they can offer themselves to the world without thought of personal cost.

One could use the analogy of believing in Santa Claus—as offensive as that might be to some—to make the classification clearer. If you still believe Santa is going to drop down your chimney and bring you presents, you're in Stage Three. If you have found out there is no Santa and you're still mad at your parents for lying to you, you're in Stage Four. If you have started playing Santa for your children, you're in Stage Five. If you've set up a national charity through which parents are able to access gifts and necessities for their children, called it Santa's Workshop, and donated your income to it, you're in Stage Six.

By numbering the stages, Fowler obviously had an idea about which was more highly valued. It's very likely you do too, because Fowler's right. While we'd like to say there is no hierarchy when it comes to stages of faith, I believe it is not inappropriate to acknowledge that at the higher stages, as is the case with Maslow's hierarchy of needs, individuals are introduced to possibilities for greater empathic response and are better able to respond to them. The capacity for compassion is preferable to the lack of capacity for compassion. Similarly, responding compassionately is preferable to not doing so. Those who have, however painfully, come to realize that their worldviews were myopic and damaging are more likely to see themselves as able to connect on a broader level and expand their acceptance of others beyond tribe.* Higher stages correspond to a greater likelihood of an empathic response. Surely we can acknowledge without argument that the empathic response is the wiser and more responsible one.[5]

What has often not been understood in regard to stages of faith is that they are dependent upon information and context, not maturity. For most people, the information has not been transmitted to them, so the context doesn't matter. They simply haven't been told everything about the faith stories they live within, in the same way that children are often not told the truth about Santa. The option to choose has not been theirs. That option always belongs to those with the information. Similarly, in the progressive work we've undertaken, we are talking not about spiritual development standards that some achieve and some don't—a sort of spiritual maturity, with a bunch of immature believers hanging on tightly to the "safer" regions of supernatural theism—but about access to information and the willingness to accommodate it. Imagine some people living without any awareness that electricity has been invented. Their lives would be incredibly different from ours. But you wouldn't think they were immature, stupid, or backward. They just don't have the technology. Give it to them, wire their houses, install washing machines, and as far as the Vatican is concerned, you'll have at least the women feeling liberated.[6]

Now think about the Amish. Obviously, some people are aware of the technology of electricity but choose to reject it. That doesn't make them immature, stupid, or backward either. They are simply availing themselves of information they wish to use and respectfully setting

---

* I intentionally use the word "tribe" to tie our propensity to gather in communities based on similarities of worldview, values, and preferences to our early origins, when our capacity to maintain the cohesiveness of our tribe determined our survival. The word is not used in reference to specific ethnic groups, which may continue to use it to describe community groups.

aside information they don't wish to use. But they don't go around unplugging others from the electrical grid or blowing up transformers. They don't sabotage the efforts of others who wish to learn about and use electricity.

Many Christians have never been told anything about historical or critical perspectives on the Bible and Christianity. They have only ever been told that the Bible is the authoritative word of God for all time (TAWOGFAT), and that it says anyone who suggests otherwise will find him- or herself in line for God's worst plagues (Rev. 22:18, 19). The smart course, as far as these Christians are concerned, is to stay away from anyone who's trying to tell them something different. Quite frankly, I don't blame them. The world feels like a safer place when you believe that the supernatural god, God, is taking care of it. It isn't safer, but that doesn't take away from the fact that it feels safer. If someone is able to set anxiety aside when the suggestion is made that the Bible might be wrong, he or she may well be on the way to a progressive perspective on Christianity.

Faith development is not about maturing. Certainly you need to be mature enough to open your mind to new ideas, but that is a necessary reality if we want to be able to change our opinion on anything. Painting the dining room red might seem like a good idea until you learn that red makes you feel hunger and want to eat more. If you struggle with weight control, you might change your mind about the colour. But it doesn't mean you're more mature if you paint the room café au lait or less mature if you go ahead and paint it red. The decision to incorporate new information into your worldview is up to you, and it's dependent upon your context and your will to do so. It's only when you get to this stage, however—after the information has been attained, understood, and assimilated—that you can even remotely begin to explore facets that prevent individuals from moving to new stages of Fowler's system. Many people, for many reasons, simply cannot. But many, many do.

What my colleague and I noted during our core beliefs program was that although we, as clergy, believed we were passing contemporary scholarship on to our congregations, people, for some reason, weren't picking up on it. Despite the theologically liberal or even progressive non-theistic perspective of many clergy, Christianity in the minds and hearts of most churchgoers remains the Christianity of their Sunday school classes. With no information to shift their understanding—private conversations with clergy, continuing education, or an exposure to contemporary scholarship on Christianity—most believe what they've always believed. God lives in heaven. He sent Jesus to live on earth. While on earth, Jesus, who is really God, was also really human. Some believe that he died for "our sins," others that he was put to death because he fought for justice. Sin is described in vague, Ten Commandment–type references, rather than in relation to our complicity in the world's ills. If we go to heaven, we will be with God, Jesus, and all the relatives we have loved. If we don't . . . well, we don't generally talk about that, preferring instead a bit of fuzziness around the doctrines of hell and the "finally impenitent."[7] And all of this is somewhere in the Bible—the Holy Bible, the word of God, God's word to us, TAWOGFAT—which is known to be an old book and so is believed to be the best book, or at least a very good one. What I learned over the course of those two years was that clergy, although trained in critical scholarship and fully cognizant of the human construction of the Bible, simply weren't getting the message across. The people in the pews in front of us didn't know what we knew, even though we thought we'd been telling them for years. What was that all about?

I returned to my congregation determined to figure out what was blocking my message from getting to the people I so wanted to reach.[8] It didn't take long to figure it out. In fact, I started my next Sunday with it: the opening prayer. Well, the opening prayer and pretty much everything that followed it.

You see, the whole Sunday morning thing continues to unfold according to a traditional theological paradigm, an old-core narrative: the readings, the prayers, the hymns, the wording on the offering envelopes, the person in the fancy clothes up front assumed to be the only one in the room with special access to God. It didn't matter what I believed or what I was saying, as long as everything else reinforced that old, old story—that God in heaven, who is holy, almighty, all-knowing, and everywhere, is going to keep us safe, somehow, now and in the end. Because God is. God does. God helps. God cares. God loves. God blesses. God saves. God punishes (yes, we need to include this). God guides. God answers. God promises. It's God we pray to and God that responds. This is the story of elementary Christianity, and it comes from the Bible (although it's nestled in there among less flattering descriptions of God and God's activities). However close all that comes, or doesn't come, to your understanding of god, it perfectly matches much of the language in the prayers and hymns and biblical readings used in the average church. And long after people forget a minister's message, or even the minister herself, they still remember the Lord's Prayer, the favourite old hymns, and the memorized Psalm or Bible verse. When I realized that—and it was a watershed moment for me—nothing was the same. It couldn't be.

## CORE KEEPERS

I was trained to be a core keeper, to protect the core narrative of our faith. The course of instruction is challenging, but it gets the job done. And how! Over the course of a solid liberal Christian education, those preparing for leadership in the church grapple with new concepts, stretch them over previous paradigms, and come to completely new understandings of things they had thought they already understood. And they did understand them. It's just that they understood them differently. Exposed to a breadth of scholarship that both challenges and reinforces beliefs they arrived with, students very often leave with those understandings completely reoriented. Sometimes, even their beliefs have changed. But the words used to describe radically differ- ent ideas ("radical" in the sense of what is at the root of something) stay the same. Learning how to do that seamlessly is an integral piece of the liberal theological education.

I would be quite surprised, in this day and age, if as I was being wheeled into surgery, the anaesthesiologist leaned over me and said, "I'm just going to cover your face with a cloth soaked in chloroform now and you'll pass out within seconds." And I'd be puzzled if, hav- ing been told that, I watched her inject a liquid into the tube attached to my arm and felt myself falling asleep before I could ask where the cloth was.

Doctors have it easier than clerics. Chloroform is chloroform. They don't have to cope with words taking on whole new meanings. And so rather than telling us one thing when they mean another, they get to tell us what they really mean: "I'm going to inject you with the sedative Pentothal and you'll feel yourself get drowsy." When they stopped using chloroform to put patients to sleep, doctors stopped telling patients they were giving them chloroform. It wouldn't have made sense to do otherwise. Yet here we are, in our religious institu- tions, stuck trying to say new things with all the same old words. It's no wonder so many of us end up on stress leave or quit before we've barely begun.[9]

As we prepare for surgical procedures or begin taking new pre- scription drugs, we realize we don't know everything there is to know, and so we ask questions of our doctors and we find out. But very few people ever ask ministers what they mean when they use the word "god," because they believe they already know. Susan thinks the min- ister is talking about whatever it is Susan thinks "god" means. Jefferson thinks the minister is talking about whatever it is Jefferson thinks "god" means. And Amandeep thinks the minister is talking about whatever it is Amandeep thinks "god" means. And a great many Susans, Jeffersons, and Amandeeps think the word "god" describes an invisible being or spirit that has existed since long before time, created the world, and has supernatural powers (regardless of whether she or he chooses to use them). It never occurs to them that their clergyperson would be thinking of anything different than that. They have no idea that the core narrative taught in liberal theological colleges has shifted so dramatically beneath the verbiage, and so they do not know that when a clergyperson or church official in the liberal church says the words "Jesus Christ, our risen Lord," he or she may not be talking about a bodily resurrection or a supreme ruler upon whom our lives depend.

Through the process of higher education, students are exposed to contemporary scholarship within their field, whatever that field may be. Medical students do research in new areas as our collective understanding of the human body grows and changes. Engineering students prepare for careers in which they will use technology to solve problems that don't yet exist. Art students experiment with new media, some of which have only recently been recognized as appropriate for the purposes of art. Law students preparing for their bar exams review decisions that are mere hours old, handed down by justices advancing the law inch by excruciating inch.

Despite appearances in the average mainline church, it's no different in theological colleges. Sure, we want the church's one foundation to appear to be solid and secure; the illusion of constancy is one the church has worked hard to maintain. But it is just that: an illusion. Every year, as students bend over compulsory texts in the hallowed halls of their theological schools, seminaries, and Bible colleges, scholars are adding to the volume of material future students will review. They explore the roots of biblical literature, apply new historical methods to our understanding of church, include emerging cultures in theological discourse, and basically rewrite beliefs once thought to be constant and secure. Like the best medical, engineering, law, and art schools, the best theological schools expose students to the work of contemporary academics and researchers. Much of it takes them beyond the understandings with which they arrived, forcing them to catapult the simple "God up there, us down here" theologies that may have ordered their world to that point. What they learn strips the Bible of its presumed authoritative voice, tarnishes the ecclesial pedigree, dishevels the perfect image of Jesus, and topples God's mighty throne. It's a hard learn.

Upon graduation from an institution of higher learning, students who have allowed their education to open up their worldviews are eager to share what they have learned. They want to engage their clients and peers on the same transformative level on which they were recently engaged. Doctors reach for the latest pharmaceuticals not only because they have free samples but also because they want to find the most effective options available in the quest for their patients' health. Bio-engineers have little use for outmoded climate research when working to preserve the protective mangrove forests along tropical shorelines. Artists best affect their audiences with fresh inter-pretations of their subject matter, surprising them into understanding. Lawyers build their clients' cases on decisions that will stand today, not on something overturned late yesterday afternoon.

But what happens to graduates of theological colleges? Like other new graduates, they too want to use the best of what they've learned. The problem is that the best of what they've learned is often light years beyond what the congregations they will serve have been exposed to. Only in the few minutes assigned each week to preaching will they have the opportunity to make any headway. What they squeeze into that sliver of time is entirely encased by a liturgical architecture that rivets them to the past—hymns and prayers, rituals and symbols steeped in images of a supernatural deity who loves, cares for, and will protect his children.*

And so the references they make to god are crafted in such a way that they will offer parishioners, no matter where they are along the continuum of Christian understanding, something that reflects that understanding. A minister may describe redemption, for instance, in a nuanced way, drawing a picture of a redemption that is necessary only because of the pain caused by our complicity in the brokenness of the world around us, of a redemption that is possible only through the human gift of compassionate love. This explanation will soothe those who have slipped beyond conventional core narratives, but the minister's use of the traditional Christian code word "redemption" will pacify those who have not yet found need for theological shift.

Marcus Borg, a fellow of the Jesus Seminar, biblical scholar, prolific author, and former professor of religion and culture at Oregon State University, argues in his latest book, *Speaking Christian: Why Christian Words Have Lost Their Meaning and Power—and How They Can Be Restored*, that losing the Christian language is akin to a people (he uses the example of the French) losing their language. He is passionate about reclaiming the language both because he fears the loss of it as this cue to identity, and because it has been—for him as an Episcopalian—a deeply nourishing gift in which he has been saturated most of his life.[10]

Borg is so right to be concerned about identity. Identity is one of

---

* I know that many evangelicals don't like the word "liturgy" because it makes them think of rote prayers and responsive readings and is grounded in the idea of there being two distinct actions necessary for worship to be acceptable to God—the action of the priest and the action of the people, the latter of which is known as the liturgy. I use the term to refer solely to the sum of the many elements within a worship service, to talk about the "flow" created. I regret the lack of another word that encapsulates that as simply, and hope this explanation helps those who oppose to the use of the word move past some of their objection.

the major reasons movements succeed or fail. The revival of Hebrew in the mid-nineteenth century helped to define the Jewish people. Modern Hebrew is now one of the official languages of Israel and is spoken by most of the country's almost eight million people. A clear, well-defined identity that sets a group apart from the culture in which it exists will better ensure its survival than a regular influx of lottery winnings.

While I too have felt and been nourished by the common language that is Christianity, its complexity and the very familiarity Borg and I have with it makes things very convenient for clergy and (although not so significant for our purposes) academics. It means we clergy can still talk about god without ever having to tell our congregants what it is we really mean when we use the term. If we *are* light years ahead in terms of our knowledge of critical contemporary scholarship, it will be an enormous challenge to bring them up to speed—and not just for them. We rely, subconsciously or otherwise, on the assumptions being made about what we believe and on the unlikelihood of our ever having to clarify ourselves in any way. What the people don't know won't hurt them—at least not within the parameters of our comfortable new theologies.[11]

When challenged, we clergy are often too happy to make excuses for not telling our congregants what we believe by arguing that sharing such information with them may damage their faith, destabilizing the happy assurance that they live in a world overseen by a benevolent being. It creates this nice little protective bubble that allows us to survive the constant challenges of congregational ministry without getting into any threatening theological quarrels. Those quarrels, sitting as they do atop the exploding array of twenty-first-century pastoral concerns (tight fiscal realities, reduced volunteer resources, and rising personal stress), have the potential to set their costs exclusively at the feet of those clergy who enter into them whose livelihoods will be threatened if parishioners feel their comfortable pews rattled. Given the potential fallout, it's no wonder clergy keep silent.

## FEEL THAT STRETCH

If those who have found nurture and shelter within the church were to imagine themselves fleeing its cataclysmic ruin, having only the time to reach into its vast store of real and symbolic religious accoutrements and draw into the future those elements most central to their Christian life, it would be interesting to see what we'd find they had taken with them. Many would grab their favourite music, although C3 Exchange, a radically progressive Christian community led by Ian Lawton in Spring Lake, Michigan, has left hymn singing behind. Justice and social action—two key elements of mainline, socially aware denominations and congregations—would certainly be grabbed and stuffed into pockets on the way out. Were people to find themselves outside without having managed to save prayer as well, though, would they still identify themselves as a church? Participating in prayer is a defining characteristic of people who call themselves religious. It is also a defining characteristic of organizations that call themselves religious.

Faced with the imminent downfall of the church (we're pretending here—sort of), people are influenced to take with them whatever is important to them. Those seeking to bring new ideas to the fore will be happy to leave the old ones behind. They might race out of the building with empty pockets altogether, eager to free themselves of what they have felt as constraints, and perhaps even recognizing the collapse of what was as the potential for creating something new and exciting.[12] Those seeking to enter the future nourished and sustained by the wisdom of those who came before might want to carry larger loads, including much of their doctrine, ecclesial architecture, and yes, practices such as prayer. I'm not on one side or the other of that argument. Take what you need and what works for you. My concern is for those who are currently shut out of the church or silenced within it. We're racing toward the future at something more than a thousand kilometres an hour, depending upon where we're standing on the globe. If the church is going to influence that future in any significant and positive way, I think it is important that we put our best thinking to the work of what we take and what we leave behind. From my perspective, the best thinking is not locked in by assumptions; it is freed by wonder, speculation, creativity, and reason. It cannot be framed by models such as the Wesleyan Quadrilateral.[13] Thinking through an assumption that no longer stands—the Bible is TAWOGFAT—is faulty thinking. We must think cleanly into the future. Cleanly and courageously.

Progressive (or as the business community currently calls it, "innovative") thinking requires that we shove our preconceived notions to one side and try to open ourselves up to new frontiers of understanding. Humans have unlimited powers of self-deception, and anyone holding on to an old idea (for example, that the bible is the authoritative word of God for all time—TAWOGFAT) will argue that a new one, even in the face of proof to the contrary, is either delusional or needs more proof. Challenging the way we think is even more difficult when we are not aware of the worldviews that inform our perspective or do not understand why we are being obstreperous. Without knowing the frame of reference within which we operate, we are unable to get outside that frame to see and understand anything differently. It's the old but oh-so-true story of Plato's cave.[14] We never recognize that we are merely seeing shadows until we're able to break free of the chains that hold us to that understanding. We have to be open to new ideas, no matter where they come from, if we are going to move thought, in any discipline, forward.

While great advances in any field can result in incredible challenges from status quo believers, the opposition to shifts in thinking about belief is particularly stubborn. It seems to have more emotion behind it, as though there is more to lose. In many ways, there is. A worldview that is based in revelation from a supernatural source has all the answers, and those answers are believed to be always right—no matter who says otherwise; such a worldview distrusts and often maligns those who question its source or denies evidence that might challenge it. In particular, challenges to moral concerns are easily dispensed with when a divine entity has pronounced on such matters. We don't need to get our heads around new interpretations of right and wrong when we hold such a viewpoint. Threaten that worldview and the whole thing risks collapse—at least in the eyes of those who have staved up their opinions, choices, and prejudices with it. Question it and you'll be, at the very least, charged with being irreverent and summarily dismissed.

The most constant threat to a worldview carefully constructed of "revealed" truths is reason. In a reasoned world, the idea of truth is dynamic. It hasn't been revealed once and for all, and so opening up the doors to new ideas and concepts is part of everyday life. Reason distrusts revelation in the same measure as it is distrusted by revelation. It "relies on observation, reflection, critical thinking, and testing by experimentation, and it builds on what is learned in this way from generation to generation to expand knowledge and understanding."[15] Ideas based in reason don't shy away from the demand for proof; either they have it or they find it. And if ideas can't be proven, they are set aside without threat of destabilizing the whole worldview.

Once we have caught the scent of another way of thinking about or seeing reality—assuming we don't shut it down entirely because our worldview is threatened (remember, you might not even be aware that's happening)—we are that much more likely to think progressively about it. This is especially the case if we bring a reasoned approach to it and can be passionate about finding its source, its truths. Often the mere freshness of an idea can impassion us. Passion challenges us. It refuses to let us sit idly by while engaging conversations, new insights, or captivating thoughts are being shared around us. If those thoughts are doing laps in our own minds, we'll be captivated by them night and day. So thinking innovatively requires openness and passion.

It also demands creativity. Those laps taking place in our minds aren't merely for exercising the grey matter. We're working our way toward something, rubbing dissonant ideas and experiences up against the hard, resistant edges of our belief systems until they work themselves into a pearl of wisdom that takes us that step forward. No progress was ever made without a creative mind being applied to a problem, a blockage, or a system that no longer fulfilled its intended function.

Progress, in my understanding, is not about bigger and better, faster and farther. Rather, it is about facing the concerns of the times and pushing ourselves to find new solutions for them. It filters out the noise and distraction of the obligatory rigmarole, the hassles and the pleasantries, "the way we've always done it" in whatever our field happens to be. We feel the passion of the idea, the latent creativity waiting to be released, and we begin to search for the tools we need—the brushes and paints, the pixels and code, the hammers and nails, the words and wisdom, the instructions and instructors—to bring it into being.

Yes, progress can get out of hand. Yes, we make mistakes. We're bound to whenever, in our excitement or lust for "more," we embrace the new idea as the *only* idea. Diana Butler Bass, in *A People's History of Christianity: The Other Side of the Story*, reminds us that "ancient tradition, deeply formed in the ideal of spiritual progress, insisted that progressive faith was about humility.... [P]rogress is a journey, not a destination."[16] I don't know a single progressive thinker who believes he or she has arrived at a destination, although I do know Christians who have argued that Christianity is not a journey; Christianity, they say, is all about a destination. Most progressive thinkers I know say,

"I've come this far. Go further. We need to go further." That's the refrain I'm used to hearing. As long as we have not yet achieved justice, a humane response to every human condition, a world community in tune with the needs of the planet, we will need to push our thinking further, be more creative, be more innovative. Those who think they've arrived at the end of the journey aren't thinking progressively anymore. They may have brought us a long, long way, but the journey isn't over. For future generations, it hasn't even begun. How can we stop here?[17]

Yes, we need to move wisely. Movement may not be the only option when where we are now is about to disappear, but it's the only one we'll survive. I understand the challenges in using the word "progressive" and appreciate that despite the risks, we need to collate all the best, latest, and greatest information we can, sift it through our emotional reaction, find its good options and its bad options, dream it into countless possibilities, and then figure out what to do.[18] Opening ourselves to the process lets us step forward into the future with openness, creativity, and passion.

As we do, we get to acknowledge whatever tools have helped us make it this far, and to sort through those tools and choose which ones we're going to need for the next leg of the journey. Which experiences from the past will help us shift out of the conundrums we currently experience—personally, communally, globally? What is worthy of a new tomorrow and what is just baggage? In one of the Buddha's well-known parables, he likened his teachings to a raft constructed by a monk so he could cross a turbulent river from a side where there was great danger and uncertainty to a side where there was peace and safety. The monk crafted his raft from materials available to him and paddled his way, using his hands, to the other side. The Buddha asked his students whether it would be wise for the monk to carry the raft on his back from then on, grateful that it had brought him to a place of safety. His students said that would not be wise. So the Buddha suggested that the monk leave the raft on the shore, thanking it for the safety it had afforded him, and again asked his students if that was wise. They agreed that it was. The Buddha then told his students that the raft was like his teachings, which were of practical assistance for the crossing but were not to be seized and held forever. The truth was in the arrival on the other side, not in the mechanics of what got the monk there.

Prayer, for many, has been like that raft. It has helped them cross very difficult periods in their history and in our history, both communal and personal. Like the monk, we are wise to express gratitude for what prayer has done, but we should not cling to it as the final antidote to our insecurities. As we sort through what prayer has been for us, with our focus on the truth to which it carried us, we will recognize that a great deal has been carried purely out of loyalty to the practice. Leave it in a heap and step away. Our instincts keep us too close to see clearly. Stepping away allows us to get the perspective we need to make careful and deliberate decisions about our core narrative and those aspects of our lives it influences.

## THROUGH A GLASS DARKLY

There's one difficult thing about those who step away: sometimes they keep right on going. When they go far enough, their whole worldview changes as though once they're not inside the old picture, they don't see life through its imperfect and aged glass. Not that their glass is perfectly clear—but whatever peculiarities now mar their view, they aren't the same ones that blemished the view they had from inside the box. Although diverse viewpoints have been covered by Christianity's wide umbrella, it's still important to consider views that come from alien voices, other traditions, and those who have moved beyond the stickiness of church.

I am not a scholar in the fields of philosophy, religious studies, biblical studies, theology, or any of the social sciences. I am a minister. That makes me a practitioner: a helper, a counsellor, and a teacher. But beyond that, I am someone who, like you, is deeply interested in the whole subject of life—the nature of it, the living of it, the living of it well. So it is important to me to know what is being said by others who also take life seriously. I want to consider various points of view and think about what's being claimed or suggested. Reflect. Challenge my present views, if need be. Discuss them with others. Challenge their views, if need be. The good parts I'll try to incorporate into my life and work. That's essential to my own growth, and one of the most important responsibilities in my work.

Scholars in many disciplines have written works relevant to prayer, some of them in almost ordinary language. Psychology, anthropology, sociology, and history—all these fields address religious beliefs in their study of human beings. There's also the psychology of religion, the sociology of religion, the history of religion, etc. Philosophy, long considered the "handmaid" of religion, today still analyzes and reflects on religion as it explores those intriguing conversations on what is real, how we know it's real, and what is ethically good. The philosophy of religion applies those branches of study directly to religion—what does religion claim is real, how can it claim that, and what are the things that it says are good (this is *not* always the same thing as what is ethically good). Religious studies is an interdisciplinary consideration of beliefs, activities, and institutions, focusing on what they are or what they do.

And of course there's theology, the study of religious faith, practice, and experience. Theology is not the same as religious studies because it examines its topic—what's inside the box—from the perspective of someone who remains in the box even as she seeks to examine it. Her beliefs are supported by inside-the-box assumptions. But those who study something are decidedly and indelibly influenced by their own place in relation to their subject. Although the word "theology" literally means discourse on the topic of god with no assumption of belief one way or the other, theologians rarely study from such a perspective. In fact, theology's place as an academic discipline has been challenged of late because of its presumption that god exists, and that belief in god is basic to human existence. It is simply not neutral enough to qualify as academic for some, despite the many variations in understandings of god professed within the discipline.

Even the very thin versions of theology, those that come closest to eschewing a theistic, supernatural god, are still grounded in some sort of religious belief—that is, a belief that does not meet the ordinary academic requirements for proof, rational or empirical. Queen's Theological College, where I achieved my M.Div., has just changed its name to Theology at Queen's School of Religion—perhaps an acknowledgment that objectivity is essential in academia, and perhaps, too, that theology is a discipline on the wane.

Worldviews, perspectives, context, interest, and respect or appreciation for a subject all work to influence what scholars record. And these things further influence the people who read or choose not to read a scholar's work. Even in the academic world, even at the more objective-sounding Queen's School of Religion, no one writes "neutrally." No one has *no* beliefs. It is particularly complex when we're writing about religion; the writer is someone *with* beliefs writing *about* beliefs, or about practices founded on beliefs, such as prayer. Some writers will believe the beliefs they are writing about and some will not; some will try to suspend their own beliefs and some will not. But whether they do or don't still influences the work they do. Add to that the additional filter applied to the work by its reader and, well, the glass gets darker and darker.

The Christian beliefs that undergird the work of many authors who write on the topic of prayer make their claims particularly difficult to plumb for accuracy. Rather than furthering our understanding, their beliefs may erode our confidence in their findings. Most books on prayer are written by those trying to teach its benefits and how to achieve them. Massive assumptions underlie such works; the most fundamental of these is that prayer has the ability to change reality.

Nevertheless, we need to try to suspend our judgment, especially when we're passionate about a subject, and expose ourselves to the best of the best information, even if we initially (or perpetually) disagree with it. There are innovators—scientists, educators, and artists—at the top of every discipline who, like those whose lectures are shared through the TED (technology, entertainment, and design) conferences and made freely available to the world through its online portal,[19] launch us into new realms of discovery and hone our understanding of areas we are passionate to explore. We rise alongside them, move our intellect outside of its previous confines, reach up (way up, sometimes), feel the stretch, and begin to move forward.

## Qualificationally Disqualified

Many argue that religion can be studied *only* by someone who is religious. *The Penguin Dictionary of Religions*, edited by J. R. Hinnells, argues that "religions cannot be studied successfully by one who is not a religious practitioner."[20] Christianity, Hinnell would suggest, gets a fair go only if those who are studying it are Christian theologians; they understand the implications of what they study better than those who aren't Christians.

To disavow insights that come to Christian practice and theology from a source outside its cloistered walkways suggests a suspect defensiveness. Eliminating "inside" authors, however, means it's impossible to find a "clean" perspective that isn't non-Christian. Claims of my bias in this work are sure to be forthcoming. We all know that the only person who can call a football game is someone who doesn't have a vested interest in it. At the same time, that person needs to be familiar with the rules of the game. We need to remove the accusations and emotion from the examination of prayer and—rather than heatedly arguing against non-religious perspectives (often referred to as "atheist" in an attempt to discredit them)—recall the principles of progressive thinking. They require that you let go of assumptions. Belief in the efficacy of prayer is an assumption.* In our endeavour to determine what we are doing when we pray—that is, what happens to us, what we yearn after, and what we get out of the experience—we must explore it from a variety of different perspectives and different disciplines.

That said, those who study religion from the perspective of an "outsider" can miss incredibly important aspects of the religious experience. Contemporary scholars looking at a religion or elements within it (say, fundamentalism, charismatic experience, or prayer), never having experienced its essential nature for themselves, are exploring a topic they can never really "get." How often have researchers studying the great apes or dolphins wanted to know what their subjects were thinking and why they made certain choices? To confine the study of religion to mere observation reduces it to the level of laboratory analysis, something that can only ever be a portion of what we really need to know.

---

* Please don't try to argue that the belief there is no benevolent (or otherwise) supernatural being looking out for the world is as big an assumption as the belief there is such a being. It's not. Clean and simple. As the savvy ad campaigns of Freethinker organizations have argued, extraordinary claims require extraordinary evidence. It's not extraordinary to assume there is no one present when we have no evidence of someone being present. And no, we do not believe an account of someone being present just because a witness has a personal experience he or she interprets as someone being present. It's logical to assume that a space does not contain something invisible to us, despite what an individual might say. It is illogical to assume that a special force changed something if we cannot see the changes. If the space looks empty and you want me to believe there is something there, you're going to have to give me some proof—just as my grade eleven physics teacher did. The opposite is not true. Let's move on.

If we are going to come to an understanding of what prayer is and what it does, it is important to look to the works of both those who are not predisposed to assume the existence of a supernatural theistic being and those who are. An outside view is often more able to provide a useful perspective on the nature of prayer, within either the Judeo-Christian tradition or the traditions of other faiths, and an inside view will help us understand the impetus toward it. Even so, I believe truth is more likely to live in the wreckage of an outsider's attack than in the perfectly manicured gardens of a blatantly sympathetic argument. Psychology, sociology, philosophy, and anthropology all legitimately have something to add to our understanding, despite the fact that many who write from within those disciplines are not religious.

## THE SUBJECT AT (FOLDED) HAND(S)

Speculation about what prayer means and does has most likely been around since the first person watched someone else slip into what was, back whenever, a posture of prayer. As long as questions about prayer remain unanswered—or the answers that come are rejected—that quest will continue. As Immanuel Kant noted in the opening of his *Critique of Pure Reason*, we are captivated by questions we can neither solve nor ignore.[21] It is almost as though there is a part of our brain that doesn't turn off until it has all the numbers clicked into the right places, all the thoughts sorted and put into retrievable files. The nature, purpose, and efficacy of prayer are among those things we have been unable to resolve unequivocally. It's like we're stuck in a loop, trying to figure out where prayer starts and where it ends, mesmerized by the inexplicable forces that keep us orbiting our subject.

The study of the history of prayer—how it came to be, what was its impetus, where it began—that story is much shorter. We'll start by looking at the period in which interest in prayer was particularly keen: the end of the nineteenth century, when the rise of scientific inquiry less fettered by religion was beginning to wear on the hearts, or perhaps more accurately on the minds, of believers.

### Are We in Dreams Awake?

Exploring the two realms he believed were at the base of human inquiry (because they were biological realities that faced every person), English anthropologist Edward Burnett Tylor, working in the early years of the twentieth century, connected sleep and death to the idea of prayer.[22] Tylor wrestled with the strangeness of these two distinct conscious states, wondering how people could be lying in their beds and yet moving about in their own and other's dreams. What happened to that part of us that seemed to be able to be experienced by others after we died? And what was the relationship of all that to the experience of prehistoric peoples, who were still, in Tylor's time, understood as "primitive" and "childlike"? He developed a theory of the soul as "a thin unsubstantial human image ... the cause of life and thought in the individual it animates," which was "capable of leaving the body far behind, to flash swiftly from place to place ... appearing to men waking or asleep as a phantasm separate from the body of which it bears the likeness." This phantasm, Tylor theorized, continued to exist after death and was able to enter the bodies of other people, animals, or things.[23] It made sense to Tylor that prehistoric humans must also have pondered these same issues, and that they would have felt it important to be able to converse with such a significant and lasting part of themselves, with their ancestors, and with other animals and plants—all of which must, he figured, also have had ghost-souls. And there, according to Tylor, it was: the birth of prayer!

### Magic? Religion? Science!

Social anthropologist Sir James George Frazer developed Tylor's thinking further. Frazer argued that magic was an early form of science, one based on the belief that two objects that had at one time been together continued to be able to influence each other through the use of ritual or prayer. He also argued that magic, of course, didn't work, and that prehistoric humans were smart enough to figure that out. So Frazer came up with another hypothesis: religion was a refinement of magical thinking, one that accessed the power of gods or spirits through prayer in an effort to make happen the things magic had failed to realize. Believing his contemporaries had figured out that religion didn't work either, Frazer championed science as the ultimate authority, as did the whole of Europe in those days. It is helpful to remember, however, that at the time of enthusiasts like Tylor and Frazer, anthropology wasn't really considered a science. It was "less a profession than the hobby of a number of gentlemen of leisure."[24]

## We Can't Know but Let's Try Anyway

Friedrich Heiler's *Prayer* was originally published in German in 1918.[25] While Heiler asserts that "there can be no doubt at all that prayer is the heart and centre of all religion,"[26] he is upfront with the fact that we can't possibly know the origins of prayer. "[Petitionary prayer] is an echo of that primitive prayer which once—when and how we know not—broke from the lips of prehistoric man and opened devotional communion between him and the divinity."[27]

Heiler recognizes the intimately personal nature of mystical prayer, through which the supplicant seeks union with God, and notes that communal prayer must have evolved through a different avenue. Although he had previously described the communal nature of primitive and Greek prayer, he now identifies prophetic prayer as that which leads to "public worship," naming the Hebrew prophets as proponents of the model.[28] Prayer included in public worship within the Abrahamic tradition is certainly rooted in the early cries of the psalmists and Israelite prophets, but the desire for the welfare of the community will have predated these later developments by centuries. Heiler is describing his subject territory subjectively—that is, as a Christian—a perspective that, unfortunately, contaminates his observations.

## Look Out! You're Too Close!

American psychologist and philosopher William James, whose *Varieties of Religious Experience* continues to be a standard reader in the study of the experiences of religion, attempted to bring scientific inquiry to his study. Try though he did to distance his findings from the reality of his own Christian faith, he appears to have had a difficult time disentangling his assumptions from his conclusions.

The lasting interest in James' work may be because of the nature of it. Rather than a theological study, or even an anthropological interpretation, his book was a recounting of individuals' personal experiences in regard to religion—"a descriptive survey," as one scholar puts it.[29] In the conclusion to his work, which relied solely on the recorded experiences of others, he sets out his belief that "prayer or inner communion, with the spirit thereof—be that spirit 'God' or 'law'—is a process wherein work is really done, and spiritual energy flows in and produces effects, psychological or material, within the phenomenal world."[30]

James set out to bring to the fore the experiences of those who were rapt with religion, those he called the "pattern-setters to all this mass of suggested feeling and imitated conduct."[31] He appears to have struggled as he realized the proximity to Christianity of the beliefs exposed in his conclusions, perhaps because, at the time, he was working to find his footing in a world absorbed by the critical scientific method. In a postscript in subsequent editions of his lectures, he sought to tone down what he recognized would place him in the same camp with many whose understandings of Christianity he would eschew. He wrote,

If one should make a division of all thinkers into naturalists and supernaturalists, I should undoubtedly have to go, along with most philosophers, into the supernaturalist branch. But there is a crasser and a more refined supernaturalism, and it is to the refined division that most philosophers at the present day belong. . . . Refined supernaturalism is universalistic supernaturalism . . . the "crasser" variety . . . admits miracles and providential leadings, and finds no intellectual difficulty in mixing the ideal and the real worlds together. . . .[32]

Even today, theologians often absent themselves from the crass supernaturalism to which James refers. They prefer, as did he, the attributes assigned to "refined" supernaturalists, because they believe that by sidling over to that side of the room, they can rid themselves of some of the more profane ramifications that taint the higher ideals they would attain. While they think no one sees them, they are all still in the same room.

*Almost . . . Almost . . . Almost . . . Ohhhh! Too Bad!*
Working under the direction of his uncle and fellow sociologist, Émile Durkheim, in the early years of the twentieth century, Marcel Mauss took on the challenge of studying prayer from an objective perspective. Mauss ventured into the realm of prayer and, had he actually completed and published his thesis, may have raised the bar beyond what those writing from within the faith have been able to achieve. Like Heiler, Mauss found the origins of prayer impossible to trace but reasoned that it had evolved from a mechanistic form to a purely interiorized, mystical form.

Mauss, like James, was intent on studying varieties of religious experience, and although he never finished his work, his contribution was significant. He argued that it was difficult, if not impossible, to get a clean look at the roots of prayer because many traditions were imprinted by a pervasive Christian ideology, noting that even as those in the field gathered new evidence, they were trampling it by their own faith traditions.[33]

We do not have the final pieces of Mauss' work on prayer. For a reason unknown to anyone but himself, he abruptly stopped his work on it and never returned to it. Some suggest it is because further ethnographic material became available to him, and that material either undermined or overwhelmed his research. Others think the difficult relationship he had with his uncle damaged his ability to complete his thesis. Whichever it was, we know that in some corners of academic endeavour, the examination of prayer strayed far from the protective corridors of theological seminaries, despite the common argument that the study of it or any other religious practice was the exclusive domain of those schooled within it.

## In Cloistered Halls

Originally published in 1969, also in German, Joseph Jungmann's *Christian Prayer through the Centuries* works its way through the significant epochs of Christendom, reflecting on the development of prayer through a study of the materials communities used as they practised this part of their faith life. It is a comprehensive exploration of prayer by a Catholic theologian and scholar.

For that very reason, *Christian Prayer through the Centuries* is, unfortunately, limited to being exactly what it purports to be: a comprehensive exploration of Catholic prayer. The chapter "Passage to the Modern Era" devotes but a paragraph to the effects on prayer of the Reformation and the Humanist movements of the sixteenth and seventeenth centuries. Jungmann's truncated assessment of these enormous shifts in perspective is in line with the official doctrine of the

Catholic Church. Luther, after all, was excommunicated for suggesting that the individual could have a relationship with God unmediated by the church. Non-Catholic prayer—that is, prayer without the intermediary action of a priest—is no prayer at all. Similarly, Jungmann offers no review of the history of prayer within Orthodox Christian communities, themselves out of favour with Rome following the East–West Schism of 1054 CE.

## Draw the Circle Wide

The tone of Philip and Carol Zaleski's *Prayer: A History* is set by the opening sentence "The story of prayer is the story of the impossible: of how we creatures of flesh and blood lay siege to heaven, speak to the Maker of all things, and await, with confidence or hopeful scepticism, a response."[34]

The Zaleskis circle their massive topic with examples, experiences, and deductions, and bring a considerable weight of attention to it. They explore what is said of prayer in a timeline that extends from Palaeolithic findings to contemporary situations, examine the writings of those who have wrestled with the subject down through the ages, delve into the many different kinds of prayers in which people engage, share biographies of individuals who exemplify various practitioner styles, and end on a note of mystery familiar to any who have sought to understand prayer.

Like Heiler and unlike Jungmann, the Zaleskis are not dismissive of other traditions; in fact, quite the opposite is true. They willingly and sometimes boldly embrace and celebrate the prayer experiences relayed by Buddhists, Jews, Hindus, Muslims; the Zaleskis even remark on Haitian voodoo practices and explore instances where magic and prayer intermingle. The religious perspective from which Heiler approached the study of prayer allowed him to presume the existence of the soul, and so made a way for his Christian beliefs to undergird his scholarly writing. The Zaleskis are Christian writers and teachers, and bring no apology with them to their work. Their beliefs simply inform their perspective in a manner they do not find exclusive or unhelpful.

While both Heiler and the Zaleskis carefully validate the prayer experiences of those who practise religions other than Christianity, they are able to do so because they share belief in a supernatural god, being, or force by which prayer is answered. In other words, they share a *supernatural interventionist* perspective and align themselves with others who prefer to keep people who are not actually practising prayer away from its study. Although assenting to the possibility that science may have something to offer, the Zaleskis assume that its findings can only ever take a back seat to the personal experience of those in the praying inner circle.

## They Certainly Prayed

Historian Rick Ostrander wrote *The Life of Prayer in a World of Science: Protestants, Prayer, and American Culture, 1870–1930* to correct what he saw as an omission in the historical study of that particularly vibrant period. Ostrander notes that Protestants "may or may not have been interested in how many authors wrote Genesis, [in] whether humans were descended from monkeys, or in the Social Gospel," but they certainly prayed. "Yet while historians have devoted ample attention to the Protestant attempts to meet the intellectual challenges of biblical criticism and Darwinian evolution, not to mention the cultural challenges of a modern industrial society, the history of prayer" seems to have drawn little consideration.[35]

Ostrander unravels the struggle that occurred in Victorian England and beyond her shores as the impact of scientific knowledge breached the gunwales of the church. Those who sought to examine religion critically often found that their Christian roots overshadowed their desire to remain objective and, as we have seen, influenced their findings. It is as though religion was too sensitive a topic to be ravaged by the raw and burly truths of the youthful scientific method.

But it wasn't just scientific method that was conquering new territory during the Enlightenment period. A whole new understanding of historical method was also unfolding. As Ostrander explores the controversies surrounding prayer, he considers sources, examines context, critiques narratives, and tells us, to the best of his accumulated knowledge on the subject, what he thinks happened. We expect that of our historians. But in the late nineteenth and early twentieth centuries, arguments raged over how historical methods should be applied to religion and specifically to Christianity. One side asserted the right to study scripture in relation to the contexts in which it was written, and the other denied that context could have any effect whatsoever on the eternal truths contained in the Bible. Perhaps these uncomfortable challenges, highlighted in the magnificent theological war between Union and Princeton theological seminaries and the heresy trial of American Presbyterian theologian Charles Augustus Briggs,[36] sidelined the study of the history of prayer until a later school could examine it more objectively.

## DISSENTERS: THE ONES WHO DIDN'T KEEP SILENT
"Great believers and great doubters seem like opposites, but they are more similar to each other than to the mass of relatively disinterested or acquiescent men and women." So observes historian and poet Jennifer Michael Hecht, author of *Doubt: A History*.[37] The thinkers who disturbed the status quo, who opposed a received tradition in part or in whole, who proposed another way of seeing—these have cared as much about truth as those who clung to older formulations. In some cases, the doubters held to truth even more than their believing compatriots. Which truth was being pursued, of course, depended on whether one considered it to be defined by a supreme authority

and mediated through earthly agents or to grow out of the human heart and mind. Believer or sceptic, authority from beyond or authority from within—each pursuit has always been one of passion.

It often comes as a shock to my audiences to learn that the progressive Christian understandings I am talking about are not new. Despite the "progressive" label, much of what undergirds my argument for change has been offered many times before by thinkers both within and outside the church. Church history, like most history, is generally told from the perspective of the victors, those who made the rules and reinforce them. Those who dissented from the accepted beliefs of their time—often risking infamy, isolation, academic shunning, ridicule, or death—are depicted as heretics and traitors to the faith. History is told to discourage us from finding affinity with them.

If we were to explore history from the vantage point of those who were seeking to define truth without any preconceived absolutes, however, it would look very different from what is normally understood to be the story of our faith. Indeed, I am convinced that twenty-first-century progressives would not be seen as renegades brandishing cavalier ideas if that history of dissent were better known. We could take our place in church history alongside those persistent voices arguing that doctrine must be open to critique. In truth, to read what our forebears argued on behalf of critical thinking in the past is humbling and not a little humiliating. Why has it taken so long for us to offer the argument in ways that can be accepted by the church and by the too many who have already left it?

Many thinkers and scholars risked everything over many centuries to push forward ideas that countered the church's claims of supernatural authority.[38] When someone asks me why I do what I do, these people come to mind. But then, those around the world who continue to live under belief systems that posit authority in a supernatural source—and its ugly twin, tyranny—are also in my mind. Each time someone shares with me his or her personal experience of breaking free of that tyranny, it is justification enough for what I, and all progressives, do.

The characteristic beliefs of Christians who identify themselves as progressives have much to do with the human construction of religion, god(s), sacred texts, and beliefs, as well as our right and responsibility to critique them. Those who have laboured to bring awareness of these assumptions have understood the importance of rational inquiry. Their work has, many times, exposed the hypocrisy of the church. Yes, it is humbling for those in the church to learn that ideas they are just discovering are hundreds of years old, but they can remind themselves that ideas are often not admitted to our worldview until we are ready to accept them.

New Zealand theologian Lloyd Geering is one of the most "out there" progressive thinkers on the block. He believes that nothing that can be called "god" exists, and he would argue that a new secular religion—one that points us not heavenward but toward the earth we inhabit[39]—would be about working together to achieve "the highest and best of human ideals." His colleague Don Cupitt, the controversial English philosopher of religion, puts it this way: "Religion is a communal way of reimagining and remaking the self and the world. It is what we are to live *by* and what we are to live *for.* . . . [W]e need religion as much as ever. We need it as human, value-creating *activity.*"[40] Is this what the progressive thinkers of the past thousands of years were pushing us toward, the acceptance of responsibility for our own lives in the cosmos? Can we survive the existential angst that lambastes us as we let go of the cosmic supergod?

In that, we know we are in good company. Through the ages, those who bravely expressed dissent, pressing and prodding Christianity forward, looked to their fellow humans as they argued their ideas. A greater compassion was their guiding principle, and that lies as a single thread through all their work. To this task, I too am committed. If our religions cannot call us there, then I want nothing more to do with them. But if our religions can be a way to reimagine ourselves and the world—as Geering argues—then I believe that is an endeavour worth undertaking, and I thank and honour all those who have challenged us to do so.

It may be, in fact, that those in the religious world who are conversant with core narratives and the worldviews that grow from them will be the ones to offer them. Once out there, these new stories will be assessed by a rightfully suspicious non-religious world. If they are worthy of being accepted, perhaps they will be the gift religion can give a world too fractured by individualism and too controlled by corporatism. Or it may be that religious frameworks have had their day and can no longer be trusted to serve the world and not themselves. Perhaps Hollywood, with its ability to weave ancient human struggles into contemporary blockbusters—*2001: A Space Odyssey*, *The Matrix*, *Avatar*, *Inception*—will offer up the new myth. We do not know. But I yearn for a narrative that holds us in community, holds us to a deep responsibility to and for one another, and recognizes and honours the gift that is life, in all its permutations and complexities.

Should such a narrative be born of our current challenges, we will immediately be confronted with the realities of sharing it, daring communities and individuals to live up to it, and creating all those structural supports that have, in every age, been both the greatest strength and the greatest weakness of human organization. The rules and the courts we currently acknowledge within religious and secular systems will undoubtedly have to be reconfigured as we choose ways to be together. Then we will have the challenge of determining how to apply those rules. But my hope is that the core narrative will generate and celebrate the rich diversity created by our individual and very personal experiences of life. It will, I hope, honour and protect the rights of all to engage life fully and to express themselves freely in ways that allow others to engage life fully and to express themselves freely in ways that ... and so on, and so on. ...

What I believe we must do is apply these principles of progressive thought, the same principles we applied to the concept of god, to prayer—that is, to consider the implications of non-theistic, non-supernatural thought on this particular element of our communal and private faith lives. I want you to approach the topic of prayer without assumptions—no matter where those assumptions came from, no matter how long you've held them, and no matter whether you've found them meaningful in your life. We can encourage each other, perhaps even comfort each other, whenever a treasured belief starts to shake or a cherished practice starts to look oddly different to us. You can always reclaim your assumptions and the perspective you base them on at the end of our time together.

As we explore, I'll take responsibility for being respectful. I didn't mention respect when I was sharing the principles of progressive thought. It may not be an obvious principle, but it is essential. If I can't convince you while offering my perspectives with respect, then I don't deserve to convince you at all. Similarly, when you go from our time together, having read this book, it will be your turn to be bound by that same principle. Because the way we live is more important than what we believe.

The concept and practice of prayer cannot be immune to the demands made by modern (and not-so-modern) critique. Christians have used prayer to stifle complaint, feed our arrogance, and lay the blame for horrific events in the conveniently restricted realms of "failed personal piety." It would be nice if we could point to that behaviour as something that happened in the past, and demonstrate that we have come a long way since the days when prayer was used to cause people pain. The truth, however, is that Christians continue to use prayer to galvanize people around the oppression of groups whose race, gender, or sexuality offends them;[41] to remove responsibility for evil and pain from humans and hand it to Satan;[42] and to invite religion into halls of government around the world.[43] And it's all because of a core narrative with staying power.

3

# TRACING THE INFLUENCE
# OF CORE ASSUMPTIONS

When someone sinks to her knees, folds her hands, lights a candle, or touches her forehead to the floor, there is a very stable foundation of belief upon which she is relying. That foundation, however stable it may be, is constructed entirely of core assumptions about god.

## VARIATIONS ON THE THEME

The Greek word *theos* means "god." The term *theism* means a belief in the existence of a supernatural god. In its broader sense, this could be any god. In the narrower sense, it refers to the supreme, personal, all-powerful, all-knowing, all-loving creator and sustainer of life, "God, if you will."[1]

Those who are uncomfortable with traditional theism but still want some sort of god have options. *Deism* is the idea that it's pretty obvious when you look at the world that God created it, and just as obvious that he backed far away afterward, leaving it to run according to laws he designed. *Pantheism* (pan = all) sees god and Nature as the same: everything is god. *Panentheism* (pan + en = all + in) conceives of god as personal, alive within every aspect of nature, but also beyond it, giving it life: god is in everything. Process theologians are comfortable with all the bad stuff the god, God, is remembered for, because he was just a kid once, too. But he's growing up, so they're happy to be theists. Or pantheists. Or panentheists. Depends whether they believe God's still a bit of a kid, an adolescent, or a mature adult.

## NON-THEISM

Non-theism rejects theism. I learned about non-theism from a host of writers and found it extremely helpful to my thinking and my practice, although I'm aware that it is heavily criticized by strong proponents of theism, especially at its most narrow description. But in truth, there are some process theologians who might argue that a really grown-up god is a non-theistic one.

In my previous book, I used the concept of non-theism to analyze and critique traditional church doctrine on the subject of God. I shared the view, common within liberal, mainline denominations, that scripture was not the authoritative word of God for all time (TAWOGFAT), a supernatural revelation, or a repository of authoritative truth, but rather a humanly constructed collection of writings by an ancient people attempting to relate their authentic experiences of life *as they interpreted them.* Those experiences are necessarily filtered through their assumption of the existence of a Supreme Being with supernatural qualities (and a few pretty unflattering natural ones as well). This view doesn't mean they were wrong; it means I don't have to say they were right. And it's also perfectly appropriate and actually advisable in many cases for me to challenge their version of reality, including their construction of the very god who was supposed to have revealed it all. Non-theism helps deconstruct and critically examine this constructed theism, challenging claims of truth and asking whose voices are reflected in those claims and whose are left out, whose power is protected and whose marginalized. Protecting belief in that worldview has covered not only acts of oppression but also a more subtle paternalism and life-diminishing judgment and exclusivity. It also helps mine much of what is relevant and valuable for personal and global issues today. We get to keep what works and leave the rest as history.

The term "non-theism," however, in the hands of those seeking to gracefully retreat from the more troubling aspects of supernatural theism, has often been reduced to nothing more than terms of endearment in the place of God's name. Compassionate One, Hope of all Hope, Beauty beyond Naming, Miracle's Beginning, and so on, are all very creative, but they don't get us past the idea of a separate and distinct being who had personality. As much as I honour everyone's right to choose whatever concept of god helps them live a loving life, it has become important for me to be even more specific about my beliefs than the term "non-theism" is able to imply.

## REALITY CHECKS

We need to go directly to a discussion of the nature of reality if we are to explore the underlying assumptions of prayer without the taint of either a privileged or a prejudiced perspective. Reality is a big topic. I'm a practitioner, though, not a theologian or a philosopher, so the reality conversation I bring to you is likely, in the eyes of either of those, dreadfully abbreviated.

### Does It Exist, and How Would I Know?

First, there is the question of what *is* real, of what exists. Then there's the question of how we are able to know that what we *think* is real really *is*. Back in my first year of an undergraduate program at Mount Allison University, I walked out of my philosophy course a week into it. Those two questions made no sense to me at the time. I mean, can't you see what is real all around you? And aren't I smart enough to know that the way I know it's real is because I can see it or touch it or smell it? Come on! What more is there to talk about? Well, believe me, I wish it were that simple, but I'm still glad I dropped the course. I was no way ready for that at seventeen.

## Evidence

The complications start cropping up when we're asked to prove something is real. And pointing to it, much as you'd like, isn't proof enough. That's just half of the deal.

The two most common types of evidence are facts and logic. Factual evidence, called *empirical*, is something you can register with your senses—sight, hearing, touch. It's a "Just look and you'll see for yourself" type of proof. Logical evidence, called *rational*, is a matter of mental reasoning, something I wasn't very good at back then. It's the "Hmmmm, I see" type of proof, when "I see" means you've followed a couple of thoughts through to a conclusion. Facts and logic sound solid and trustworthy, but what seems a fact to one person may strike another as opinion. Reasoning can be valid or invalid, and we've all been swayed by the arguments of a good salesperson whose presentation of reality isn't quite what we ended up with. We don't have to go around doubting everything we see, or holding all conclusions as tentative, but it's important to remember that while we can trust our senses and reasoning abilities for most of our everyday living, we're also quite capable of assuming something is absolutely true based on evidence we think is solid but isn't.

Science and philosophy use specific terms for various ideas about reality. If we believe that everything we see, hear, and feel around us is real—that is, really there—then we are realists.* If there's a tree on

---

* The term "realist" is normally used to mean someone midway between an optimist and a pessimist. Unfortunately, this is one of those situations where the technical use of the term is not the same as the pedestrian use of it. This doesn't contradict my argument that we should not use words that have baggage. It is always possible to clarify which of two definitions you are using. It is not always possible to clear away the baggage brought to a word by another person.

a hill and nobody is there to see it, there's still a tree on the hill. Our presence has nothing to do with it. There's a real world and a real tree, and that's just plain common sense.

But there are two different kinds of realism—naive and critical—so things get a little more complicated. Naive realists, also more flatteringly known as direct realists or common sense realists, believe that the things we see are *exactly* as they appear to be. Apart from optical illusions, we can trust our senses absolutely. If something seems real, it is. If someone disagrees with us, like my first-year philosophy prof, he is wrong.

Shocking as this may seem to us, however, we are not infallible. Critical realists believe there's a real world out there with real things and real people, but since our perception of these things may not always be accurate, we need to be willing to critique them (hence the "critical"). And since we're always interpreting things through "lenses" that have been conditioned over a lifetime by everything from our DNA to our hometown, our interpretations may be off too. We could get the tree right but be wrong in thinking that it's about to fall down. Or that if it fell, it was pushed down by a bear or an extra-terrestrial.

Now, I'm afraid I must also share with you the startling news that there are people living on this planet who believe that this planet—and everything on it, for that matter—does not exist. Not even themselves. Not really. Or at least, they think none of it exists independently of our picture of it in our mind and our expression of it in language. Non-realists ask how we know that we're not imagining the whole thing, that it's not all a dream, that it's not all being projected on the screen of our mind. Of course, they also drive real cars, walk real dogs, and make sure a real chair is underneath them before they sit down—just like the rest of us. But when it comes to proof, they argue there is none. It's not just that perception is fallible—of course it is—and that we interpret in socially conditioned ways—of course we do—it's that there's no way to get *outside* ourselves, outside our own perceptions to check out that they're telling us something true about the outside world.

So we have naive realists (the world is all real, no interpretation required), critical realists (there's a real world, but our interpretations of it are only sometimes right), and non-realists (it's all interpretation). There are significantly different perspectives on what exists and what doesn't, and on what we can know and what we can't. It's crucial that we be aware of what we're saying when we make both kinds of statements, especially when it comes to less tangible things—that is, things we believe but cannot prove empirically and sometimes even logically.

I believe love is real because I've experienced it. But I'm not saying that love exists somewhere and I can pick up a fresh supply when I run low. I may be able to show my children that I love them, and if I do that consistently, they will know that I do. Love will be real, but real in our relationship, not real somewhere beyond us. I don't go to the depot, get some love, and take it to them. I love them—it's a way I feel internally and a way I behave externally. I might still speak of the existence of love, however. It probably doesn't affect much if I do. As long as I continue to love.

Claiming love exists, is alive, is engaged in activity apart from us, and holds the secret meaning of life . . . well, that's a different thing. And the most common proof for that different thing is too often "I just know." For this conversation, that's just not good enough.

Guess where we are. That's right. We're now talking religion, god, and prayer.

## Religious Reality Checks
Religious thinkers have adapted the terms "naive realist," "critical realist," and "non-realist" to describe types of belief. Just add "religious" to

the concepts and you've probably got it figured out. *Religious naive realists*[2] are utterly comfortable believing that supernatural forces or beings exist, just as described in the Bible (contradictions notwithstanding), the *Koran, The Urantia Book, A Course in Miracles*, and other spiritual and religious documents, as well as by religious and spiritual leaders. There's nothing fallible about perceptions here, because naive realists don't even have to "perceive"; they intimately know. God just is.

*Religious critical realists* believe there's probably something real beyond the natural world, a type of spiritual dimension—maybe god, maybe something god-like, or maybe even the god, God. Yet they acknowledge that, given our limited and limiting language, we can't really comprehend god or say anything really accurate about god. We can use poetry and imagery, but we don't really claim that our words are so much true as they are meaningful.

*Religious non-realists* believe that many of the religious claims about the supernatural are invalid. The real world is the natural world, nothing more. In it is much we don't understand, and much that defies description. But since it is within the natural world that we wrestle with meaning, religious non-realists advise we keep our speculations within that world and not turn to supernatural explanations to explain what we do not understand. Although I wasn't sure I was with the philosophical non-realists, who denied me the reality of my morning coffee and argued me into the second piece of cake because it didn't really exist, I'm definitely with the religious non-realists when it comes to doctrinal beliefs. Most of the doctrine of the church relates to another dimension, another reality, despite having been constructed by human minds trying to express and describe human experience. It is a non-realist perspective that can most clearly reveal to us what we need to acknowledge, revise, remove, and replace with regards to our religious system of beliefs.[3]

Critical realism attempts to save the language of religious realism by reinterpreting it—providing a glossary, as it were, of new meanings for old words. Religious non-realism, on the other hand, calls for reverting to the inherent values and experiences that precede the doctrine and its language. Doing so brings along none of the tainted concepts, the baggage against which so many have rebelled out of hurt and disillusionment.

Confusion occurs when religious non-realists continue to use archaic theistic language. Yeah, I know. Total disconnect here. While arguing that no supernatural realm exists, they retain language that has been used—sometimes exclusively—to describe that supernatural realm. In order to be very clear, I'm going to use the term "theologically non-realist." Not only do I not believe a supernatural realm exists, but I especially don't believe that there is a being who rules over it and, through it, over us.

## SUPER!NATURAL ASSUMPTIONS LEAD TO SUPER!NATURAL EXPECTATIONS

The theistic god, God, is a supernatural being living in a supernatural realm. I'm not going to take on the existence of a supernatural realm here. Although I am content to see everything, no matter how bizarre, as part of the natural order, I also readily acknowledge that there are things we can't explain, yet or ever, and I'm open to staggeringly new discoveries that may undo what we know today. But when it comes to a supreme being benevolently ruling our world from another dimension, "I'm reticent. I'm reticent." Well, okay, I'm not reticent on rejecting it, just on assuming it, but I had to get in there that great Hermione Gingold line from *The Music Man*.

### The Theistic God Is Perfectly Good (Remember, We're Talking Assumptions Here!)

At any rate, the theistic god, God, being supernatural, has supernatural qualities, all of which you can list in the margins, if you wish. (It's a long list.) The supernatural god has everything we need and is the answer to all our problems. In traditional prayer, based on the assumption of theism, the expectation is that because God is perfect and loves us, God will share the wealth. We expect goodness from a supernatural god. God is the supernatural *source* of all goodness: of life, of love, of courage, of wisdom, of strength, of joy, of peace, and of comfort.

### The Theistic God Is Active in Our Lives (More Assumtions)
The theistic god, God, thinks, feels, chooses, decides, and acts. All in love and according to his will. God is active, involved, engaged in our lives—he is an "interventionist," breaking in from the supernatural realm and making something happen in our natural realm. When we need help, God will act. When things are difficult, God will help. When we don't know what to do, God will enlighten. When we're lost, God will guide. Nothing is impossible with God. In traditional prayer, based on the assumption of traditional theism, we expect God to intervene, to act on our behalf as the supernatural *agent* of goodness.

### The Theistic God Is in Control (Yes, More Assumptions)
The theistic god, God, is also in ultimate control, and has an overall purpose for life. Although God gave us free will, he is still sovereign and will accomplish the plan for your life and the plan for the whole world, regardless of the forces pitted against them. Each denomination, each religion, has a different way to interpret god's will, although finding it in any clear, consistent form or convincing others of the correctness of our own interpretation is an ongoing challenge. There are currently over twenty-five faith-based wars or skirmishes occurring in the world.[4] We are to rest assured of God's unconditional love, perfect wisdom, and overall control, trusting that even when things go wrong—even very wrong—it will still all work out in God's long-term plan. God has a reason: his ways are not our ways. "God is in his

heaven; all is well with the world." In traditional prayer, based on traditional theism, God is the supernatural *promise* of goodness.

### So Good, Good, Good, Good Assumptions

Theism, then, assumes the god, God, has the market on goodness. God is the supernatural *source* of goodness, the *agent* of goodness, and the *promise* of goodness. Belief in God, in theism, means these qualities can be expected to be operating at all times. Prayer turns to God because God is the source of what we need, because God will act for us, and because God is the promise that all will be well.

## SUPER!NATURAL EXPERIENCE: IT WAS GOOD FOR ME! WAS IT GOOD FOR YOU?

The experience of prayer with the supernatural *source, agent,* and *promise* god varies according to the individual. Even those for whom prayer has been a treasured, even crucial component of their lives have experienced times of frustration. Cavernous silences. Oppressive guilt. Desperate helplessness.

On the whole, however, people who engage in traditional prayer to a theistic god—to the one they expect to be the supernatural *source, agent,* and *promise* of goodness—seem to share similar positive experiences, validating prayer for them as a worthy pursuit. Acknowledging the *source* of all goodness can bring a sense of wonder, awe, amazement, and reverence for its immense power, wisdom, strength, and creativity. It also provides a sense of identity and belonging as God's child, the object of God's personal love. Praying to the supernatural *agent* of goodness produces hope for change, and reinforces the faith needed to believe that God will act to make things better for us or for others, or at least cause us to be able to handle our difficulties better. Praying to the supernatural *promise* of goodness gives me assurance that things are not out of God's control, that there is a higher meaning for this world and my life in it. We can give thanks for a "yes" and adapt to the "wait" and "no," because we trust that God always knows what's best and always chooses what's best. When all looks dim, we trust in God's promises of eventual peace and harmony. Meanwhile, everything happens for a reason, God's reason. We are *comforted*.

Wonder, identity, belonging, hope, help, meaning, assurance, and comfort—all human needs and aspirations. In theistic prayer, they are attached to, enmeshed in, and dependent upon the concept of a theistic god. If that works for you, keep doing it. Religious non-realism allows that these things don't have to be dependent upon a theistic God, though. We can seek out wonder, identity, belonging, hope, help, meaning, assurance, and comfort in myriad ways without tying them all neatly back into a scriptural or religious referent.

## There You Have It: Cause and Effect!

Believing in a theistic, supernatural god who is perfect, active, and effective, we *expect* that this theistic god will be the *source* of goodness for us, the *agent* of goodness for us, and the *promise*, now or eventually, of goodness for us. As a result, we interpret our experiences in ways that line up with that triad of "truths." If something good happens, it was because God is good and chose to intervene in our lives to give it to us, and wants us to know that it stands as a token of a future filled with goodness. Conversely, if something bad happens, it cannot be a God-problem, for God is good, active, and effective, so it has to be either a problem with us or a mystery. The framework through which we have experienced prayer—our assumptions and the expectations based upon them—are the very things we can use to explore it.

So we'll head out to church now to look for signs of the theistic god setting up our expectations and colouring our interpretation of experience. We won't be contesting anyone's experience, but we will rigorously shake up what leads to the interpretation of that experience. The shaker will be a non-theist, theologically non-realist perspective. The purpose of the shaking is to sort out what to leave behind and what to bring along. For goodness' sake.

PART TWO

# IN A WORLD
# STILL TIED TO BELIEFS

4

# IN-SPIRED: PRAYER
# IN THE AVERAGE CHURCH

*Our Father, who art in heaven, hallowed be thy name . . .*

We commonly think of the Christian church as comprising a bunch of different denominations, but that hasn't always been the case. After the legitimating of Christianity by Constantine in the fourth century, "the church" (in quotations because there wasn't a single entity that could be called the church) was hard pressed to come under a banner of unity, and early councils sought to achieve consensus among the geographically dispersed and theologically diverse communities. Throughout the first millennium of Christianity, it developed its theology, ecclesiology, and Christology without having to answer to any external authority other than God, capable as he was of "lording it over" temporal kings and power brokers. Of course, from time to time, one pope would excommunicate another, making the job of discerning which whatever-it-was-God-was-saying was the right whatever. Still, ecclesial authorities wrote, collected, and collated the authoritative texts, creeds, and doctrine that decided what the faith really looked like. In some cases, the biblical witness was given the upper hand. In other cases, extra-biblical witness and revelation were used as the cornerstone of doctrine.

It's hard for us to imagine the stark simplicity of early Christian prayer life. We know from the Didache, an instruction manual for the Gentiles dated by many scholars from the turn of the first century, that disciples were required to pray three times daily, and that their prayer was to include the Lord's Prayer.[1] It was otherwise basic, its purpose—focused on achieving God's gracious gifts in either this world or the next[2]—disposed of through the recitation of a few words. Its rote nature was often directed at bringing an individual closer to (and thereby under the protection of) God, and there was no better way to do that than to use scriptures believed to have been designed by the deity himself. The desert fathers—early ascetics who were the forerunners of monasticism, and who sought to observe uninterrupted prayer through every hour of the day—used the Psalms to direct their prayers.[3] Singing the Psalter was a development that saved people from being lured into heresy by hymns thought to have been written for that purpose.[4] Later practices added creeds to the recitation of the Psalms,[5] and in the Middle Ages, monasteries began including biblical readings from beyond the Psalms to their prayer hours.[6] For hundreds of years, prayer rested on these biblically based texts, as people (both laypeople and those within ecclesial orders) worked their way through the various postures prayer demanded.

But things broke open early in the sixteenth century when Martin Luther, himself a devout Catholic, blew up over some of the extreme practices the church had developed—practices that, as far as Luther was concerned, took the church's authority way too far. In particular, Luther objected to a new issue of indulgences meant to raise funds for the building of St. Peter's Basilica in Rome. Those who bought the indulgences were promised a complete remission of sins and also had the assurance of further absolution on two occasions of the purchaser's choice, participation in church fellowship even in a state of sin, and the freeing of a deceased relative from purgatory into heaven.[7] Along with asserting that the sale of indulgences, and the church's teachings in relation to them, was outrageous, Luther argued that the church itself was making it impossible for the true Gospel to be shared by the people. His argument rang throughout Christendom and brought the authority of the Bible—rather than that of the church—to the fore.

The whole of Protestant Christianity rests upon that authority—and has since its first steps away from the Mother Church under Luther's tutelage. Many Protestants don't question the simplicity of the argument that the Bible is the foundational document for their denominations. But for denominations whose primary training centres encourage or even require the exploration of contemporary scholarship—I'm thinking of the United and Anglican churches of Canada; the Uniting Church of Australia; the Episcopal, United Methodist, Metropolitan Community, and United Church of Christ denominations in the United States, among others—and whose leaders are aware of the Bible's slender claim to absolute authority, it's not so clear. Perhaps reviews of doctrinal statements that pertain to the Bible's authority will become the norm among diverse denominations as contemporary scholarship continues to seep into the pew and is met with affirmation rather than a fearful rejection by clergy. As we look at the prayer practices of different denominations, we will have to pull apart the language used to frame them. Only that will allow us to assess all of prayer's implications.

## THE ROMAN CATHOLIC CHURCH

> *Prayer is Christian insofar as it is communion with Christ and extends throughout the Church, which is his Body. Its dimensions are those of Christ's love.*
>
> —CATECHISM OF THE CATHOLIC CHURCH, PART FOUR, SECTION ONE

The oldest ecclesial institution is the Roman Catholic Church. Using language that is highly symbolic, the Catechism of the Catholic Church speaks of prayer, God's gift, as covenant and as communion. Reminding us of Augustine's claim that "man is a beggar before God,"[8] the Catechism describes prayer as the "encounter of God's thirst with ours."[9] It is also identified as a "response of faith to the free promise of salvation and also a response of love to the thirst of the only Son of God."[10] Prayer outside of that relationship with the gospel of Jesus Christ would not be recognized as prayer by the Catholic Church.

This acceptance of only "insider" prayer supports the concept of the covenant it purports to create—joining humanity with God through Jesus. Although the whole person prays, adherents focus on the heart, mentioned so many times in the Bible, as the part of the person that actually engages in prayer. "If our heart is far from God, the words of prayer are in vain." The covenant is made in the heart as the "place of decision." "It is the place of encounter" between humanity (well, not all of humanity, only those who are "in Christ") and God.[11]

Describing prayer as communion further restricts it to those who are part of the identifiable group. Those who are "in Christ" and engage in prayer find themselves in the presence of the "thrice holy"—God the Father, Jesus Christ, and the Holy Spirit.[12] That communion, believers are promised, is always available to them because they were baptized into union with Christ. Of course, many were not. Despite an agreement among all denominations that "there is one baptism," Roman Catholic school boards in Ontario sometimes require children baptized in Protestant churches to undergo "rebaptism" before they are accepted into the publicly funded "private" school system.[13] One wonders whether individuals baptized in Protestant churches, then, could, according to the Roman Catholic tradition, really engage in prayer. Perhaps they could, but what of those outside Christianity? Apparently not. The Catechism reminds us that prayer is exclusively Christian. It is possible only insofar as the "communion" created through baptism is a reality. No "real" baptism means there can be no communion; no communion means there can be no prayer. End of story.

The significant question here is whether the individual has been the recipient of an "invisible grace" (the definition of a sacrament from the Council of Trent). Without that "invisible grace," one cannot be in communion with the Father, Son, and Holy Spirit, and as we've seen above, Catholic theology argues that if you're not in communion, you're not praying, regardless of what you might think you're doing. No, as far as the Roman Catholic Church is concerned, if you aren't doing it right, you have no right to do it.

That's exactly how the Roman Catholic Church played its position in Brisbane, Australia, in 2009. Having celebrated baptisms at St. Mary's Catholic Parish in South Brisbane for twenty-eight years, Father Peter Kennedy, with the help of Father Terry Fitzpatrick, had woven the parish deeply into the heart of the community and, with energy and enthusiasm, had built a vibrant, mission-oriented church that defied many of the statistics that identified decline as the norm for parish participation. One of the parish's mission projects, a social-justice initiative dubbed "The Micah Projects" in reference to a biblical passage often quoted by Christian social-justice activists, had grown from the passion of a handful of parishioners into a multi-million-dollar, publicly funded support centre for thousands of Brisbane's poor.

But Kennedy and Fitzpatrick had studied theology. And they'd studied Christology. And they'd studied ecclesiology. And they'd studied Catholicism. And they'd studied church history. Roman Catholic church history. And they'd come to understand that ministry is less about what hierarchies say is true and more about what circumstances reveal as true. So things had a way of changing at St. Mary's to reflect the needs of the community that surrounded it.

One of those things that changed over the course of the years was baptism. As everyone knows, a baptism involves at least two people— one doing the baptism and one being baptized—some water, and a few special words. Both Peter Kennedy and Terry Fitzpatrick used water, and there was always someone to be baptized. It was the words that came to be the problem. Well, the words and the fact that the priests weren't wearing the right clothes.

Kennedy and Fitzpatrick believed their parishioners, in order to be sustained in the work they were doing—in order to come truly "into communion" with one another and those beyond their doors—needed to be captivated, convicted, and edified by the language of baptism. The words used needed to be more a contemporary restatement of the intention inherent in the symbolic act in which they were partici- pating and less a doctrinal formula. So at St. Mary's in Exile, the words changed. And the procedure changed, too, so it could be a radically inclusive event. Everyone who wants to participates in the baptism may do so by saying, "We baptize you in the name of the God who is Creator, Liberator, and Sustainer of Life." The words call the people involved to a radical—in the sense of getting to the roots of some- thing—engagement that is understood by this community to be their witness to the Gospel. As an additional sign of the communal nature of the sacrament, the priests are not the only ones to place water on the forehead of the individual being baptized; members of the gath- ered community, friends, family, visitors, men, women, and children, all come forward and participate. At St. Mary's, baptism is an event that celebrates and reflects the community's reality.

Not good enough. The Vatican and most denominational bod- ies within Christianity hold the view that during baptism, only the phrase "I baptize you in the name of the Father, and of the Son, and of the Holy Spirit" will ensure that a "sacrament" has taken place (that is, will ensure that the "invisible grace" really comes to be present). A sacrament isn't possible with just any words. They have to be exact. Shift them around, make a mistake, confuse the order, read something backwards, and there is no sacrament. No sacrament means there can be no invisible grace; no invisible grace means there can be no communion; no communion means there can be no prayer. End of story.

The Vatican barred Peter Kennedy from St. Mary's in the spring of 2009 because of his refusal to use Vatican-sanctioned formulas for baptism and the Eucharist. He and Terry Fitzpatrick began holding mass in a local Trades and Labour Council Hall, and several hundred members (that's almost everyone) of the St. Mary's congregation joined them. Although officially named St. Mary's South Brisbane, the community is commonly known as St. Mary's in Exile.[14] Having been spontaneously invited to assist with the Eucharist while visiting the congregation in Brisbane (me, a Protestant woman), sharing prayer and song with them, and listening to their children recite the same prayer led by children at West Hill, I know first-hand what a deeply moving experience it is. Even if the Vatican says nothing was happening.

The requirement to use specialized words sounds a lot like something you might come across in the classroom of Severus Snape, the potions master at Hogwarts. A magic rite, a secret code, an incantation at exactly the right moment, wearing exactly the right clothing (almost forgot that part), and you have that invisible grace you need. Your spell works. You're saved. The parallels are uncannily convenient.

Of course in *Harry Potter*, J. K. Rowling makes sure we know if the spell worked or didn't. There's proof. Someone is hurt or someone is healed. Something disappears or something suddenly shows up. Something hurls through the air or something stops dead in its tracks. There's proof—fictional, I know, but proof nonetheless—when a magic spell is cast. Shouldn't there be at least some proof where such vitally important things as sacraments are concerned?

We once had a request for an infant baptism at West Hill United from someone who was not a regular attendee. The administrator advised the woman that we'd be happy to celebrate her child's life with her and then gave her the date for the next scheduled baptism—a couple of months away. Stricken, the woman argued that it had to be done right away. Her baby wouldn't sleep through the night, and she was convinced that baptism would make her nights instantly quieter. Much as I'd have liked to offer those kinds of results, they just aren't part of the package.

We don't see the result of a "sacrament" and we don't see the result of "being saved." We don't see the results of our "prayer," either, regardless of whether we're praying as a bona fide "invisible grace" Catholic or as a stammering first-timer who's just found herself in a terrifying situation and has no idea what else to do. We can look for signs and support ourselves and reinforce our choices with what we subsequently witness unfolding before us, but we have never been able to predict the efficacy of prayer, and unless some scientific, reproducible effect is uncovered, I expect we never will. (Scientific approaches to prayer will be explored in the next chapter.)

The reality is that the church reinforces the framework of a supernatural *source*, *agent*, and *promise* god by stating that sacraments have some particular effect. Those who take part in the sacraments reinforce that framework by agreeing to agree with the church despite the lack of substantiating evidence. The other reality is that we can decide to withhold our agreement, and many Roman Catholics do; individual Catholics hold a wide range of opinion on almost every single doctrine. And because that range of opinion challenges the authority of the church, the Vatican comes down from time to time on one side or the other of a debate in order to keep the lines clear.

## THE ANGLICAN COMMUNION

*O God the Father, Creator of heaven and earth,*
*Have mercy upon us.*

*O God the Son, Redeemer of the world,*
*Have mercy upon us.*

*O God the Holy Spirit, Sanctifier of the faithful,*
*Have mercy upon us.*

*O holy, blessed, and glorious Trinity, one God,*
*Have mercy upon us.*

—OPENING RESPONSES FROM "THE GREAT LITANY,"
*THE BOOK OF COMMON PRAYER*

The Anglican Communion, overseeing Episcopal congregations in more than 160 countries, has had its share of challenges over the past few years. It has struggled to remain united, even as its members rally around radically different perspectives regarding women and lesbian, gay, bisexual, transgender, and queer (LGBTQ) individuals and the roles they are permitted to play in the church. Throughout and because of these struggles, the Communion has sought to bring districts and communities together in a covenant document.

Approved in November 2009 for distribution to all Anglican congregations by the Standing Committee of the Anglican Consultative Council was a text that seeks to invite churches back into a covenantal relationship. Prayer is identified as one of the significant elements necessary for that work to be fruitful.

To spend time with openness and patience in matters of theological debate and reflection, to listen to and study with one another in order to discern the will of God—these are essential features of the life of the church as it seeks to be led by the spirit into all truth and to proclaim the Gospel afresh in each generation. Some issues that are perceived as controversial when they arise may well evoke a deeper understanding of the implications of God's revelation to us, while others may prove to be distractions or even obstacles to the faith. All such matters therefore need to be tested by shared discernment in the life of the church.[15]

Prayer appears to be a tool for assisting in that discernment process, accessing wisdom that is believed to come via revelation from a remote god. If there is any question about what exactly constitutes prayer in the Anglican Communion, a catechism currently in use in the Anglican Church in South Africa is available on the organization's website. It states that "[p]rayer is responding to God, by thought and by deeds, with or without words," identifies nine different kinds of prayer (adoration, praise, thanksgiving, penitence, oblation, intercession, petition, meditation, and contemplation),[16] and challenges its adherents to know what distinguishes each kind.

Prayer in the Anglican Communion is dominated by the Book of Common Prayer, a collection of formal liturgies for use in services of worship. Originally published in the mid-sixteenth century, the Book has been revised for more contemporary use in most churches. In the preface to the 1955 Draft Book of Common Prayer, prepared for the Anglican Church of Canada, the editors used the archaic word "liege"—a word Canadians would have heard during the induction of Prince Charles as the Prince of Wales in 1952—as an example of the fact that language changes over time. They were introducing changes they knew would not be taken lightly.

In his book *Rites for a New Age: Understanding the Book of Alternative Services*, Michael Ingham, now the bishop of the Diocese of New Westminster in British Columbia, pointed to the Anglican Church's resistance to change in the past, reminding readers that the original compilers of the Book of Common Prayer also had to contend with "furious theological attacks." In reaction to that prayer book's publication, riots took place in Cornwall, England, and in London, and some were hanged for their opposition. "With an irony characteristic of our tradition ever since," Ingham wrote, "Anglicans in those days demonstrated more visible concern about the language in the new Prayer Book than they did about the takeover of the church by the state."[17]

Although I am of Cornish stock, I cannot be counted upon to argue the retention of archaic traditions. As far as stated beliefs of the church go, the changes in the Book of Common Prayer made little difference. If the concern of the church is, as it was understood to be then, the salvation of souls, it would seem important to widen the circle as far as possible. The revisions were meant to do that, but people neither heard nor understood that. They *felt* the changes. They experienced loss.

Ingham uses two stories to illustrate the widely different emotional reactions Anglicans had when the Book of Alternate Services was made available for public worship in 1985. Different concepts of religion led to differences in the impact of innovation.

One participant in his congregation, a surgeon regularly inundated with change and new technologies, wanted his church to be the one place where things were always the same. His security lay in the details he witnessed each week: "the candles in exactly the same place on the altar," the same words recited, and the same hymns sung. They were familiar to him from his childhood and were a balm in an otherwise overstimulated life.[18] His was an extrinsic religiosity.

Another member of Ingham's congregation, a woman of eighty-three, looked at ecclesial changes quite differently, perhaps owing to her longevity. As she got closer to death, she found herself becoming more "passionately interested in life," and she experienced the new services as opportunities to be more free and joyful than she'd been in the past. "It helps me cope with myself," she said, arguing that as long as she was changing, she knew she was alive.[19] Hers was an intrinsic religiosity.

It seems that if we want or need "stability and permanence in a troubled and changing world, a sanctuary of tranquility and spiritual peace, a haven from the tumult of worldly life,"[20] then we might resist any slight change in language, particularly a change to the language of prayer, experiencing it as the crumbling of our source of security. If we want relevance in a world of trouble and change, then we might want the church to "remain open to new insights and developments both in the church and in the world itself,"[21] and perhaps even in the language related to prayer. The average congregation is made up of some who want the stability and some who want the change. The split, in fact, may even occur within the same person. Often, that's just where it does its most destructive work: in the hearts of those trying to balance what they know with what they want to believe. But then, that's where that split always hurts the most, and not just with issues of theology.

## THE PRESBYTERIAN CHURCH

*Dear Lord,*
*We ask that You would show us Your will for our lives.*
*We acknowledge to You, Lord, that we cannot live without*

> *Your guidance*
> *and we ask You to lead us where You want us to go.*
> *Amen.*
>
> —FROM "PRAYER GUIDE FOR PRESBYTERIAN ELDERS,"
> THE ELDERS INSTITUTE (CANADA)

The Westminster Confession of Faith originally set out the beliefs of the Presbyterian Church in the mid-seventeenth century. At the end of the nineteenth century, debate raged in America as to whether it was appropriate to revise the confession to reflect more contemporary beliefs. American theologian Charles Briggs, whose heresy trial was the hot topic of the day, argued that the church had moved so far from the original theological principles of the confession that the document had been virtually revised anyway. While the Presbyterian Church USA (PCUSA) has since revised its statement of faith, the Presbyterian Church in America—which was founded in 1973, making it the youngest of the Presbyterians—appears to hold on to the oldest articulated beliefs. In both its oldest and its most recent renditions, the statement of faith presupposes that the same basic assumptions underlie Presbyterian prayer: God is the supernatural source of goodness, the agent who will bring goodness our way, and the promise that goodness will be ours either now or in eternity.

In the Book of Order, the PCUSA lists prayer as the first element of Christian worship and at its heart. "In prayer . . . people seek after and are found by the one true God who has been revealed in Jesus Christ. They listen and wait upon God, call God by name, remember God's gracious acts, and offer themselves to God." The book recognizes the several ways in which its members respond to God: adoration, confession, supplication, intercession, and self-dedication. Prayer is about drawing near to God, becoming more aligned with what God, as a remote, loving being, wants. (I was heartened to see that in its official documents, the PCUSA pulls from the biblical record permission to participate in prayer using a variety of means. One of them is clapping! Whoever said the Presbyterians were staid? I'll applaud any denomination that encourages clapping in church and give a standing ovation to one that says it's appropriate even during prayer!)

Communion brings with it a deep sense of participation within the Presbyterian churches. The people are understood to be invoking the Holy Spirit to "lift them into Christ's presence" and to "unite them in communion with all the faithful in heaven and on earth." Through communion, the community renews the vows its believing members take at baptism. Although the vows taken at baptism within the PCUSA (professing faith in Jesus Christ as Lord and Saviour and renouncing evil) bear no resemblance to those made at a service celebrating the life of a child in the community I serve (commitment to a journey to find and nurture wholeness within themselves, their children, and the world), we share the connection between the vows we make and our participation in communion. Having committed to such a challenging journey through baptism, we recognize the importance of community in sustaining us along the way; communion becomes the symbolic action of recommitting to be present to one another on that journey toward wholeness.

The Presbyterian Church in Canada publishes a monthly folder, "Presbyterian Prayer Partnership," with prayer suggestions offered for each day. The month of November 2011 begins with prayer requests "for farmers in Nicaragua as they learn to increase their crop yield, make organic fertilizers, and grow vegetables through support from Presbyterian World Service & Development." The month concludes with prayer requests "for those who find it difficult to pray," asking that "they be supported by the prayers of others." There is a certain solidarity in the idea that potentially all other Presbyterians in the country are, on the same day, focusing their energies on the same thing for which you are invited to pray.

# THE UNITED CHURCH OF CANADA

*We believe that we are encouraged to draw near to God,
our Heavenly Father, in the name of His Son, Jesus Christ,
and on our own behalf and that of others to pour out our
hearts humbly yet freely before Him, as becomes His beloved
children, giving Him the honour and praise due His holy
name, asking Him to glorify Himself on earth as in Heaven,
confessing unto Him our sins and seeking of Him every gift
needful for this life and for our everlasting salvation.*

—BASIS OF UNION 2.13 ARTICLE XIII OF PRAYER (1925)

The United Church of Canada (UCC) continues to poke and prod itself about what it believes. Having survived the process of creating a new, more poetic statement of faith, known as A Song of Faith, at the 2006 meeting of its General Council, it wrestled at its subsequent meeting, in 2009, with a request to have the powerful Twenty Articles of Faith removed from the Basis of Union. These articles, part of the original document created by Methodists, Presbyterians, and Congregationalists in the years leading up to union, have remained at the heart of the church's doctrine despite the affirmation of a newer statement in 1940 and the widespread use of a much-loved shorter piece developed for liturgical use in 1968. Those Twenty Articles speak specifically of prayer and set a dated, though welcoming, tone, encouraging us "to draw near to God . . . in the name of His Son, Jesus Christ." The purpose is to pour out our hearts on our own behalf and on the behalf of others. The answers to our prayers will lie within God's "unsearchable wisdom," which is to say that although there is no guarantee your prayers will be answered, they'll at least fall into the realm of what God wants. There is no indication that there is any way you'll ever know what that really is.

The updated 1940 version of the Twenty Articles of Faith, which took close to fifteen years to write, placed upon the church's members the responsibility to pray for the church and for the "common life where the will of God for the well-being and peace of men shall be done over all the earth." The most recent version perhaps assumes that we know what prayer means, for it states that our only responsibility in regard to it is that we pray "for the deliverance from evil." "Our prayers of deepest longing" are offered by "the Spirit," recasting a much-used passage from the Epistle to the Romans in the New Testament: "We do not know what we ought to pray for, but the Spirit himself intercedes for us with groans that words cannot express"(Rom. 8:26).

The only reference to personal prayer in A Song of Faith is succinct enough to be included in its entirety here:

> God transforms,
> and calls us to protect the vulnerable,
> to pray for deliverance from evil,
> to work with God for the healing of the world,
> that all might have abundant life.[22]

Thus the perspective of the most progressive Christian denomination (on the planet), despite its partnership tone, is that God is remote, can offer us protection, and will work for the healing of the world.

## THE UNITING CHURCH OF AUSTRALIA

*Assurance of Forgiveness*
*"There is one mediator between God and humankind, Christ Jesus, himself human, who gave himself a ransom for all."*
(1 Timothy 2: 5, 6a)
*This undeserved good news is that in Jesus Christ we are*

> *forgiven.*
> *Thanks be to God!*
> —THE REV. DR. MOIRA LAIDLAW, UNITING CHURCH OF AUSTRALIA

The Uniting Church of Australia (UCA) brought together the same denominations as did the United Church of Canada, but it did so more than fifty years later. Its statements of faith, then, are much more contemporary than the statements that drew together the Presbyterians, Methodists, and Congregationalists in Canada. But the UCA has already seen revisions necessitated by the growing awareness of the importance of language that does not privilege based on gender.

There is little mention of prayer in the Basis of Union document of the UCA, and so, we can presume, no doctrinal understandings are required. From the website of its Mission Resourcing Network in South Australia, however, we can glean a variety of perspectives, including the belief that prayer is an opportunity to offer praise to God and to request that God's presence offer strength and wisdom. Prayers are asked in Jesus' name, a biblically grounded formula meant to strengthen the power of the prayer, or at the very least, to ensure it gets God's attention.[23]

The Rev. Dr. Moira Laidlaw has offered lectionary-based liturgies online for many years. I know that because many years ago I used to pull up her webpage when I needed something in a pinch. I found it especially good for creative children's interactions. But the rest of the material is very heavily theistic, grounded in the concept of a supernatural, interventionist god who is in control of the universe. Laidlaw's prayers reflect the belief that this god will act on our behalf according to a long-standing promise made to his people. Although the resources may save time-strapped pastors from needing to write their own material, and I heartily approve of using web-based resources from time to time, I suspect that this gifted writer could fly if she unbuckled the lectionary's concrete boots and set herself free.

## THE SOUTHERN BAPTIST CONVENTION

> *You can impact the nations with powerful prayer. Simply put, Jesus said, "Go." There are still multitudes of people around the world who have never heard about Jesus. When you connect to an unreached people group by researching, praying, giving and going, you join the journey to bring the Gospel to all peoples. Today you can pray for hard-to-reach people who live in darkness with no chance to hear the name of Jesus.*
>
> —INTERNATIONAL MISSION BOARD OF THE SOUTHERN
> BAPTIST CONVENTION, "MY PRAYER JOURNAL:
> ADULTS TO IMPACT AN UNREACHED WORLD"

Recognizing that the most "supreme" need for the world right now is the teachings of "the Lord Jesus Christ, Prince of Peace," the Southern Baptist Convention (SBC) challenges all to pray for his reign and the coming of the Kingdom of God. "The Kingdom of God includes both His general sovereignty over the universe and His particular kingship over men who willfully acknowledge Him as King."[24]

These statements come from the most recent version of the Southern Baptist Convention's Statement of Faith, embraced at the beginning of the millennium, in the year 2000. Entrusted with the challenge of bringing the Statement of Faith to a place of significance for its members, a "Blue Ribbon" committee presented it with this preamble:

New challenges to faith appear in every age. A pervasive anti-supernaturalism in the culture was answered by

Southern Baptists in 1925, when the Baptist Faith and
Message was first adopted by this Convention. In 1963,
Southern Baptists responded to assaults upon the authority and truthfulness of the Bible by adopting revisions to
the Baptist Faith and Message. The Convention added an
article on "The Family" in 1998, thus answering cultural
confusion with the clear teachings of Scripture. Now, faced
with a culture hostile to the very notion of truth, this generation of Baptists must claim anew the eternal truths of
the Christian faith.[25]

Throughout its history, the SBC has responded to developments
outside of the church and the resultant tidal surges that have hammered it, by issuing statements clarifying and drawing tighter the
scriptural basis of the faith. Baptists stand firmly in the tradition of
the Reformed churches, turning, in every possible situation, to the
authority of scripture to determine their way forward. There is no
room within the SBC for anything other than the supernatural god,
God, who reigns over all, and is the *source, agent,* and *promise* of goodness. Any threat to the supremacy of that doctrinal belief is swiftly
responded to with more and tighter doctrine.

In fairness to the Roman Catholics, it must be said that the
Southern Baptists and other evangelical Christians like them also
argue that unless you are in a proper relationship with God through
Jesus Christ—that is, unless your first prayer is to affirm the lordship
of Jesus and accept his death as an atonement for your sins—you simply will not be heard. Evangelical Christians believe that for prayers to
be heard and answered, a personal relationship with the god to whom
you are praying is fundamental. Any who are not saved, not redeemed,
not born again—who have not accepted Jesus as their personal Lord
and Saviour—are just making so much noise.

## DENOMINATIONAL DILEMMA

Most denominations have accepted practices that safeguard their established doctrinal standards. Through examination of candidates for leadership and ongoing peer or hierarchical supervision, the doctrinal standard is maintained at a level acceptable to the denomination. Denominations exist not only to support their congregations and members but also to protect the purity of their beliefs.

That's the quandary. Denominations are faced with the challenge of allowing new concepts and understandings to grow up within them, even as they are doing the proverbial work of "defending the faith." It is a thankless position to be in, with critics fast to pronounce upon both their least efforts and their grandest gestures. If liberal denominations are going to survive as local and globally effective forces for good, they are going to have to be attentive on a variety of fronts and work their way through the complex demands brought to them by their constituents and the world they serve—that is, those on the inside and the outside, and those undecidedly on the border.

It is no surprise, then, to find nothing of great controversy regarding prayer in denominational documents. The image of the god they appeal to remains a supernatural source of all goodness with the capacity to affect outcomes and everyone's (at least everyone in the denomination) best interests at heart. (Of course, history would lead us to question whether, indeed, that god has a heart. . . .)

# 5

# SUPERNATURAL ACTS

We have learned to be sceptical of claims of universal authority or truth. Postmodernism has taught us to critique, critique, critique. Yet there are some human responses that seem universal. Among them are awe, gratitude, guilt, and need. What prompts each response may be dramatically different from one person to the next, but we do seem to share these capacities. In fact, those who don't may find themselves labelled with a pathological disorder of one sort or another.

In traditional prayer, these four impulses are directed not inward to ourselves or outward to others, but "upward," if you will, to God. It is God we are to adore and thank, God we are to confess to, and God we are to ask for what we need. Formal prayer in traditional churches is built on these basic human responses: adoration, confession, thanksgiving, and supplication (ACTS). Some, I know, will argue that the religious teaching of these things came first, and that we learned these responses because of our faith. If that is so, wonderful. If it is not, wonderful too. No matter how we have done so, the important thing is that we have.

It is true that these prayerful activities go deep into the origins of the purpose of worship: reminding the community of the great strength and awesome grandeur of its god; recognizing the damage that has been done to the community's relationship with its god by the behaviours and choices of its members; expressing relief and gratitude that the god will not abandon them even though they have not served it well; and asking it to remain constant in its attentiveness to them. Liturgies are created to flow through adoration, confession, thanksgiving, and supplication (ACTS), and even the most progressive of services often contain traces of these elements. I believe that one of the reasons the congregation at West Hill United has been able to move as far into a progressive, non-exclusive perspective as it has is because much of the feel of the service remains the same—it is framed within the same elements as a traditional service, although the language used within each section is very different. Those comforted by the symbols and rituals kept them; those who found language a stumbling block experienced a service free of such challenges.

All prayer can be filed within these four folders. Whether practised by individuals or offered in congregational and group settings, adoration, confession, thanksgiving, and supplication reflect the manner in which people are invited to approach prayer—with their experiences of awe, guilt, gratitude, or need met in the undertaking of ACTS.

## ADORATION

*Like the whispered softness of the perfect morning,*
*it falls soft upon my head—*
*subtle, gentle, exquisite.*
*Still, its urgent strength*
*arrests all other considerations.*
*I am lost in wonder.*
*Amen.*[1]

It is early morning on the coast of the Gulf of Mexico. Awakened to the pounding rhythm of a tropical rainstorm, I emerge from my room to find the sun shining, waves lapping the beach, rain persistently beating the sand. An enormous rainbow is a bridge between the open sea and the dancing fronds of the landlocked palms. Tears, the ones that come from nowhere, rim my already blurry eyes.

There is little in the morning's weather to stir me so deeply, yet it sends me clear to that place of wonder, of questioning, and of struggle. The question "Why?" with its characteristic impertinence, pushes itself to the fore. Why am I here—not Gulf of Mexico here, but here in the crux of time and place that is my life? Why not two centuries ago, when I most surely would have been dead long before the age I've reached today? Why not the Persian Gulf, where the passions that are mine may have been put to radically different purposes? Why white, female, straight, middle-class, educated, Christian (yes, in that order)?

The questions head out beyond the limits of my personal space and forage around in the larger seas of wonder. What is truth and what denies it? Why can't we humans—sharing the earth, its resources, its beauty—see one another with eyes that understand and sow the seeds of honour and dignity by which we might all live? Where are we headed, each one of us fragile and uncertain, yet as a species, a hard and destructive force upon the earth?

Despite the wonder that wells up in my heart, it is no wonder at all that it does. We are and have been, probably since before recorded time, captivated by what the earth is, offers, does, provides, and destroys. Moved by the power and majesty of what we behold, both on the earth and far beyond it in the skies, we have turned to express a whole host of emotions in the practice we call prayer. Sometimes that awe is manifest in the silent slipping of one hand into another. Sometimes it is the wondering pause that comes when a head is bowed over the eyepiece of a microscope. Sometimes it is tear-stained fury in the aftermath of the capricious realities of nature's power over a vulnerable planet and the fragile life forms dependent upon it. The unfolding of any hour offers up untold possibilities and untold opportunities.

In the mid-nineties, I had the opportunity to take a tour of Israel and explore many of the sites visited by Christian tour groups. Well into the week, our bus finally approached Jerusalem. It was amazing to see, and we viewed it from outside its walls at our first stop, the Garden of Gethsemane. Ancient olive trees stood guard over the garden, and it was easy to imagine deep, reflective, turbulent moments taking place there, real or fictionalized.

As I walked through the garden, Warren, another tour participant, and I exchanged reflections on the experience we'd had. Neither of us felt that—despite the many wonderful sites we had seen, the stories they represented (most of the sites are "It would have been something like this, not this actual site"), and the weight of history and faith that was visible upon them—we had really experienced any "Oh my God!" moments. It was almost as though we were touring downtown Anytown with some older buildings thrown in for good measure. Nothing enormously special. We'd each expected to be blown away by the intensity of it all, and while we weren't feeling disappointed, we noted that it hadn't been what we thought it would be.

And then we stepped into the Basilica of the Agony, also known as the Church of All Nations. Once inside the door, in a room lit predominantly by the soft light of alabaster windows, I needed every ounce of strength I had to keep from falling face down on the floor, forcing a major pile-up in the doorway. The intensity of the place hit me straight in the centre of my chest—fast, unexpected, almost with what could be described as a targeted force. I moved to the front of the church and sat on the exposed rock foundation, utterly mesmerized not only by the architecture but also by the atmosphere of that incredible—in the true sense of the word—space. Years later, I real-

ized that the rock I'd sat on is the one attached by legend to Jesus' last
prayer. The tour guide may have told me so, but in the rapture of
the moment, I heard next to nothing. Eventually, I pulled away and
absorbed myself in the beauty of the rest of the basilica, wonderful
and awe-inducing under its navy-blue domes of golden stars.

*That* was adoration and very probably my first experience of it.
It wasn't focused on any one thing, but it did exactly what adoration
is supposed to do: reorient, realign, redefine. It takes away arrogance
and hubris and replaces them with humility and awe, carving onto
your heart a script that owns you in some mysterious way. It makes
you part of something instead of allowing you to see yourself as too
big, too smart, too independent, too wealthy, too witty, too cosmopoli-
tan, too refined, too educated, too good for anything or anybody else.
Adoration simply dissolves all that "too" stuff and levels the playing
field. It's one of the most powerful things I have ever experienced. I
now see that moment as the opening of another part of me, a part
that invites me, in the ordinary days of my life, into adoration—on a
walk, in a conversation, while listening to the exquisite harmonies of
an orchestral arrangement or the emotive words of a country music
song. Adoration is everywhere.

It is the very personal experiences of things like my morning on
the Gulf of Mexico or my afternoon in the cool beauty of the basilica,
coupled with our need to have those experiences affirmed by others,
that both drives the enormously popular contemporary praise worship
experience and, in a dramatically different form, creates the atmosphere
of reverence and ceremony that frames the early portions of more traditional services. The opening segments of each style of service are dedi-
cated to creating a sense of profound wonder and supporting belief in
the majesty of the transcendent and immanent Creator God who knows
each individual intimately, yet presides over the whole of an expansive
and expanding universe. While worship leaders might not be able to

replicate a rainbow-lit shoreline or alabaster windows and star-painted ceilings, they know participants will be looking for a similar emotional impact—the desire, bordering on need, to be driven to the acknowledgment and adoration of something far larger than themselves. The creative liturgist will work hard to ensure these opening moments are perfectly choreographed to meet that need with precision. Once that has been accomplished, worshippers will be united in their focus and prepared to move on.

The act of invocation is the first thing in a traditional mainline worship service that requests something of God. It isn't necessary when people are lost in exaltation on the shores of an ocean, or when they're in a room throbbing with the energy of dozens, hundreds, or thousands of others already "experiencing" God directly through the emotive words and harmonies of what is known as praise music. Although we often think of prayer as asking something of God, the opening acts of adoration and praise are completely without any need for action on the part of the deity. Participants simply offer God their devotion, love, or attention. But here, in the middle of the opening words, is a request that *God* attend to *them*, listen to them, be present to them as they gather. It's written into innumerable hymns and sets the stage for the sense of sacred presence that is to unfold throughout the rest of the service.

I don't need to tell you that in church, no one actually waits for a sign that God has listened and come into attendance with the congregation. We aren't channelling, hoping that the curtains will rustle or the candles flutter to convince our patrons that the spirits are with us. Evangelicals don't need a sign either, because they *know* God is present (although sometimes that presence is more evident after a particularly emotive praise chorus followed by "Jesus, we jus' know you are with us . . ."). But there does seem to be a presumption in the expediency with which mainliners dispense with the request, moving as quickly as they do into whatever comes next in the service. No bated breath, no hesitation, no moment of silence—just the next thing. And if not a presumption, at the least a discourtesy is inherent in ignoring the arrival of the most important and crucial guest, the one for whom the whole affair has been struck.

Perhaps we move so quickly through the moment of invocation in our services because those of us who have inherited a liberal understanding of Christianity are uncomfortable with what we're asking. If we actually believe God is the supreme ruler of the universe, we also have to think it's very likely that she or he is needed somewhere else. Our demanding an attendance might be seen more as an arrogant affront than an invitation to the beloved. Or perhaps because so many of us in leadership within my tradition understand the word "god" to mean "love" or "ground of all being" or "that sense of goodness that convicts us and calls us back to what is right, not only for ourselves but for others and the planet"—or anything else we might use to describe something other than a supernatural being—we may realize that asking it to "come" to be with us is utterly nonsensical. So we surge forward into the next thing in the fervent hope that the curtains *don't* rustle and the candles *don't* flutter. What would we do if they did?

In these opening moments of the communal worship experience, as in the crashing waves of awe that tumble upon us in our solitude or build in the most intimate moments of relationship, we are being opened to the possibility that there is something much greater than ourselves; opened to the reality that our own desires pale in comparison to the desires of that possibility; opened to seeing who we really are when placed in the presence of that greatness; opened to whatever it is the worship leader, the universe, the person who holds us rapt might offer. Opened and, in our openness, made completely vulnerable.

## CONFESSION

*In the depths of winter,*
*Your stillness covers the land, Holy One,*
*protecting it from the harsh cold of existence.*
*Deep asleep, the fruits of the field*
*and the strength of the forests*
*rest through the crispness of the morning.*
*Help us to still ourselves, too, Holy One.*
*Our hearts, too, need rest*
*from the excesses of cold, of lists, of hurrying about.*
*May we find in the centre of our hearts,*
*those places where stillness pours over us*
*like a running summer brook*
*that we might be refreshed and made new.*
*As Light into Light, we pray.*
*Amen.*

While some may argue that believing in Jesus as the only begotten Son of God is the single most important principle one has to hold to be a Christian, there are those who would beg to differ. In its 2008 edition of the *Oxford Junior Dictionary*, Oxford Press eliminated the word "sin." Explaining that the company had solicited feedback from experts in the field and reviewed millions of books for words children would regularly encounter, the publisher said it was utterly comfortable with the decision; not so those in the Christian church, who argued that without the word "sin," Christianity becomes meaningless.[2]

They have a point, and a big one. The basic premise of Christianity—that Jesus came into the world to be our saviour—emanates from the idea that sin came into the world through the fall of humanity in the Garden of Eden. Christianity offers, in each of its far too many iterations, ways for individuals and communities to get right with God despite that deep stain with which, the church argues, we have all been born. The United Church of Canada's Song of Faith uses the word "sin" in relation to personal and systemic brokenness while declaring all of creation good, setting aside Fall theology and its stamp of inherent sinfulness. Nevertheless, the UCC continues to present sin as universal. "We are all touched by this brokenness," reads the Song of Faith, something that we might agree on, but that I believe neither the UCC nor any other church or institution has the right to pronounce. The Anglican Church in Canada asks those being baptized to commit to repent when they fall into sin—something the liturgy seems to suggest happens irregularly. But the church's daily offices, a litany of devotional prayers that can be said by individuals at their homes and away from the church, include the Lord's Prayer, which contains its own abbreviated version of a confession. Similarly, the Anglican Church's weekly Eucharistic services contain confessions of sin. The theme seems to be that if you are living and breathing, you're going to be falling into sin on a regular basis. This idea underscores virtually all of Christianity. Despite Oxford's editorial choice to clean up the dictionary, if you take sin out of our vocabulary, Christianity takes a massive hit.

That moment of mythic intrigue, when Eve exercised her right to dissent, purposefully reaching beyond the rules laid out for her, and passed the fruit-never-identified-as-an-apple (check it out) to her earthling counterpart, is argued to have destroyed the perfection God had created, tumbling humanity into a vortex of sin out of which it could not extricate itself. Indeed, it is only the divine gift of salvation offered through Jesus Christ or God's own grace that can pull any of us from the pit—or so the story goes.

Many of us console ourselves with contemporary biblical studies that offer interpretations taking us beyond the typically Fall-driven

misogyny of the second chapter of Genesis, perhaps engaging us in
the story by referring to it as myth. Lyn Bechtel is one of those scholars
who takes us there. Recognizing that there's no reference to the Fall anywhere in the Hebrew scriptures and working from the contemporary
understanding of Genesis as myth, she argues that it is an allegorical
story of human maturation.³ She supports her arguments with in-depth
examinations of the use of language, mythic symbols, and the deliberate placement of particular elements of the story.⁴ In his novel *Putting
Away Childish Things*, American biblical scholar Marcus Borg uses the
fictional Dr. Katharine (Kate) Riley, a brilliant and attractive assistant
professor of religious studies, to share some contemporary understandings of Genesis.

> Kate took them through a handout that treated the story of
> Adam and Eve as the story of all people. It described how we
> begin our lives in a state of dreaming innocence in the pres-
> ence of God. Then, with the birth of self-consciousness, we
> enter a world of separation and self-concern, hubris, exile
> and violence. We all begin our lives in Eden, but end up liv-
> ing our lives east of Eden.⁵

Borg, a prolific author in the area of contemporary biblical interpretation, uses this new genre, fiction, to bridge the great gap between
what many believe the Bible says and what scholars, for a very long
time, have been arguing it means. His choice will position the scholarship in a section of the bookstore more likely to be visited by the large
numbers of people who say they believe in God but do not attend
religious services. Perhaps in this way, up-to-date scholarship might
seep more effectively into contemporary culture.

Still other scholars, many of whom are feminists, dispense with
discrediting the conventional interpretation of the story altogether,

arguing instead that it is the misogyny we must rise above. In so doing, however, they continue to reinforce the "original sin" theology for which the story is so famous, and in this way extrapolate its effects far beyond the sacramental washing-away of this original stain. Many Christians and congregational leaders, happy to agree with contemporary scholars that the story is a myth, nonetheless continue to present without question its concepts of sin and forgiveness, as well as the Christian imperative that we live without sin or risk the rejection of God. If you have any doubt of this, attend a Eucharistic mass, a charismatic revival, a sedate Ash Wednesday service in a liturgically hip liberal congregation, or any kind of Christian service you might routinely find being offered across the land, and you will see what I mean. Even those who have celebrated the work of theologians like Matthew Fox—who, with his book *Original Blessing*, sought to find a dignity and beauty inherent in all living beings, and in each new birth a cause for celebration rather than the determined cleansing of sin[6]—often find themselves bound by the language of liturgy and the weight of tradition.

## *You Just Wait 'Til Your Father Gets Home!*

Perhaps the prayer of confession has served as a crucial avenue back into that warm relationship with the divine parent that we long for. Our understanding of god influences the kind of confession into which we enter. Those who believe in a theistic god will find that their willingness to enter into the practice of confession will be influenced by what they perceive the nature of that god to be. If we see it as something warm and forgiving, then we may be eager to return to its embrace. If we see things more negatively, our own psychological health may be at risk.

[I]f confession carries with it the expectation of disapproval from a wrathful God . . . slow to forgive, I am less likely to admit certain wrongdoings to myself, let alone to my Maker. Those ... who like to see the world in complex greys are more likely to view God ... weighing rights and wrongs, offering arguments and counterarguments in order not to leave any stone unturned.... God as a fair judge is more likely to give us the benefit of the doubt. Though we are guilty of sin, God here finds a way for us to do penance or make restitution ... and restore our sense of well-being.[7]

Sharon Hymer, author of the article cited above, links confession with the disclosure of secrets. Secrets create splits between us and others in our lives. Confession, she argues, provides the opportunity for us to make whole what has been broken. In fact, according to the supernatural *source, agent,* and *promise* god worldview, it is God who is going to have to do the work of making whole what has been broken.

The requirement to offer an annual confession, demanded by Pope Innocent III at the Fourth Lateran Council in the thirteenth century, turned the practice back onto the individual, demanding a level of personal introspection that previous communal prayer had not. Hymer connects the Roman Catholic tradition of silent, introspective prayer and the Protestant tradition of prayer diaries to modern-day psychotherapy, suggesting that these practices served to provide the benefits of self-examination.

## Putting the Fear of God into You

A flip through the pages of any art history book will give you a glimpse into the pit of hell that Christians of the last millennium believed was awaiting them. Those classical images of the netherworld—emaciated men and women, skeletons, flames, and monsters—live on, and not only in the work of contemporary cartoonists who use them as a convenient shorthand to identify where certain political leaders are going.

Whether classical or contemporary, those horrifying images of hell remind us how real are our fears of the next life, many planted during times of communal vulnerability.

Jonathan Edwards, an early evangelist to Native Americans and considered America's "most important and original philosophical theologian,"[8] spoke in his 1741 sermon "Sinners in the Hand of God" of those who had not turned away from a life of sin and depravity by being born again. He compared them to miserable insects being held over a flame.

> O sinner! consider the fearful danger you are in: it is a great furnace of wrath, a wide and bottomless pit . . . that you are held over in the hand of that God whose wrath is provoked and incensed as much against you, as against many of the damned in hell. You hang by a slender thread, with the flames of divine wrath flashing about it, and ready every moment to . . . burn it apart; and you have . . . nothing to lay hold of to save yourself . . . nothing that you ever have done, nothing that you can do, to induce God to spare you one moment. . . . [A]ll of you that were never born again, and made new creatures, and raised from being dead in sin, to a new state . . . are in the hands of an angry God.[9]

Now, personally, I don't really get the "tell me you love me or I'll send you to hell" message such preaching promotes. If demonstrations of love to my husband were the result of threats he'd made to my well-being, I'd recognize him as an abusive brute and also be thinking he was some sort of twisted if he really thought the "love" he got through such intimidation was of any value or meaning. If we believed in a benevolent Creator of the Universe, we would be even more surprised at such behaviour, yet it continues, to this day, to be a significant characteristic of the Christian deity.

Of course, it is easy to point fingers at those on the radically evangelistic edge of Christianity and the vengeful god they portray. Those with more liberal hues will argue that portrayals of hell such as those in Edwards' sermons are no longer valid, and that the liberal church should not concern itself with them. While we might think that softening our position on sin in the liberal church is a new phenomenon, it was 1953 when theologian Richard Niebuhr denounced the elimination of sin from the liberal Christian message. "The liberal gospel," he wrote, "consists of a [g]od without wrath bringing people without sin into a kingdom without judgment through a Christ without a cross."[10]

While liberal Christians may be all too familiar with the benign preacher in the "never die" cliché ("Old preachers never die—they just ramble on and on and on"), the message offered by an evangelical preacher is never quite so bland. Every evangelical revivalist or Christian schoolteacher who's ever preached a message of damnation has done so with the sole purpose of haunting people to the grave, in the fervent hope that, even at the last possible moment, they will influence someone to give his soul to Jesus and so find his way to eternal bliss.

Listening over the past few years to those whose stories of childhood faith experiences are littered with such images has suggested to me that the liberal church has a very important role to play in this area, however, and cannot simply carry on ignoring the persistent presence of damnation. Indeed, the idea of hell as a consequence for sin continues to pervade not only conservative Christianity but also, according to a 2008 Pew Research Center study, the beliefs of 59 percent of the general American public.[11] Although that's a dramatic slip from the 71 percent shown in a 2001 Gallup poll, you can bet that those who have switched categories for reasons other than their personal introduction to whatever afterlife accommodations do exist (i.e., death) continue to suffer from the stories they once held to be true.

Here's just one example: An email correspondent wrote to me of an extremely distraught woman with whom she'd had a conversation following a Sunday service in an Anglican church. Having read *23 Minutes in Hell*, a book by Bill Wiese, who purported to have spent that many minutes in hell accompanied and protected by Jesus, the woman was horrified. The book had convinced her that her recently deceased husband was being subjected to the fires of hell because he had not been born again. I could only wonder how her clergyperson's pulpit theology had let the woman fall victim to such a book at all. You may think this is a book easily dismissed as quackery, but consider that it consistently and dramatically outranks Marcus Borg's *The Heart of Christianity*, a book eagerly studied by mainline congregations across the country, on Amazon's bestseller list.

In his 2005 documentary, *The God Who Wasn't There*, Brian Flemming, a filmmaker and former Christian, describes the depth of the fear he experienced while he was a student at a private Christian school. Taught that the one unforgivable sin was disbelief in the Holy Spirit (Mt. 22:31, 32), Flemming was terrified that if the thought even crossed his mind, he would spend eternity in Hell.[12] In the documentary, Flemming returns to that school to exorcise some of his demons. Not all are as successful at finding liberation.

## The Good Thing about Hell Is . . . ?

Some work hard to argue that belief in hell isn't all bad. In 2004, researchers at the Federal Reserve Bank of St. Louis, in a stunning break from the normally dry content of economic reports, included in their July quarterly review the results of a study they had done to explore the relationship between a belief in hell and economic prosperity. Drawing on work by outside economists, they concluded, "In countries where large percentages of the population believe in hell, there seems to be less corruption and a higher standard of living."[13]

After all, the United States, with (at that time) a reported 71 percent of its population living in fear of eternal damnation, and Ireland, with 53 percent in the same category, were both high on the economic prosperity index. Of course, because they had no statistics regarding the religious landscapes of sub-Saharan Africa, it was impossible to determine if that region's beliefs about hell had any bearing on its comparatively low GDP.[14] Also not included in the study were Muslim states such as Saudi Arabia and Afghanistan, where close to 100 percent of the population very likely believes in hell. Since those countries share what the Federal Bank of St. Louis argued is a crucial indicator of economic success, why are Saudi Arabia's prosperity levels thirty-two times those of Afghanistan? And why, we might ask, were the United States and Ireland both hit so hard by the recent financial downturn? The belief in hell, one would assume, has only risen as a result. Perhaps some of the more troubling issues of the report were pointed out to the researchers; it is no longer available online.

Most of those who are hell-haunted come from evangelical or sacramental churches, where salvation is believed to hinge on the actions of the individual—choose to accept Jesus as Lord over your life or participate in the sacramental acts of confession and absolution. You might be quite justified in saying that the image of sin I am conjuring does not reflect the way it is understood in many liberal churches. But when people break away from the guilt-inducing theology of a fundamentalist congregation, they are often looking for communities in which they can find healing for their faith-inflicted scars. If those communities continue to use the word "sin" without considering the heritage with which it arrived upon their doorsteps, they shut out any who hear more than what is intended. This is true not just of the word "sin" but of *all the other words linked to it*: "guilt," "shame," "evil," "hell," "judgment," and yes, even "grace."

## You Should Be Ashamed of Yourself!

As children, when we're behaving badly, we learn one of two things: either we'll get into trouble or we won't. Those who don't get into trouble are on their way to any number of relationship challenges as they grow up. Those who do might learn one of two other things: either they can make things better by saying they're sorry and doing whatever they can to fix the situation, or they can never make things better because it's who they are, not just what they did, that's bad. The first response helps us get things back into balance—cancels the debt, so to speak. The second doesn't ever let that happen.

That's because we're no longer talking about guilt; we're talking about shame. Guilt is attached to action, to something we have done wrong. It may or may not be something we can fix or for which we can make restitution, but it exists as something distinct from who we are. Shame, on the other hand, goes to one's self-understanding and esteem, and it's bred in children who are blamed for *being* bad, not just acting badly. Shame shifts the focus beyond the particular action and highlights what the person comes to see as his or her essential badness. It identifies that badness as what caused the behaviour. Fear of having being exposed as unworthy, bad, or evil is an essential element of shame. Consequently, unlike guilt, shame is only exacerbated by any attempt at confession, since confession demands exposure.

This poses a particularly difficult situation for the church, whose theology often engenders shame (related to self-esteem) but hides that shame under the banner of guilt (related to action), and in so doing neither addresses shame nor allows its participants to deal with it. In his intricate examination of the topic, *Shame: Theory, Therapy, Theology*, theologian Stephen Pattison reviews the contributions made by those within the Christian tradition to the understanding of and therapeutic responses to shame—and finds them shamefully wanting.[15]

Pattison explores the blurred line between feelings of awe, praise, and devotion and those of shame engendered by the impossibility of ever meeting God's expectations or achieving the perfection of the models Jesus and Mary. He argues that the images of the god, God, create incredible dissonance between the individual's understanding of what is good and what he or she is or can ever hope to be—God does not have a body with bodily functions and physical desires; God is pure and holy; God does not need anything from humans, etc.

Reflecting on the work of psychologist Alice Miller as it pertains to children and abuse, Pattison points out the "worrying degree of similarity and resonance" revealed by a comparison of the attributes of the Christian god and the belief characteristics that lead to the development of shamed children—a feeling of duty produces love; hatred can be done away with by forbidding it; parents deserve respect simply because they are parents; children are undeserving of respect simply because they are children.[16] Pattison writes, "The Christian God as imaged in the majority tradition and still described, discussed, and worshipped is in many ways a guarantor and contributor to abusive parenting. This God continues to be the 'official' deity of Christianity, ever to be worshipped, honoured, and adored, even by the most shamed members of the human race."[17]

While Pattison recognizes that not all who encounter the monarchical god of the Christian scriptures will incorporate its characteristics into their psyche as shame, he argues that "religious images and ideas can have a baleful effect upon the minds of people who are receptive to them," and that "the uncritical propagation of images and ideas that can harmfully fund and reinforce the shamed imagination as well as legitimating shaming practices and attitudes in families and wider society cannot simply be uncritically accepted."[18]

## Kinder, Gentler Sin?

While the concept of sin within Christianity is inextricably bound up with the theology of the Fall, a different understanding has grown up in reaction to a distaste for original sin and its implications. Sin has come to be understood, particularly within liberal, mainline Christianity, as the result of a direct, responsible turning away from God—the result of actions we choose to participate in that are directly against what we believe God would want us to do. I can remember preaching sermons on the importance of making decisions based on one's baptismal vows. The implication was that in anything we do, we must first consider its impact on our relationship with god, even if we hold a non-theistic understanding of what that term means. The intentionality of this kind of sin stands in contrast to the original sin purported to have been ladled into our hearts long before we were born.

A young woman once wept in my office as she struggled with what she feared were the implications of higher education. Having completed a second degree and failing in her attempts to conceive a second child, she believed she was being punished by God for her "self-centred choice." Even liberal worldviews might construe an experience like this one as God's way of being heard in her life, asking questions such as "What do you think God/the Spirit is saying to you through this experience?" Despite her intellectual rejection of a vengeful God, the woman—a long-time member of a mainline denomination—continued to be haunted by her strong evangelical background, which had convinced her she had failed to live up to the expectations God had for her as a woman. Of course, had she had a second child before going back to school and never accomplished her professional goals, she would have been equally able to assert that she had not met God's expectations for her. God's expectations (more commonly referred to as "God's will") are always too easy to hang on our own understandings of guilt, shame, and the things we really want to do. It's as easy to rationalize that our choices are bad as it is to rationalize that they are good, and our humanly constructed God stands in the wings ever willing to play the perfect foil for those rationalizations. Liberals may like to think that they've done away with the nasty aspects of a judgmental god, but the experience of those who wrestle with him is often that he is just as harsh and judgmental as ever.

## Squirm, Baby, Squirm

*Let us confess our sins before God.*

Just the other day, I sat through a prayer of confession given by a prominent American religious leader. It was a good five minutes long and addressed many things that are deeply important to me—the challenges inherent in our society and the sense of despair I often feel in not being able to address them or reduce my own impact on the world, its resources, and its people to the extent I believe might finally make a difference. That's the thing about a good prayer of confession. It's an opportunity for us to unburden ourselves, to face the realities from which we too often shy away, to acknowledge that we are not all we wish we were; the reality of *that* is, simply, that we cannot do it all. Because the words envelop an entire community, they can, even as they condemn, ease the personal burden. And for those who haven't felt it . . . well, a good prayer of confession can be a real wake-up call.

But many congregations are doing away with the prayer of confession because they find the theology that supports it problematic. Often, that's terribly true. Put it in the wrong hands, frame it with the wrong intent, fill it with the wrong set of wrongs and the prayer of confession dis-eases in many ways.

Perhaps, like many, you find prayers of confession insulting. Rare is the person who wants to sit in a room with a bunch of other people and either listen to someone else tell her sins or be handed a bulletin outlining them so everyone can join in together and read them out loud. We feel uncomfortable being lumped in with all the other sinners in the world. Besides, we know what we've done wrong or where we've fallen short this past week, and it's been a long time since whatever *that* was actually showed up in print. Most of the time, what we're handed to read doesn't seem to have anything to do with us, and even if it does, it's so remote as to not disturb us that much. Because most of the harmful actions we perpetrate upon one another and the planet are unintentional, we don't see the sin in which we are encased until long after we've committed it.

To raise a contrasting, more biblically grounded perspective, I'd suggest that perhaps we are discomfited by prayers of confession because they stare at us with a constant accusation: we're indifferent to the ultimate condemnation of our brothers and sisters, whom we have not brought to the mercy seat.[19] If we have even a shred of belief that God's forgiveness is essential to right relationship, then to refuse to proselytize to those who do not seek that forgiveness is to consign them to a life that experiences neither healing nor hope.[20] It suggests to us that we do not care about our brothers and sisters. True, I'm baiting you here, but you don't get to have it both ways. Either God's forgiveness is necessary, and you seriously attend to the task of bringing your sinful companions to confession so they can get into right relationship with God, or it isn't necessary. Period. Participating in a prayer of confession every week suggests that confession and absolution of some kind are essential. Sacramental Christian denominations reinforce the belief that this is so. If you agree that's the case, get out there and haul your friends into the pews. If you believe that's not the case, you're participating each week in a prayer that goes contrary to your belief. No wonder you get antsy.

## Justice or Justice?

A prayer of confession, like most theological constructs, is much more complex than the unsuspecting layperson might expect. Set up to bring individuals back into right relationship, confession can be understood to mirror the processes of justice and therefore function in either a retributive or a restorative manner. Of course, as is more traditionally argued, confession may have nothing to do with justice at all but simply be the obligatory element leading to the outflow of God's mercy; in other words, confession is the recognition of our complicity in whatever is wrong with the world and/or ourselves, and once that recognition is brought before God, it's met with a benevolent love. Are prayers of confession and the apparent readiness of God's mercy just a simple way for us to let ourselves off the hook? Or are they a complex playing out of a process of justice that helps us find a way toward wholeness in ourselves and our relationships?

In retributive systems of justice, a wrongdoer is expected to make reparations to the state, the government, or the king or queen—whoever is keeping guard over the civil practice of the land. Those reparations are to be made at a magnitude that roughly equals that of the offence.* The state enforces the justice system by bringing offenders to it, clarifying their guilt, meting out punishment commensurate with their crimes, and overseeing the discharge of that judgment. Someone accused of stealing the property of another may be sentenced to time in prison, leaving the wronged party with little or no expectation that she will be repaid or her property returned. Reparation for the offence is made to the state, despite the fact that the original offence was made against an individual.

In a restorative system of justice, the impact of the crime on the victim and on the offender's family and support network are the objects of assessment. Establishing a way to right those broken relationships is the key to restorative justice ideals. Agreements are forged between

---

* "An eye for an eye" is the biblical imperative shared by so many faith traditions. It sets the tone for a retributive justice system, but in its most primitive form, it leads to gross abuses of human rights.

those who have been harmed and those who created the harm as to how the affected relationships can best be healed. If someone has had his or her property stolen, that individual would be a significant participant in the discussion regarding the punishment of the offender, and that punishment would likely include either the return of the stolen property or restitution equivalent to its value.

The payment for sins against God has appeared through the ages to be more retributive than restorative, but a closer examination would suggest otherwise. In most situations of sin, the defendant—sinner—is accused of having offended God, not just the community or the church. The offence is seen as a direct action against God.

Restitution for such an offence has always been understood to have been made to God—that is, in legal terms, directly to the plaintiff. That suggests it is restorative rather than retributive. The process, regardless of the punishment meted out, is an attempt to bring two parties back into relationship.

Even in situations that present the bleakest examples of Christian extremes—inquisitions and heresy trials—the actions of the officials of the church can be interpreted as attempts to get the guilty party to confess and be reconciled to God and to the community. Someone accused of heresy and found guilty by ecclesial authorities, for instance, would often be sentenced in a manner that sought to bring him back to the church and into right relationship with God. Penance, confession, silence, banishment, and torture could all be used in an attempt to effect change in the individual and extract a confession. Death was the sentence only when all other attempts didn't work. Abhorrent though they truly are, even current laws enacted by governments seeking to control the sexual lives of their citizens by restricting the practice of homosexuality could be argued by proponents to be attempts at spiritual and communal reconciliation.

Many of the so-called offences against God are those that once threatened the most important elements of a community's life in the period during which its religious systems developed. It is very likely that because of the importance of community in early societies, any behaviour that led to a breach of communal values or threatened communal harmony would be considered an offence against the deity to whom the community paid homage. Beyond being understood as the mere settling of disputes between neighbours, such wrongs achieved a greater, cosmic importance. Changing the plaintiff—that is, making the deity the offended party rather than an individual or group or community—ramped up the seriousness and the perceived consequences to the community. With God offended, everyone was at risk. Any issue elevated to a cosmic level demanded extreme, costly compensation. The guilty party could be physically maimed or killed, or a member of his or her family could be killed.

A community evolves, though, and what threatens its stability and cohesion changes over time. Laws that are considered to be against a god or gods, or that are thought to have an impact on the cosmic order, have a much higher staying power than other laws. Because of their particularly costly punishments, such laws can end up being counterproductive to community, destroying rather than enhancing what they were meant to preserve.

In Nadeem Aslam's novel *The Wasted Vigil*, all the situations described, although woven into a fictional story, actually happened in Afghanistan during the course of the Russian occupation and the Taliban regime. In one vignette, Marcus, an English expatriate, is forced to watch the stoning of his wife, Qatrina, an outspoken doctor revered in the community. She is stoned in the town square, her burqa tied in a knot and used as a bag to drag her body away. Married twenty-nine years earlier by a female imam during a time that celebrated and worked toward strengthening the rights of women, Marcus and Qatrina are victims of a shift in religious understanding. The Taliban refuses to recognize women in leadership roles, and the marriage of Marcus and Qatrina is therefore considered invalid. Since anyone who has sexual relations outside of marriage is committing adultery according to Islamic law, the consequence for Qatrina and Marcus is her death by stoning.[21]

At one time, the law that prohibited sex outside of sanctioned marriages may have been a good law, inasmuch as it preserved the community. Remember that without the ability to stick together as a community, humans would never have survived the chaotic and harsh realities they once were up against. Though seeming severe to us, the penalties for breaking such a law may be the very reason we're around today. To make sure behaviour with such potentially catastrophic consequences was eliminated from fragile community networks, leaders elevated it to the level of an offence against God. In some of the more heinous acts of "justice" now meted out within human community, reparations on a cosmic scale are being made for offences that are no longer the divisive threats to human community they once were. It does not matter whether the relationship is a productive or stabilizing factor within the community, as the relationship between Marcus and Qatrina was.

Although what was essential long ago is not essential now, some transgressions are still identified as offences against God. Rather than being dealt with privately or in relatively minor litigious ways, these breaches of the law continue to demand the same penalties as were required in that previous milieu. Such a scenario can be imagined only inside a religious framework and carried out within a religious fundamentalist state. The establishment of God as the plaintiff turns any law into a worst-case scenario. Unless a community is willing to retract what it has previously said is important to God, it will be unable to reduce the penalties associated with laws that are no longer in the best interests of its members.

*Go to Hell. Go Directly to Hell.*
*Do Not Pass Go. Do Not Collect $200.*

In Roman Catholicism, the gravest sins are mortal sins, those that are offences against God. They tear at the relationship between the individual and God, and if reparation is not made, the offender is ultimately consigned to hell. Fortunately, according to Catholic teaching, you can't commit a mortal sin by accident. You have to know and understand the consequences and willingly commit the offence. (If you didn't commit the sin on purpose, it is reduced to a venial sin, the kind that will not cause someone to lose eternal salvation.) The only way someone who commits a mortal sin can make it to heaven is through confession and absolution.

Sins named by Paul and referenced in the Roman Catholic Catechism include "[a]dultery, fornication, uncleanness, lasciviousness, idolatry, witchcraft, hatred, variance, emulations, wrath, strife, seditions, heresies, envyings, murders, drunkenness, revellings, and such like" (Gal. 5:19). The Roman Catholic Church does not publish a list of mortal sins, but anything it determines to be a "grave matter" (that is, related in some way to the Ten Commandments) is subject to the same consequences.

While readers may conjure up murder and rape when they think of what could get someone cast into hell by the Catholic Church, many will also know that masturbation and homosexual relations, once considered threats to the life of the community, were understood as offences against God. Any sexual behaviour that did not plant the male seed—believed to contain the whole human being—where it could have the opportunity to be nurtured into a viable baby became an offence. Although our scientific understanding has long since set aside this archaic belief, the Roman Catholic Church cannot simply choose to overlook a "crime" it has repeatedly argued to be a sin against God. Catholics have bound themselves so closely to their doctrine that, with the exception of a few historic retractions, they have found themselves unable or unwilling to disentangle themselves, even when it becomes clear that it is no longer a positive influence on the life and health of the community.

From time to time, the Vatican decides on other "grave matters" and creates new mortal sins that have arisen out of contemporary civilization. In March 2008, seven new deadly sins were added to the list: environmental pollution, genetic manipulation, accumulating excessive wealth, inflicting poverty, drug trafficking and consumption, morally debatable experiments, and violation of fundamental rights of human nature.[22]

I invite to you consider some other grave sins identified more recently by the Congregation for the Doctrine of the Faith (CDF). In July 2010, the Vatican issued a statement clarifying its terms for dealing with sexual abuses against children by members of the priesthood and outlining the moral consequences of such abuse.[23] Once again, however, it neglected to pronounce upon its own grave error, that of covering up cases of abuse, and even refrained from accepting responsibility for inadequate oversight. It also failed to offer any changes to the ordinances regarding the priesthood that many felt worthy of consideration—eliminating celibacy, for instance.[24]

In its statement, the CDF made another grave error by naming two more actions as mortal sins. Listed alongside—and thereby linked to—the sexual predation of children by priests are the recording and disclosure of sacramental confessions, and the attempted ordination of women to the priesthood ("attempted," of course, because the church denies such a possibility). One has only to consider the speed with which information can be shared globally on social networks to realize how dangerous the disclosure of confessions might be to any individual's reputation. But is it worthy of eternal damnation? That's another question. Is it on a par with the sexual predation of children? Certainly it would have to be a particularly heinous disclosure to approach that level of depravity. And the ordination of women? It might be obvious to some why this is a threat against community, but I believe it has more to do with the threat to a male power-archy than the fear that suppressed or ignored maternal instincts would threaten the continuation of the tribe. Naming it a grave sin to participate in activities that raise this issue before the church and its people reinforces just how threatening the idea of women's ordained leadership continues to be to the patriarchal system.[25]

### It's Not All Bad

There are aspects of forgiveness and the role of the confessor that can be of significant support and healing in an individual's journey. In the Roman Catholic confessional, with a priest acting as mediator and God as the symbolic plaintiff—the injured party—prayer can serve as the first step toward wholeness. While the terminology is outside the traditional Catholic theology around the sacrament of confession, we could say that the individual is psychologically moved into the "healing circle," where the confessor may attend to the broken relationship between her or him and God. In this manner, with the act of confession serving as a component of reparation, the laity participates to the furthest extent possible in the process that will bring him or her back into right relationship with God. It is the priest, through the consecration of the Eucharist, who completes the transaction, symbolically placing the person's sins on Jesus while his crucifixion is taking place, and thereby including the sins in those for which Jesus died. The individual, through this intense act, is absolved and moved back into right relationship with God and the community.

### Mainlining Confession

Mainline denominations have been perfecting the communal confession of sin for generations, a form perhaps meant to offer a participatory feel while dealing with all sin in one fell swoop. Perhaps it is often a dreadfully lacklustre part of the service because shared intonation of sin is not exactly a cause for enthusiastic effort. Or perhaps the sins listed are far from the shallow pettiness and self-centredness that would truly convict most of us. The five-minute prayer of confession I mentioned earlier listed a whole gamut of ailments within society, not one of which I was directly challenged to do anything about (nor would I have been *able* to do anything about). It referred to huge motherhood issues—poverty, distant conflicts in the world, and generalized convictions about my being "too hard on myself." I have written, read, and sat through confessions that were blistering damnations of the world's chronic problems but, upon reflection, served to clear each person present from even the slightest culpability.

If I participate in a communal prayer of confession that decries our penchant for material goods, our selfish wants in relationship, our callous attitudes toward the needy in our society, and the impact of a global economy on the marginalized in our communities and around the world, I am being offered an opportunity to look at my complicity in systems that continue to oppress individuals, groups, and whole nations. But if I am not also offered ways in which to change my participation in those systems, the prayer alone is too often deemed to be enough. A lack of tangible accountability and the rote recitation of impersonal prayers, even within a framework that posits a perfect, judgment-seeking god, can ease us away from any personal ownership of the issues raised. At the conclusion of the eloquent prayer of confession in which I participated, the liturgist absolved me—and everyone else present—of all sin in the name of the Trinitarian God. Whether we'd given two seconds of thought to the concerns raised or not, we were forgiven. It is standard practice to do so. But what does it accomplish other than to separate us further from the concerns? I am encouraged to believe that I don't need to do much about any of those crucial issues beyond think about them in a confessional way on a Sunday morning—as though merely bringing our own shortcomings and humanity's failures to mind is so burdensome and painful that, having endured it, we can be absolved there and then.

But even if, in real terms, little productive change is brought about by a confessional system that absolves us merely by virtue of our participating in it, there may be some liturgical truth to its liberating value. Recall the concept of restorative justice. In that system, God as plaintiff becomes a participant in our "hearing," in the circle of reconciliation. Our confession, which is very personal and private, and the penance we are asked to make through prayer become the tools that repair our relationship with God and, through that, with the community. Using a model that demands concrete action on the part of the defendant, the ritualized confessional prayer serves as that action. It is the symbolic act that works in the same way as real acts do in a restorative circle: it helps us become whole through the process.

If we are trying to "make it right with God," then perhaps that is enough. If, however, what we are hoping to achieve is more intimate and more global—if we are attempting to return to right relationship with ourselves, others, and a community that is integral to our spiritual and psychological well-being—then a liturgical squaring off of our debts is not enough. For many of us, as we come to recognize the depth of our complicity in the issues facing the world—global warming, inequity in food distribution, the growth of corporate power and its effects on communities and cultures, etc.—our level of cognitive dissonance reaches a critical point. How do we keep working toward healing relationships and a sustainable planet when our energies are finite, and our personal needs, and those of the individuals around us, are urgent and cannot be dismissed? The corporate prayer of confession can no longer address the brokenness we experience and of which we are a part, but I am convinced that the church has a role to play as we work toward wholeness as individuals and as a global community.

## THANKSGIVING

*When I walk through this world all alone, You are with me.*
*When the song that I sing's not my own, Your voice lifts me.*
*So I know You're not just there, in the great beyond somewhere,*
*For Your voice, Your love, Your song have found me here.*
                                                *Evernear.*

Christian thanksgiving has traditionally poured out of hearts that believe the source of all the blessings in the world, the granter and promise of goodness, is the loving, benevolent, all-knowing God. An eighth-century collation of the Psalms, meant to assist monastic prayer, identifies more prayers of thanksgiving than any other type. Early monastics practised reading and reciting the Psalms in the order in which they were found in the Psalter (often as quickly as possible, with a view to getting through as many as they could). One early guide to praying the Psalms, the eighth-century *De Psalmorum Usu*, divides them into categories to assist the devotee in choosing the correct one for the situation at hand. In the breakdown, in addition to the Alleluia Psalms, there are thirteen that deal with thanksgiving—by far the largest category.[26]

In mainline churches today, thanksgiving prayers distinguish themselves from prayers of adoration by focusing on what has happened in the individual's life or in the life of the community or world, rather than on the attributes of God. The general nature of the category allows thanksgiving to pop up in a number of different places in a standard service: in response to forgiveness following a prayer of confession; as a celebration for the gift of scripture before the readings are presented; as a general reflection on God's benevolence; or as a response to specific blessings experienced in one's life. Thanksgiving is often a significant portion of what is referred to in many churches as the pastoral prayer. (In mainline denominational congregations, a single prayer known as a pastoral or community prayer often brings together prayers of thanksgiving and supplication, with the latter broken into intercession and petition. While these prayers are similar in their underlying assumptions, they each offer a different perspective to the congregational gathering.)

The prayer of thanksgiving is one of the few opportunities in mainline denominational worship, outside of hymnody, for congregants to identify the goodness they have experienced and to celebrate the place of God in that goodness. Because we experience goodness in a multitude of ways—personally, communally, and in situations unfolding around the world—the prayer can cover a wide range of topics. While usually read for the congregation, it often includes a time of silence, when the participants can name their own thanksgivings.

The Great Thanksgiving, which is included in a communion service, reflects the earlier tradition of thanking God for belief and forgiveness. Typically, it moves through the creation and salvific history of the world as seen through the eyes of a believer. Beginning with an offer of thanksgiving for the act of creation, it carries on through the history of God's fidelity to the Jewish people; expresses gratitude for the undeserved gift of Jesus as experienced through his life, prophetic ministry, and the act of atonement made possible through his death; and culminates in thanksgiving for the ongoing gift of the Spirit, poured out upon Jesus' believers. All of this is unmerited in the eyes of the believer, and gratitude and thanksgiving, mingled together with praise, spill from the lips of the liturgist, who is intent on ensuring that these feelings also well up in the hearts of participants. The prayer concludes with a narrative of the Last Supper and the intoning of the sacrificial words attributed to Jesus at that final meal. It is drama of the highest order, meant to twin with and build upon the early praise section of the service.

Our own thanksgivings usually veer toward the ordinary, as celebrated in Sarah McLachlan's "Ordinary Miracle" in the hit movie *Charlotte's Web*. The sky snowing, seeds growing, a sun that rises every day, and a night that folds us into darkness—these are the subject of much of our personal thanksgiving on ordinary days. On days that are not so run-of-the-mill, thanksgiving can turn to the news of a job after lengthy unemployment, a peaceful death at the conclusion of a healthy, celebrated life, the birth of a child, or the winning of rights or freedoms for the oppressed. These are the kinds of things often pointed to as signs of God's goodness. Our fragile confidence is bolstered by insubstantial proofs, however, even as we bask in simple gifts such as these. Yet because of the innumerable times things *don't* work out for us, gratitude toward a personal deity is troubling.

## Free Grace, Cold Comfort

Perhaps the first time I was really struck by the impact of the word "grace" was while watching Susan Nelles, a young nurse, address a gathering of her colleagues, her peers, and the press. Nelles had just been cleared of murdering four infants at the Toronto Hospital for Sick Children. After years spent defending herself, she reflected upon how vulnerable anyone in a caring profession is and asked those in her audience to consider the ordeal she had just been put through and recognize their own vulnerability. In an effort to bring home the "it could happen to you" reality of her situation, she asked those gathered, should they ever see someone similarly accused, to remember the familiar phrase "There but for the grace of God go I." It is a statement of thanksgiving for a perceived divinely granted protection.

That phrase has become a cliché. We think it when we read news of tragic accidents and houses burning down, when children are born with physical ailments that will limit their lives to a few days of pain and suffering, when someone develops early-onset Alzheimer's or macular degeneration or cancer. Even when we wouldn't dare say it out loud—in the presence of someone who embraces life despite incredible physical limitations or shies from it because of chronic pain—it runs through our minds. And both when we say it aloud and when we don't, those who catch our eyes nod in agreement and understanding.

The cliché "dodged the bullet" allows us to share the relief we feel when we are lucky enough to avoid a fate we certainly wouldn't choose. "There but for the grace of God go I" seems to say the same thing, but in stark contrast to the camaraderie of the bullet remark, the implication here is that the other person has not merited grace, has offended God, is deserving of affliction. It is Job's friends come to needle him into acknowledging his guilt, the reason for the death of his livestock, the demise of his children, the destruction of his world. In essence, the approved, acknowledged, acceptable state to be in is a state of grace; God has noticed us and bestowed grace upon us. If we have not been noticed by God, we are outside that grace. If we have lost God's favour, we have fallen from grace—and we've lost God's protection. By linking her arrest for the deaths of infants to the phrase, Nelles implies that it happened because God refused to provide her safe passage. Exposed, bereft of God's grace, she fell into the pit. Without that grace, the phrase suggests, any one of us would.

When we use the idea of grace in our thanksgivings, we find ourselves back on the topic of sin. Grace is the flip side of the sin coin. But when we're talking about sin, it's better to be an operative—that is, to have the responsibility for making your own decisions about your actions—than to have your actions pronounced upon by a remote deity with no choice in the matter. Being a pawn in some game or a puppet on a cosmic stage, jerked and bumped around to amuse the gods, like those who are suddenly cast from grace into darkness—

that's harsh. It's something they have no control over, and, like Job's, it's much bleaker terrain than one they might have made of their own choosing. Christian doctrine pertaining to sin and grace assumes our primal sinful nature and so justifies a worldview in which we can be the recipients of tremendous harm at the hand of a capricious god. When we use the phrase "There but for the grace of God go I," we place ourselves on that cosmic gameboard, claim the victor's position, and denigrate—unwittingly, for the most part—those who need our compassion, not an ugly theological justification for their realities.

## Getting Our Lines Crossed

Prayers of thanksgiving and supplication reinforce the premise that God is the provider of all that is good. Everything good—from the cessation of conflict in a war-torn area of the world to the recovery of an individual after surgery—can be seen as the work of God's hand. It is a warm and beautiful way to see the world, and very comforting.

On too many occasions, a direct line can be drawn between our gratitude for good things that happen to us or around us and our despair at those things that tear lives apart. One winter evening, a small boy perished in a tragic fire in one of the cities that rings the metropolis in which I live. The radio news clip included an interview with a neighbour at whose home the child had played the previous evening. Devastated, she shared the intensity of the family's grief.[27] At the conclusion of the piece, the news anchor introduced the next story by saying: "And now, from tragedy to triumph . . ." Unwittingly, one hopes, he drew that disastrous line. The next item, about a woman who was lost in a snowbank for many hours and had not been expected to be found alive, also included a clip. This one was from the woman's husband. In it, he shared his belief that his wife was still alive only because God had reached down his hand and wrapped her in it.[28]

I have no right to take issue with someone finding solace, encourage-ment, strength—even the reason for an outcome—in his or her faith. I do have a problem, however, with a national broadcasting service legiti-mizing such a belief by airing it in a news piece. And I have a seriously big problem when that piece is juxtaposed with a story of tragedy, creat-ing the implication that God didn't intervene in the former event, either because he was oblivious to the suffering or, worse, because he chose out of indifference not to respond in a catastrophic moment of need. The worst implication of all is that God made that catastrophe happen as part of a grand, unrevealed plan, using a child and a woman as pawns in order to teach someone else about the strength of his power. When we tell these stories as if God were looking out for the woman and not for the child, we reinforce our personal sense of security. One person has God's blessing; another doesn't. If we say the kind of thing the much-relieved husband said, we need to be aware of the implications; when we get right down to it, what we're saying is that all we really care about is that God take care of us. Of course, that's what religion has always been about.

Our prayers of thanksgiving reinforce a system of religious belief that melds together our real world with ideals we attribute to a divine being. Philosopher Bertrand Russell, writing over a hundred years ago in his essay "A Free Man's Worship," explored how we weave the two together, *mis*placing all our ideals into the hands of a created god. He posits that we came to adulate power out of the impotence we felt in the face of nature. Having created a supernatural god as power's ulti-mate form, we must find ways to appease it, and it makes sense to do so as long as power is our only ideal.[29] As soon as we begin to differen-tiate other ideals—compassion, kindness, truth, peace, and joy—and separate them from the ideal of power, we find they are at odds with the often terrible and capricious power of the god we have created.

We have to either work this into our worldview or let the worldview go. Praying the old way doesn't work, because what we conjured in the past was that god of power. It is this god to whom we have appealed for strength and courage, not because we have found that it embodied those things but because we gave it the power to bequeath them.

And so, as Russell shows, one of two things happens if we cannot let go of the supremacy of God: either we refuse to recognize the importance of other ideals and continue to hold power as supreme, celebrating the survival of the fittest in its most cruel form, or we mingle God's power with the ideals we hold to be right, believing that "in some hidden manner, the world of fact is really harmonious with the world of ideals" and pushing to the fore the hand of God, for good or ill, as it writes a course of history we are incapable of understanding.[30] A woman survives an incredible ordeal and praise be to God. A child perishes in a fire and God's will be done. There but for the grace of God go I.

## SUPPLICATION

*holiness known and unknown*
*into the hollow chalice*
*of our deepest need*
*you pour yourself*
*until our*
*cup*
*is full*
*full*
*full*
*full*
*so may it be, amen.*

On the flip side of thanksgiving resides supplication, the act of entreating on our own behalf (petition) or the behalf of others (intercession). It is here the integrity of thanksgiving is tested, as we cast our needs and desires into, we presume, the hands of a benevolent being or power. If we get what we've prayed for, we can easily be grateful. If we don't, we're stuck trying to figure out what that means.

In a worship setting, we get to supplication after thanksgiving. After lives have been examined, places that might have experienced a divine touch identified, and the appropriate thanksgivings dispatched, we move on to the idea of supplication. It's the kind of prayer we most often think of when we think of the word "prayer," because it involves the request for something from God. They are prayers that focus predominantly on our responsibility to place our needs before God and God's ability to respond to them.

The dictionary suggests that supplication is about being humble.[31] I wonder if that's what Joel Osteen, author of *Your Best Life Now: 7 Steps to Living at Your Full Potential,*[32] thinks when he thinks supplication. The king of what is known as prosperity Christianity, Osteen believes in asking for things and asking big. Way big. The bigger the better, as far as he is concerned. And it's all biblically reinforced when you read the lines that tell you how generously God is going to bless you during your life on earth, and how much God wants you to ask for those blessings.

But the prayers posted on the "Pray Together" page of Osteen's website by his followers don't have the same bravado that shines out at you with his broad smile. Most of them are desperate. Fear and confusion press his devotees to distant computer screens in the hope that God will answer. Fear of abusive partners, of losing loved ones, of upcoming court dates, of financial burdens. Underneath each posting there is a little box you can check if you'll pray for that individual and a count of the number of people already praying for him or her. I stare at the empty boxes and tallies and think only of the empty hopes. Even in this forum, most are alone. The humility is there. The earnestness is there. Where, IJN,* is God?[33]

Prayers of supplication are about believing in a supernatural god who is the *source*, *agent*, and *promise* of goodness for you, and about hoping that your requests will be met sympathetically and answered with a resounding yes. Supplication is asking, sometimes pleading, for our needs and desires, or those of others, to be fulfilled. But since we are early taught that God's ways are not our ways, that God's wisdom is beyond our comprehension, and that his overall plan is hidden from our view, we're never secure about being answered with that yes. The foolproof methods and guaranteed results touted by many a television preacher or zealous author would suggest otherwise, yet when someone puts up a website on which women are posting that they and their children are being beaten by the men in their lives, there should be some accountability beyond the promise that an invisible being is going to provide the answer. Doesn't there need to be a little more offered than just hope? Joel and Victoria Osteen might, in fact, do that. Maybe they step in and provide assistance, a safe place, shelter. Maybe they see themselves as instruments of God when they do. That would be awesome, and I'd be grateful. Someone suffering abuse needs more than prayer. She needs help.

I have little illusion about the realities people face in their lives. We are overwhelmed when our own and others' psychological and emotional challenges threaten the harmony we'd like to count on. For some, that discomfort is the result of occasional disruptions in their otherwise privileged lives—economic downturns, relationship challenges, bereavement, illness. For others, disruption is a constant

---

* Most of the prayers end with IJN or IJNA: "in Jesus' name" or "in Jesus' name, amen."

shadow with which they live on a daily basis as they struggle with the challenges of chronic physical or mental illness; economic, cultural, and intellectual poverty; oppression; and emotional scarring. We often feel alone in the struggle, whether accustomed to it or not.

Prayer is a contract for hope, not results. If we don't see proof of God as the source of good or the giver of good, we fall back on the promise of *eventual* good, the assurance that everything will work itself out in the end—sometimes the very, very end—and that we'll get over this hurdle and the next and the next. Many of us are calmed if we're able to believe that the supreme ruler of the universe is watching out for us, holding us in the palm of his hand. Even if what we are experiencing is particularly horrific, handing our fear over to a benevolent god—our God—makes it endurable, helps us find our place in that cosmic story. When we enter into prayer, we become a participant in that story, a party to its contractual promise, and we can be deeply, powerfully, physically, and emotionally soothed as a result.

Some time ago, I was involved for two years in a drug trial for the delivery system for a therapeutic migraine medication. The drug itself was already approved as an effective treatment for migraines, but the study was assessing whether a nasal spray would allow the drug to begin constricting blood vessels more quickly, thereby relieving symptoms faster than a pill could.

Throughout the study, whenever I got a migraine, I was to spray the mystery mist—either the drug or a placebo—up my nose and keep track of the results. If it did not work within an hour, I could take backup medication to relieve the pain. The problem was that if I didn't take the backup medication at the onset of a migraine, it had a much-reduced effect. So I often found myself deep in the darkness of headaches from which I could get no relief. A placebo *effect*—the experience of results without the ingestion, or in this case, inhalation, of the actual drug— would have been nice. Alas, *wanting* one didn't *produce* one.

And that's the problem with placebo effects. Even if I experienced relief from the salt water I was obviously spraying up my nose, those positive results would likely have disappeared if someone told me it was only water and not the meds I needed. Prescribing placebos is an ethical minefield in medicine right now for just that reason. Some conditions respond quite favourably when patients are given only placebos. Why would you give your patient a drug—perhaps a costly one—when she can get the same effect with sugar tablets or a saltwater spray? Do you withhold from a patient information about medication you are prescribing him if his knowing what it is will mitigate its effect?

The same ethical question has faced the church for decades, if not centuries. But in its wisdom, it has doled out a placebo prescription for the supernatural *source*, *agent*, and *promise* god that has treated our insecurities, checked our anger, and kept our existential panic at bay. Having recognized that there is no potency to the supernatural pill we've been swallowing, will we lose the strength its placebo effect once gave us? Will we find ourselves paralyzed by fear? Will we unleash unforeseen levels of violence because we are no longer afraid of divine retribution? Will the very real consolation we have known disappear when we accept that its source is imaginary?

## Intercessory Prayer

Many understand the idea of intercession as the act of praying on behalf of others who are in need, whether or not they are able to pray for themselves. American Christian author Philip Yancey begins his book on prayer by relaying a story of being injured in a fall while jogging in Russia and sending out an email asking his friends to pray for him. The expectation is that those prayers—like people checking off the little box on the Osteens' website—will make a difference. Yancey—who obviously survived his ordeal—found solace and strength in the belief that friends and family were praying for him. As far as he is concerned, those benefits are directly tied to the practice of prayer.

Technically, that's not really what intercession has been about, although it is certainly the most commonly accepted understanding now. The idea of intercession grew out of the belief that there were individuals who *could not* pray for themselves—the unbaptized or the unsaved. The devout are, for these hampered individuals, the only chance for their prayers to be brought before God. In fact, in some denominations, even the devout believers themselves are considered unworthy of bringing their petitions before God and so must work exclusively through the intercession of Jesus, ever on the right hand of God to plead for his people. Other denominations teach that people cannot approach even Jesus directly, and therefore they direct their prayers to a variety of saints, including and especially Jesus' mother, Mary, who in turn may intercede for them, so that Jesus will be more inclined to intercede between them and God.

Intercession is the act of bringing the needs of someone with no right to ask for help to a person who holds the power to alter the situation. The intercessor steps into the breach, often a risky place, on behalf of someone who cannot do it for himself. In biblical lore, Abraham stepped up and argued with God on behalf of the good people who lived in Sodom, pressing his argument forward over and over again until God relented (Gen. 18:23–33); Moses railed against God's decisions as he interceded for the people of Israel (Exod. 32:11–14); and Jesus prayed for God to forgive those who crucified him (Luke 23:34). The person—or in this case, God—with all the power is approached by someone bold enough to do so. It is a courageous act.

The orthodox understanding of Christianity requires that all prayer be funnelled through Jesus as intercessor. That's the reason prayer concludes with "in Jesus' name [IJN], amen." As long as we acknowledge our dependence upon Jesus for this task, we avoid the pitfall about which Friedrich Heiler was so concerned—that we be moved to pray directly to God and thus unwittingly eliminate the need for the central meaning of Christianity. It's classic mythology/theology: a mighty and powerful god, approachable only by one upon whom he has bestowed favour. The rest of us, unworthy, can only hope that the favoured one will take our requests forward. While the Reformation removed the need for an intercessor in the form of a priest, the intercessory role of Jesus has remained an important element of Christianity.

Jesus' act of intercession takes our requests to God. *Our* act of intercession holds the concerns of others before Jesus. If the other is not saved in the evangelical tradition or baptized in the Roman Catholic tradition, prayer offered by a believer matches the traditional role of the intercessor after the manner of Abraham and Moses.

## Petition

Communal prayers of petition are meant to lift the people's own concerns before God, but these too must go through the proper channels—they just happen to be shorter channels if you've remembered to get everything lined up in advance of your need. Joseph Scriven certainly knew what to do, writing in the much-loved hymn "What a Friend We Have in Jesus" that no matter what your sins, griefs, or burdens, all will be well if you simply take it to the Lord in prayer. Jesus will take it from there.

In mainline denominations, interestingly enough, asking for something from God is the predominant form of prayer, despite a persistent ridicule by liberal Christians of the breadth of subject matter that can be found in the prayers of their evangelical brothers and sisters. While calling on God for help in some way or another is certainly a major aspect of a faith that understands God to be all-powerful, evangelicals, in fact, enhance their prayer life with far more prayers of the adoration sort than do liberals. These prayers ask nothing of God or Jesus but serve simply to acknowledge, experience, and strengthen the relationship individuals have with the one they acknowledge as lord of their life. Perhaps the ridicule comes from a sense of inadequacy on the part of many liberal worship leaders, who, because of their conflicted beliefs about a personal or interventionist God, couldn't hold a candle to the passion and integrity with which many evangelical prayers are offered.

## God! Stop the Rain!

Weather, ever the blessing and bane of human existence, has exerted its profound and devastating effects in dramatic fashion over the past few years. Flooding in Pakistan forced four million people from their homes; ten thousand schools were destroyed or taken over for emergency shelters; families, uprooted, searched for anything that could provide some stability in a country under water. Australian cities found themselves deluged with floods that swept away cars, bridges, animals, and yes, people. The year after these tragic events was even worse, with at least eight disasters topping the billion-dollar mark before half the sheets had been torn off our desk calendars.[34]

The response of religious institutions was to ask for financial aid and, through partners and aid organizations, to attempt to mitigate the overwhelming challenges facing those who had lost everything. The Presbyterian Church USA posted on its website a request for people to pray for a change in weather in Pakistan so that much-needed relief supplies could reach the areas for which they were destined.[35] It was similar to many requests and prayers raised around the world, and very close to a prayer request that, in the late nineteenth century, sparked unsettling controversy.

That discussion grew heated around the question of whether prayer really could effect changes in the material world. As the discussion ran its course, it would trigger both a growth in scepticism and the renewed evangelical fervour of the "answered prayer" movement.

The rumbling thunder began in 1860, when, during a particularly wet season in Britain, Church of England officials prepared a fairly standard prayer, similar to those often sent out to churches in situations of national concern. It called on all people of faith to pray that the rains would cease. One cleric, Charles Kingsley, a celebrated novelist and social reformer, refused the request, arguing that such a prayer was asking God to change laws that had been created for the good of humanity.

Kingsley was already known to the scientific community. Charles Darwin's *On the Origin of Species* had been published the year before, and Kingsley had been asked to review it prior to its being made available for purchase. His comments were extraordinarily positive for a member of the clergy, and Darwin included some of them in a subsequent edition, referring to him as a "celebrated author and divine."

Kingsley's refusal to read the prayer in his worship service was censured by the praying Christian public. But it also attracted the attention of the scientific community, which, at that time, was beginning to capture attention itself. As the debate swelled, John Tyndall, a physicist, wrote an essay titled "On Prayer and Natural Law." In it, Tyndall eviscerated the argument that prayer might influence the natural laws already in place, giving the nod to Kingsley in the following thinly veiled comment: "It is a wholesome sign for England that she numbers among her clergy men wise enough to understand all this and courageous enough to act up to their knowledge. Such men do service to public character, by encouraging a manly and intelligent conflict with the real causes of disease and scarcity, instead of a delusive reliance on supernatural aid."[36]

Tyndall had managed to achieve a position of esteem within the scientific community, largely through his own self-education. Reviewing the great scientific achievements, Tyndall found that many of them, such as the atomic particle theory, had been made several hundreds of years before the Common Era—that is, before Christianity had been dreamt of. Some achievements, lost for millennia, were only just becoming widely recognized again. Tyndall asked the pertinent question: "What, then, stopped [science's] victorious advance? Why was the scientific intellect compelled, like an exhausted soil, to lie fallow for nearly two millenniums before it could regather the elements necessary to its fertility and strength?"[37]

They were good questions, but Tyndall asked them, of course, only because he already had an answer: Christianity and the acceptance of the Bible's authority over all knowledge, science included, had brought a halt to some of the most promising ideas ever put forward. Thus halted, those ideas entered their own ice age. Tyndall relished the thaw and saw in it an opportunity to reproach the belief systems that, by their very pervasiveness, continued to undermine scientific discovery and debate.

A decade after England's drastic wet season and the publication of Tyndall's essay on prayer, the country was again pressed down on its knees to ask for divine intervention. The Prince of Wales (who would become Edward VII) had fallen gravely ill with typhoid, and all parishes were ordered to pray for the restoration of the health of the heir to the throne on the following Sunday, December 10, 1871. In the subsequent week, the prince was restored to health, and many in the church took this as a sign of the efficacy of prayer.

Tyndall would have none of it. In 1872, he sent a proposal to *The Contemporary Review*, a London quarterly with sympathies aligned with the church. *The Contemporary Review* was founded in 1866 to counter the more secular *Fortnightly Review*. Tyndall, whose sentiments must have been with the latter publication, intentionally emptied his quiver into the den of his opponents by offering them an opportunity to prove their theories using the rigours of scientific experimentation. He enclosed with his proposal a letter from Henry Thompson, a celebrated surgeon, who offered the "laboratory" in which the study could take place. Patients on one ward of a hospital, similar in every way to those on the other wards, save that they would be the objects of prayer, would be observed for a period of three to five years. If prayer really worked, those patients fortunate enough to have been prayed for would, after that period of time, show demonstrably lower mortality rates than those patients who were not included on the prayer lists. The proposal for what became known as the "Prayer Gauge" ignited debate far beyond the club libraries of the subscribers to *The Contemporary Review*.

But Christians, despite what Tyndall might have thought of their intellectual capacities, were not to be led quite so easily into what they perceived to be a trap. Churchmen cried foul and argued that prayers delivered to test the reality of God were not prayers at all but merely manifestations of humanity's anxieties. Furthermore, as James McCosh, a scholar from Princeton, wrote in a reply to Tyndall, "Christians would shrink from the idea of praying for the sick on one side of the hospital and not praying for those on the other."[38] Ethically, they would be bound to pray for all the patients and so would not afford Tyndall the control group against which the effects of prayer could be tallied. McCosh noted that ten years earlier, Prince Albert had died despite fervent prayer offered up by the people of Britain and throughout the empire. He even went so far as to suggest that because of her grief over Albert's death, Queen Victoria had ignored the entreaties of her advisors and so refrained from becoming involved in the American Civil War. Was that not proof, McCosh argued, that God's ways and intentions are above our own, and that the positive result of prayer may not be a return to health or longevity but the exact opposite?[39]

These and other arguments, submitted in an effort perhaps to stare Tyndall down, did nothing in the slightest to deter him. It appeared, in fact, that he had been expecting just these sorts of objections, and so was quite ready to respond, which he did in the October issue of *The Contemporary Review*. In the course of his carefully considered reply, he reminded his adversaries (ah, could they not see themselves drawn up alongside him as collaborators?) that his concern was not with theological propositions or the moral implications of prayer but merely with the physical effects religious men and institutions have argued it was able to manifest. As soon as claims were made that the physical realm could be affected by prayer, he argued, science had a right to explore those effects. That, he pointed out, was the purview of the discipline of science, not theology, and those who refused to allow it to be examined scientifically were simply exposing their beliefs as the "residue of that mysticism of the middle ages."[40]

As the line between science and religion was being buffeted about by such ire-soaked winds, the work of another man was found at the centre of the furor. In fact, Francis Galton had published his work a few months before Tyndall's response. In the secular *Fortnightly Review*, Galton claimed the "Prayer Gauge" was unnecessary. He had already dispensed with the question of whether prayer had an effect in the physical realm, he said, through the careful review of existing records. Looking to the most regularly used invocations in the Book of Common Prayer, Galton identified the subject for which prayer was most regularly offered: the longevity of the sovereign. If prayer worked, the data would already exist to support the claim. In fact, he reviewed data relating to the lives of the kings and queens of the whole of Europe, as most had similar prayers said on their behalf on a daily basis. The results of his inquiry? Royals who were prayed for by the masses had lives that were considerably shorter than the lives of those they ruled.

Prayer similarly failed to extend the lives of the clergy, also prayed for on a daily basis and assumed to be a prayerful group. Their lives were no longer on average than those of lawyers or other professionals.

Missionaries were not spared illness and misadventure, despite constant prayers being said for them, and the ships that carried them to their mission fields were no less likely to run into peril or sink.

Galton's work seriously undermined claims that prayer had an effect on the physical realm. Accessing historical material, he silenced Tyndall's detractors, who argued that any prayer raised to test God was no prayer at all and firmly positioned Galton's work in the realm of theological theorizing, not scientific discovery.

Rick Ostrander, author of *The Life of Prayer in a World of Science: Protestants, Prayer, and American Culture, 1870–1930*, creates a three-tiered model of what elements prayer might influence and uses it to help clarify the nature of Galton's attack, as well as the tangled responses to Galton and Tyndall by the defenders of prayer. Prayer, according to Ostrander, may be said to function on three levels. The first is the internal or subjective realm, where prayer might affect the inner life of the person praying. The second is external to the individual praying, affecting change by inspiring other persons; God may answer prayer by influencing the mind or spirit of the person being prayed for. In the third, prayer, should it work, would affect the physical, non-personal world; belief in such power would inspire prayer for rain or healing.[41]

Tyndall did not speak out against the kind of prayer Ostrander placed in the first realm—that which changes one's own heart or perspective. In doing so, he left room for prayer to be an important part of an individual's life. But he made it clear in his article in *The Contemporary Review* that he was challenging only the idea that prayer would result in God's interference in the physical realm—the third possible effect identified by Ostrander. In his reply to those who criticized his motivations, Tyndall coyly argued his admiration for some who regularly employed prayer in their lives.

In some form or other, not yet evident, [prayer] may, as alleged, be necessary to man's highest culture. Certain it is that, while I rank many persons who employ it low in the scale of being, natural foolishness, bigotry, and intolerance being in their case intensified by the notion that they have access to the ear of God, I regard others who employ it as forming part of the very cream of the earth. The faith that simply adds to the folly and ferocity of the one, is turned to enduring sweetness, holiness, abounding charity, and self-sacrifice by the other. Christianity in fact varies with the nature upon which it falls.[42]

In fact, Tyndall left room for Ostrander's second type of prayer as well, allowing that someone's thoughts could be influenced by God, moving him or her toward different choices and thereby into places of greater safety. Galton wouldn't subscribe to any such notion, however. He had gone that step beyond Tyndall's interest in the physical impact of prayer, arguing that the evidence he had gathered did not support its influence over even these subtle changes in thought patterns. Many of the subjects of his study would have benefited from such divinely altered thinking. The captains of the missionary ships, for instance, might have waited a day or two to set sail or charted a safer course had they been influenced by God to change their minds come the break of the day upon which peril would ultimately prevail. Galton had built an argument against the second kind of prayer as well, proving it did not work.

The experiment Tyndall and Thompson proposed, the "Prayer Gauge," was never realized, and perhaps, in light of Galton's work, it was unnecessary. Tyndall's challenge, however, continued to reverberate through ecclesial circles, and was mentioned in books and treatises on prayer for decades to come. Indeed, it's very possible that the reaction to Tyndall and Galton led to a fascination with "answered prayer." That interest became an apologetic (that is, a defensive argument) of the beliefs of the evangelical movement, which was gaining speed in the latter decades of the nineteenth century. Story after story of answered prayer was collected and poured out for the masses to read and absorb, all of it reinforcing the third kind of prayer, which both Tyndall and Galton denied held any merit. The movement gained such speed that in one of the ninety-six essays published in *The Fundamentals: A Testimony to the Truth*, a twelve-volumes series that sought to frame Christianity's absolute beliefs, Arthur T. Pierson, an American Presbyterian minister, proposed another prayer gauge, this one to trip up the non-believers and sceptics. Using as an example the life of George Müller, founder of a number of well-funded orphanages that he claimed to have supported entirely through the power of prayer, Pierson offered "A Challenge to Unbelief." He did so despite critics noting that not one of the benefits Müller attributed to prayer broke with natural laws; any of them was entirely plausible without supernatural explanation. In fact, those which would have depended upon an "act of God" had been unsuccessful. Müller's praying that the wind direction would change, thus sparing the orphans discomfort during a scheduled furnace repair, as he reported in an 1873 autobiography,[43] is one of many examples of benefits without supernatural explantion. His despair that he had prayed to no avail for fifty years for the conversion of two close friends is an example of prayer that depends on an "act of God."

Pierson put the challenge directly, inviting anyone to create the same sort of infrastructure as Müller had, but with the caveat that there be no mention of prayer at all. Thus, the power of prayer could be tested. "When we see an infidel carrying on such a work, building five great orphan houses and sustaining over 2,000 orphans from day to day without any direct appeal to human help, yet finding all supplies coming in without even a failure in sixty years, we shall be ready to reconsider our present conviction that it was because the living God heard and helped George Müller."[44] Pierson's challenge made little sense, however, arguing as he did that the opposite of appealing to God was no appeal at all. Any "infidel" who may have taken up his offer would have had at his or her disposal the benevolence of humanity to which to appeal. The impressive Müller record notwithstanding, it remains that the same results may very well have been achieved.

Although many throughout the debate argued that true prayer did not demand any change of outcome but merely aligned itself with God's will, Tyndall was quick to note that such a suggestion bordered on an untruth. The evidence within the "answered prayer" movement bore out his suspicions. For many, Ostrander's level-three prayers—those that affect the physical world (for example) that bring or stave off the rain, those that result in miraculous healings, and that mitigate the dangers inherent in a violent situation—are those most fervently prayed and most often raised by people of faith.

As prayer came under increasing attack, the whole idea of miracles also came into question. With science challenging the validity of prayer and miracles, the devout responded defensively and with a motivation similar to that often seen today: we are afraid, and the possibility of miracles mitigates our fear. We want to know that we can control even the slightest part of our universe, and prayer promises that we can, even if we don't do it well enough to secure for ourselves, personally, the response we want. If *someone, somewhere*, is getting a response, that is promise enough for most of us. If anything at all works out positively, the devout claim, God has intervened and miracles are possible.

Until the challenges raised in the late nineteenth century, Protestants had achieved a certain comfort with miracles they believed to be safely stored away between the leaves of a two-thousand-year-old book. Unlike Catholics, who regularly and confidently pointed to evidence of miracles as proof of sanctity, Protestants argued that miracles not only no longer took place but also were unnecessary. The proof of the Christian doctrine lay in the biblical witness. No more miracles were needed, said Reformation theologian John Calvin, than those found in the good book. Miracles had ended with the Apostolic Age. End of story.

Of course, the lack of miracles in the Protestant church was pointed to by Catholics as a sign of its not being the true church. John Calvin argued that the miracles cited in the Bible were performed to confirm the teaching being presented at that time. There was no expectation that miracles would continue to occur. The revelation of God, Calvin and other Protestants argued, was complete with the closing of the canon, the set of books finally recognized by the church as divinely authoritative. The doctrine on prayer was comfortable precisely because it left no unmet expectations. But as the prayer debates continued, proofs of "miraculous" healing were met with the scientific explanation that the mind was providing relief; it was not God at all.

Robert Bruce Mullin, the author of *Miracles and the Modern Religious Imagination*, points to the greater fear that lay in the hearts of those watching the debates unfold. The idea that healing was possible through the efforts and workings of the human mind brought the entire question of the efficacy of prayer to the fore, "and almost no religious figure" was willing to suggest that religious healing could be reduced simply to "mind cure."[45]

## CONTEMPORARY PRAYER STUDIES

Stories of answered prayer have never lost their foothold in evangelical Christianity and popular spirituality circles, despite the objections of those who say that real prayer doesn't demand results. Others argue that a lack of evidence undermines the credibility of the whole idea that God answers prayer. In fact, arguments for the possibility that prayer does impact the physical sphere—in particular, the field of medical health—have led to a significant expenditure of funds and marshalling of resources in the past fifty years. Mita Giacomini, professor of clinical epidemiology and biostatistics at McMaster University, questions both the wisdom and the ethics of such studies. In a 2007 article, she reviews the breadth of interest in this field of study, finding that by the early 2000s, "remote prayer research [had] joined mainstream medical research." Millions of dollars were changing hands in the pursuit of results Giacomini believes are unmeasurable.[46]

Giacomini identifies as the culprit the validation of randomized controlled trials (RCTs). RCTs were developed to assist in the study and accumulation of medical data as it relates to biomedical interventions, a well-defined subject area that falls within the realm of natural science. Within that realm, RCTs function well, assisting in the design and careful development of research to the point that they have come to be recognized as the "gold standard." If we hear that a randomized controlled trial has been done, we assume all is well. Yet Giacomini suggests that despite the glow of confidence, all is not well. Indeed, she notes that as the explorations of medical interventions cross disciplinary boundaries—that is, when they come to include aspects that do not fall exclusively within the realm of natural science—things get a bit wonky. She refers to the mixture of disciplines as a "black box" when it comes to understanding the theory behind research that increasingly includes natural sciences, social sciences, and lay belief systems.

Such is the study of the effect of remote intercessory prayer. On the surface, a mixture of religion, theology, wishful thinking, and the natural sciences presents an interesting study. But the hypothesis, if it has to do with natural science, cannot be a hybrid. Even if it explores something we do not understand, the assumption must be, and be only, that the implications fall within the realm being studied.

Furthermore, as each study of prayer serves up inconclusive results, more are suggested, each with a clear RCT outline that, this time, will supposedly nail everything down. Not so, says Giacomini. The pursuit of a link between prayer and medicine will never be able to produce results that have any meaning. She explains that research-ers in intercessory prayer trials are seeking to measure either the effect of the individual who is praying on a supernatural deity who then intervenes *or* the effect of some universal force we have not yet come to understand or been able to measure.

Looking at the first scenario—prayer to an interventionist god—Giacomini argues that we have no hope of ever controlling the parameters sufficiently to argue significant results. There is no way to counter the possibility that those in the "not being prayed for" group are receiving prayer from some distant relative in Slovenia. Nor is there any way to determine if the supernatural deity has a plan that is consistent with our assessment of success (remember James McCosh's hypothesis regarding Prince Albert's death). In medical terms, we're going to want to see a return to wellness or a reduction of disease as a sign of positive results; the ultimate failure is death. But the super-natural deity being prayed to may not agree with what we think, and may instead choose death as the best result in the situation. Our tally is distorted when we have so little control.

While the second theory—the concept of an as yet unidentified universal force—may be more compatible with scientific exploration, there remain equally difficult challenges. Without identifying the type of force (space–time warps, electromagnetic fields, etc.), researchers have no practical application for any data collected. Complicating that fact is the reality that none of the trials have identified clearly if the participants are to use prayer to a benevolent supernatural being or the prayerful influence of an unidentified force.

And so Giacomini concludes that the RCT is really just another "emperor with no clothes" when it is used to bolster applications for funding and argue for further studies that throw into the same black box disciplines that cannot be reconciled. She argues for the end of intercessory prayer trials, and says that we who have always wanted to believe that something—anything—will work have to let go of this last vestige of hope.

Not that we don't sometimes experience life unfolding in extraordinary ways. It happens to all of us. Those times when we have been convinced that something happened—by some unknown force or the hand of God—and our lives took a turn we would never have anticipated: we met the right person; we were in the right place at the right time; we found ourselves without resources and still made a go of it. Because our desire for security in the world is so deep, it's easy to believe.

## Prayer with an Impact?

My son was sick. Really sick. We were visiting my parents, having driven the three hours to get to their home earlier that day. But Izaak, our five-year-old, had begun to spike a temperature shortly after we arrived.

When I say spike, I mean it. His temperature went up at such an alarming rate that we soon realized he needed medical attention. My sister made a phone call and learned that her physician was on duty at a walk-in clinic. The doctor would see Izaak there. We bundled ourselves back into the car and made our way toward her and the help we were convinced our son needed.

Today I often laugh and tell people I'm not licensed to practise medicine in the province of Ontario even as I give them my unqualified opinion on what might be ailing them or what medication they should discuss with their physician. Actually, I'm not licensed to practise medicine anywhere. I have no training whatsoever in medicine or any other healing art. But I have come to know and understand a lot that would be considered medical "stuff." The combination of having a nurse as a mom, sharing the realities of a multitude of medical situations as a minister, and pursuing a quest for solutions to what ails me personally has probably given rise to my inflated confidence about health issues.

Izaak was my second child. He'd been born at home with a midwife at a time when midwives weren't licensed to practise in Ontario, either. I was comfortable with bodies and health and the usual childhood illnesses that can derail many a parent. I knew that temperature in children can rise quickly. I knew how to address it with acetaminophen, cold cloths, even cold baths if necessary. I actually knew how much acetaminophen I could administer safely, despite what it said on the bottle. I had homeopathic remedies at the ready and a confidence in them that many do not share. I'd comforted my first child through many a temperature with calm and control, even though she had experienced what was diagnosed as febrile convulsions, seizures related to an elevated temperature. So taking Izaak to a walk-in clinic to see a doctor I did not know was not within my personal realm of ordinary. It was way outside it, in fact. But that is how sick he was. Sick enough to frighten me—overblown confidence and all—into seeking medical attention. He wasn't just sick. He was *really* sick.

On our way to the clinic, Izaak lay listlessly in my arms. Each time we went under a street light, he cringed, though his eyes were already closed. I was certain that was a bad sign, so my fears rose proportionately to the distance we drove. At the clinic, the doctor saw him quickly, examined him completely, and determined that despite the speed with which his temperature had risen, it was still within a normal range for a child his age. She advised me to keep doing all the things I'd been doing to bring his fever down, and to keep a close but less concerned eye on him. We were incredibly relieved, though still a bit shaken, and we left the clinic and returned to my parents' home.

Although nothing much had seemed to change—Izaak's temperature remained high—the reassurance helped us relax. We put Izaak to
bed on the third floor of my parents' home and stayed within earshot
while we went about the pleasantries of familial interaction.

And then the phone rang.

It was late, around 11:00 p.m. We were just about to turn in for the
night when the ringing sent its alarm throughout the house. It was the
doctor calling to tell us that although she rarely altered her opinion
after seeing a patient, this time she'd had second thoughts. The hospital had been alerted and was ready for us. Would we please take
Izaak there? She used the word I had been thinking of but refused to
speak—a word that terrified me: meningitis.

I knew what could happen. I'd worked in a daycare and had seen
what both seizures and untreated meningitis could do to a child. This
was *my* child. He was at risk and needed my confidence. But I was facing that risk devoid of confidence and filled with nothing more than
pure, unmitigated terror.

If we thought we had panicked before, it was nothing compared
to what happened next. Izaak was still listless and responding poorly
as we scooped him up and raced down the thirty-six-and-then-some
steps and out the door, buckled ourselves into the car, and drove. Our
hearts pulsed as we rushed to the emergency department of a hospital
that was, fortunately, only minutes away. But as we arrived, an ambu-
lance also pulled in, taking priority over our child's fate. We waited,
horrified at the thought that whatever was going on in Izaak's body
would do irreparable damage to the child we cherished before he had
a chance to see the attending physician.

While we waited, Izaak roused himself enough to let us know he
needed to go to the bathroom. His father took him to the washroom
and I lowered myself into a fear-filled, intense, purpose-driven prayer.

"God! Oh, Holy One, You who have control of the universe, hear me! Sit with me in this place. Feel my fear. Know my child as I know him. Count him among the blessed ones, the beautiful ones, the most precious ones. I know they are all precious in your sight, but hear my plea. Don't let me lose him. Not completely and not bit by bit. Not even a smidgen. You created him perfectly. You created him to *be* perfect. This is not what you had planned when you made him, so I know you do not will this. Save him for me. Save him for you. Yes, that is it. I will give his whole life to you if you save him in this horrible hour. Place your hand upon his brow. Take his fever from him. Rule over the bacteria, the virus, whatever it is; take charge of it, stop it, and bring him safely through this. It is your job to do this, not mine. Mine will be to bring him up in your love and help him fulfill my promise to you. I am your servant. But you are God, and you can do this. With all my heart and body and soul, I beseech you."

My prayer tailed off and I sat there, silent, stunned, afraid, and alone.

Then he was there, back from the washroom: Izaak, sitting up, fully alert, in his father's arms. Perfectly well, eyes sparkling, face beaming, smiling from ear to ear.

From the depths of my fear, I had cried out to whatever god might be. Falling into a shaken-up version of a prayer pattern I'd learned from Agnes Sanford's book *Healing Light*, I had whispered words, fallen silent, waited. And he had been returned to me, changed, his perfect body restored.

A few minutes after emerging from the washroom, Izaak was called in to an examining room, where he played with the doctor and sat up, as cheery as could be, with few reminders of the critical fever he'd just had. I remember no signs of a fever having broken—no sweat, no clamminess, no exhaustion—just a happy little boy in a brightly lit room with two confused and much-relieved parents looking on.

So why is it that I still blame Agnes Sanford for a very dangerous children's story I told in the context of worship?

Sanford was born in China to missionary parents and struggled through a significant part of her life with cycles of depression, but she found them much reduced after she was prayed over by a Protestant minister. Later, she became absorbed with the challenge of understanding, practising, and teaching healing prayer after witnessing her child's return to health when a visiting minister prayed over him. Over the next decades, Sanford became known as a healer and spiritual guide for those yearning to unlock the power of prayer. Her book *Healing Light* has sold millions of copies and is now available as a free download from a website devoted to her teachings.

Nowadays the fables and fairy tales I grew up with, when held under the light of child psychology, feminism and gender studies, and almost any other twenty-first-century critique, come out looking pretty dangerous. Children are forced through the stories to face their most drastic fears, a process some child-development theorists believe is quite appropriate. Many parents, however, are no longer willing to expose their children to the ups and downs and dangers of life in Mother Goose's forest, despite the fact that those same children, in a few short years, will be clobbering their friends in virtual bloodbaths on the next generation of the digital game box.

We want the stories we share with our children to edify them, to pass on our moral codes, to help them process the strange realities of the big world they inhabit. The stories shared in faith communities use religious referents to do the same thing. That's what I was doing when I shared Agnes Sanford's message in a children's time geared to help them understand the mechanics of prayer: when everything is in its proper place, the story goes, prayer has the power to transform the most dreadful situations into blessings.[47]

The story unfolded in a simple illustration involving kids, water, and a bowl. I poured water from a pitcher and then had the children stick their hands into its flow to show how they could stop it from getting to the bowl

I had set beneath it. The purpose of the "object lesson," as such stories are called in the church, was to teach the children that if their prayers weren't answered, it was likely because something got in the way of those prayers getting to God. God wants to answer our prayers, so the story goes, but if he or she can't hear them because something gets in the way ... well, that can hardly be God's fault. The something that gets in the way, the lesson concluded, was more than likely a problem with the person who prayed.

I was reading Sanford's *Healing Light* at the time. In it, she argued that if we prayed and our lives were in proper order—that is, if we'd devoted our lives to being clean with everyone, including ourselves— then we would be heard by God and our prayer would be answered. If, however, as the water demonstration showed, we let something get in the way—nastiness, perhaps, or jealousy, or lustful thoughts (no, I didn't offer that one in the children's time)—we also stopped the flow of our prayer to God, who, never hearing it, could not answer. Sanford, in fact, began a personal inventory of her choices and behaviours—the things she'd said and done to others—every time she had to wait for the bus, convinced that the wait was punishment for some forgotten transgression. Clear it away, she believed, and the bus would arrive just when she wanted it to. (That should have been my first clue to the fact that something was dreadfully amiss!)

To teach the simplicity of her prayer program, Sanford gives us the example of flicking a switch to turn on a light. If the light doesn't go on, she points out, we assume there is a burned-out bulb—or perhaps a blown fuse, a wiring problem, or a power outage. We don't, she reminds us, stop believing in electricity. Her point is that if we don't get our prayer answered by God, we need to explore the connection, not stop believing in God or God's ability or willingness to answer us. And lest you think Sanford takes a unique stand, check out the scores of contemporary books on how to pray to ensure favourable answers. They're not stocked only in Christian bookstores.

Sanford is reported to have said that Jesus has stood in churches down through the centuries with his hands tied behind his back because no one has ever really believed he could do anything. I don't think that's true. I mean, I think she said it, but I don't think people haven't expected their prayers to be answered. And that's where this story goes—to the utter sincerity of the prayers of a child.

When a child's life is touched by the chaos of disease or brutality, by hunger or poverty, by divorce or death, by bullying or any one of the dozens of physical, sexual, or social manifestations that can prompt that bullying, that child often—more often than we can ever know—turns to prayer if he or she has learned to turn to God, the source of every blessing, the provider of every need, the one who promises all will be well. Quietly, often without the knowledge of a parent, a child bends her knees, or folds her hands, or bows her head, or lies silently in her bed, or reaches her arms toward heaven and offers up what can only be, in the abyss of those moments, the purest plea ever formed in the heart of one who yearned after mercy: "Help me." "Change me." "Heal my dad." Nothing can ever convince me that such prayers are unworthy or fail to meet Sandford's discerning criteria. Nothing can make me believe in a god who would refuse to listen to them. Nothing can make me believe in a god who heard such a cry and said no, or who left a child in a horrific situation until "God's time" was right.

If our theology cannot accommodate the conundrum of unanswered prayer without pointing conveniently to a higher wisdom, a greater good that made the tragedy necessary, a lesson we need to learn, a way of appreciating all our blessings by contrast, or an unrevealed plan that will stay a mystery until made clear in heaven—or perhaps worst of all, turning on the one whose prayer was unanswered to find a fault in her or his life that has not been corrected or atoned for—then it is not good enough for me and it shouldn't be for you.

Prayer should build relationship, not create and deepen a sense of alienation or plant a badly theologized guilt in the hearts of those brave enough to enter into prayer.

Agnes Sanford's electrical switch analogy is a poor one. We don't stop believing in electricity because electricity is in evidence all around us. The light in one room might not go on, but the ones in the other rooms in our house do—or in the other houses on the block, or in the city around us—and so the circle of our quest expands until we have identified where the problem lies. But answered prayers are not all around us. We don't have difficulty with our switch; it's not just that this particular prayer or that one is denied when all our other ones are answered without a moment's hesitation. Nor do our prayers go unanswered while everyone else on the block is basking in the blessings of theirs. Our experience is that benevolence, when it arrives with the precision timing believers would argue I experienced in the emergency department that terrifying night, does so only in noticeably paltry doses. Just ask the too many children who have prayed desperately for an end to their suffering or a diversion of fate that would spare someone they love. Beauty we can find, peace we can point to, health and wellness we can celebrate, but to argue that any of these merit consideration as consolation when another desperate and urgent need goes unmet demands that we are stuck placing our faith in a weak, fickle, stingy, capricious, or at least uncaring god. Headstones, broken lives, and the tears of the lonely stand testimony to this truth.

## Condemnation Within Our Intercessory Prayers

It was in a newspaper article that I first relayed the story of the shame and anger my daughter, Hazel, felt as a school-age child when her prayers went unanswered. She'd been praying for such a big thing— the life of her teacher, who had been diagnosed with a brain tumour. Lots of brain tumours are operable or respond to medical treatment.

Not this one. My daughter's teacher died a few months after being diagnosed, even though Hazel had prayed for her every day since she heard about her illness. My daughter had listened to me and offered up her little heart in the best way she possibly could. It didn't work.

Yet Agnes Sanford would have smiled at me when my son's illness disappeared in what seemed a miraculous response to my prayer and said, "See? When you do it right, it works!" The Christian Scientists who connected with me following the publication of the story about my daughter's teacher would have pointed to the precision of my language when Izaak was ill, noting that I had recalled the perfection of his body and held that up to God, slipping unknowingly into the realm of spiritual wholeness to which they are intensely committed.* A theologian would have rolled out an explanation about the immensity of God's plan, a plan I couldn't possibly understand, to rationalize the silence desperate children face in contrast to the benevolence afforded me.

Up until that point, I had operated in a leadership role in the liberal church in what I now think of as a metaphor-induced stupor. The benevolence of a divine being, the beautiful relationship we could have with it, the props and punchlines of children's talks and lectionary illustrations—all felt so normal and right in the context of congregational ministry. It was a dependency formed during my theological training, and one I believe most of my colleagues have as well, though few admit to it. We don't think about what our words and actions really mean. (What does it mean to say a commendation at the end of a funeral? What happens when we place water on a child's head during a baptism? What are we implying when we smudge a bit of ash on someone's forehead?) We deliver the message, create the drama, instil the vision, and leave it at that.

Had I awakened from that stupor earlier and asked myself some

---

* Christian Scientists, as we shall see, believe that the body exists in a whole and healthy state, and that illness is a manifestation of our fear. If we can truly believe we are well, we will be.

of those questions, I might have spared myself and others around me the angst and shame that came from the punchline of this children's talk—that is, if your prayers aren't granted, there's something wrong with you. I would have seen the horrific implications and put away the bowl and the water. I would have closed *The Healing Light* much earlier than I did and left Agnes Sanford's teachings locked between its pages. I will never know which children took my words to heart that day and now blame themselves for what hasn't come to be in their worlds, what problems they still carry or challenges they still face. The shame of not being able to get your life clean enough to have a prayer heard— the absence of a positive outcome constant evidence of your unworthiness—weaves dark threads in and out of your heart; it does not heal but, rather, harms. My Sanford children's moment continues to plague my memory and my conscience.

As a result of the article about my faith journey and the part this break with the power of prayer had in forming who I am as a church leader, I've been called a lot of things: stupid, simplistic, naive, ignorant, and spiritually immature (to name a few of the more polite ones). Some of my correspondents couldn't believe that I'd "fire" God the first time I didn't get my way. After all, they asked, what did I think prayer was? Magic?

The reality is that much of what we offer up as prayer is not far off being just that—a magical spell that we hope the spirits (in this case, a supernatural god) will respond to, fulfilling our wishes and making us happy. Psychologist Erich Neumann, in his classic book, *The Great Mother*, reminds his readers that "the original magical intention to move and influence the upper powers is preserved in almost all prayer."[47] And whether we believe that we are being attended to by that supernatural being, are caught in the flow of the universe's energy, or are the beneficiaries of unrecognizable natural convergences, if everything is in perfect alignment we get what we want from the source of goodness, who sets the rules. And if all is not as it should be, our prayers are rejected and we console ourselves with the belief that there is a much wiser being whose ways we mere mortals cannot comprehend.

## In Our Own Hands . . .

Jim Wallis, an author and self-described public theologian, drew some examples from life with his young sons—one six, the other ten—while sharing stories about his faith journey with an audience in the summer of 2009.[48] One detail in particular circled around in my head for some time after. His elder son, while praying one evening, ran through a list of ways he thought God's intervention might heal one of the world's most devastating issues (and the one that must shame us most): the astounding number of children who die daily from poverty and lack of access to medical treatments most of us simply take for granted. At first, the son asked that God let the thirty thousand children slated to die the next day live instead. But he quickly altered that prayer, knowing, as he must, that God was unlikely to do that. So he prayed instead that God make this, their last day, the best day ever. Again, he immediately realized that wasn't very likely either. Perhaps he thought that if the children were ill enough to die the next day, they were most probably too sick to have much fun. Understanding that God couldn't, or perhaps wouldn't, intervene, the boy concluded with the only prayer through which God ever proves him- or herself to believers: he asked that God help *us* find a way to fix the problem. In truth, that's not good enough.

Prayers of intercession, thanksgiving, and petition allow us the opportunity to reflect on our world and our place in it, but more importantly (and I would argue, more toxically), they maintain an image of the all-powerful God. If our response is to cringe before God in fear or bow before him in adoration—either stance in response to the idea of God's "plan"—the result is the same: we are utterly and pathetically immobilized. Liberal communities of faith that take action on many of the fronts of human suffering will not respond easily to an image of immobility. The truth, however, is that the language of prayer most often raised, even in congregations that expend huge energies in the struggle for justice, is language that strengthens God's hand and so extends permission for the same images to be used by fundamentalist believers to reinforce the very systems of oppression such congregations would end.

## FINAL ACTS

The development of prayer over the centuries has given us many rituals, symbols, and practices that touch us deeply and call many of us to a more meaningful engagement in life. Images of those engaged in prayer—the lone figure leaning over a cylindrical candle in a chapel; someone kneeling in an empty church with bowed head; dozens of young people swaying, eyes closed, some with hands uplifted and tears streaming down their faces; men on small squares of carpet, folding into a familiar posture in a busy pedestrian mall—bear witness to the profound power it holds.

Yet we have struggled for centuries to understand prayer, defending it on differing fronts as perspectives from alternative viewpoints were expressed. The rational scientific mindset would steal from us any of the transcendence we experience in prayer. The fundamentalists would use its power to strike fear and prejudice into tender hearts. So much of its history is tainted; its premise has wounded and oppressed. Still, we cannot turn away from the very real truth that prayer has been and continues to be a source of strength and encouragement for many. So we carry on with the quest for just what it is about prayer that has sustained us throughout the millennia, how it has managed to withstand the perils of contemporary critique, and what it is about it that we can't seem to leave behind.

PART THREE

# IN A WORLD
# OF EXPOSED BELIEFS

# 6

## HANGING ON TO THE LANGUAGE

Some liberal colleagues, usually those who identify themselves as progressive, argue that the god I have been talking about—the authoritarian, judgmental, capricious, up-in-the-sky god we've called "God" lo these many years—is not the god they bow their heads before. Their beliefs are more sophisticated than that, they say. In fact, they tell me, their god isn't a being that lives in *any* elsewhere, not just up in the sky. The god they believe in is less being-ish, less angry-ish, less authoritarian-ish. In fact, it's not those things at all. And it's not supernatural either. Or omnipotent. Or omnipresent. It's more a "not this" and a "not that" kind of god. Sometimes they use a big name to describe what it is they can't say about their idea of god. When you describe what something isn't, it's an apophatic description. Apophatic theology sounds very impressive.

I'm not impressed.

Don't get me wrong—I love a good metaphor, and next to poets, religious writers and theologians are at the top of the craft. We've been weaving metaphors on the loom of belief for millennia. So we know what we're doing when we beat the weft of interpretation into the unyielding warp of doctrine and come up with a pretty new design. We impress ourselves with the careful way we've tucked in all the loose ends. Heck, it's almost as pretty on the backside as it is on the front. Yep, I can do metaphor.

The straw man accusation is a metaphor that is often used to discredit arguments against traditional belief systems. Someone creates an argument by presenting as fact things they know are not true. That's the straw man. It is then easy for them to knock the poor thing over, because it wasn't real to begin with. This is a common complaint against the arguments atheists and humanists raise as well. If I describe god as a supernatural, omnipotent, all-knowing being who can intervene in both cosmic and human affairs at will when I know full well that no one really believes in that kind of god anymore, that would be a straw man argument. But people do believe in that kind of god. And not just fundamentalists. At least, it sure looks like they do.

Many clergy and theologians hold a very progressive image of god—and I appreciate that they do. Yet when they start writing about their beliefs, it all begins to look strangely reminiscent of that big straw god they argue I'm making up. Steven Law, editor of the journal *Think: Philosophy for Everyone*, captures the essence of the argument when he writes, "[S]ome say, 'Ah yes. You may have succeeded in showing that there's no 'God,' if that's how you define him. But that's not what sophisticated theists such as myself mean by 'God.' They then add, 'What we're talking about is, in truth, ineffable and beyond our comprehension. So you have not refuted my sort of theism.'"[1] Let's see.

Marcus Borg and Ross Mackenzie co-edited a collection of essays gathered from conversations shared by leaders in the liberal Christian church at a conference that brought them together in February 2000. The collection, *God at 2000*, captures the responses the diverse participants made to the invitation to discuss how their personal experiences and situations influenced their idea of God. It is an engaging read and the ideas move far beyond traditional theological fare.

Diana Eck, a professor of comparative religion and Indian studies at Harvard, writes in *God at 2000* of placing Christianity respectfully among other faiths. While celebrating the new millennium, Eck couldn't help thinking how the globalization of our technology, communications, financial markets, and businesses stood in sobering contrast to the deep fracturing of the human community caused by old and new religious identities and rivalries.[2] Even as the new millennium was dawning, we human beings were enacting our age-old struggles, claiming divine truth for our own adherents and employing the full arsenal of religious symbols to protect it.[3]

Although deeply sensitive to the variety of experience and expression related to the concept of god, Eck nevertheless speaks almost exclusively from within an understanding that celebrates the theistic language of traditional hymnody, attributes agency to the theistic gods of different religious traditions, and honours those traditions by affirming the sanctity of their practice and their endeavours to know and describe the theistic beings they worship. "God is the rock beneath our feet, the light upon our path, the shepherd who seeks us when we are lost. Our God language is as broad and rich as language itself. [W]e speak of the God who created the heavens and earth and all that is therein, who is present with us in the life of Christ, and who inspires us in the Holy Spirit."[4]

That sounds pretty big god-up-in-the-sky to me. Eck is obviously using metaphor, but metaphors stand in place of something that can't be defined. What are her metaphors standing in for? A "rock beneath our feet" suggests support, "the light upon our path" suggests guidance, and the "shepherd who seeks us when we are lost" seems a metaphor for comfort and protection. Metaphors they may be, but if god is of the ineffable stock, she's given it a lot of very interventionist sort of characteristics, making it the kind of theistic being liberals like to say no one—whoever "no one" is—really believes in anymore.

Eck's defence of theistic language might be backed up by those who believe religion evolved to preserve social cohesion *within* groups but not *between* them, but it is entirely unhelpful if we are at all interested in broadening the conversation. We don't all have to be the same, but we do have to allow space for the other within our *language* or else dialogue simply cannot be achieved. Theism and its inherent realist perspective—that is, its argument that there really is something out there and it looks like this [insert your image of god here]—continues to be a colossal obstacle to the evolution of human civilization. And prayer, offered with Eck's persistently traditional language, can only continue to purport that God, an external being, is still the source of everything good, the agent who makes it happen, and the promise that it will. If that's a straw man, I'll eat it.

Radical Benedictine sister Joan Chittister rocked the Vatican when she refused to stand down in the face of its threats of excommunication and announced her participation in the ordination of women at the first Women's Ordination Worldwide conference in Dublin, Ireland, in June 2000. Her article in the *God at 2000* collection moves away from the theistic realism of Diana Eck and presents a less theistic but still a very realist portrait of a god "big enough to believe in."[5]

Convinced that existing images for god, even those considered radical, are prohibitive—that they are, at best, "images of god foreign to the very idea of God"[6]—she comes to the conclusion that all are "graven images of ourselves." She needs a god that is bigger than all conventional images combined. Chittister chooses to believe in god as "cosmic unity and everlasting light."[7] She writes, "[My] God . . . is [a] fierce but formless presence, undying light in darkness, eternal limitlessness, common consciousness in all creation, an inclusiveness, greater than doctrines or denominations, who calls me beyond and out of my limits."[8]

We are struck by the expansiveness and beauty of Chittister's metaphors, and many people are mesmerized by such poetic words when they are offered as intimations of a deeper source of meaning and connection in the universe. So enchanted are we, in fact, that we often neglect to ask what such images really mean. What is "undying light in darkness"? What does she mean by "eternal limitlessness"? Liberal theologies are high on poetry and low on clarity, and we need to ask what that is about. Is it an image that will help me, a practitioner, support a couple intent on wounding and damaging each other? The metaphors seem to relate to attributes liberals like Chittister want to deny. Here light again suggests guidance, or perhaps hope this time, and her god's fierce presence is something like capsicum ointment— burning and healing all at once.

Chittister refuses to allow anyone to "draw too small a God for her,"[9] and I am pulled into the conversation she offers. But her god, large though she may find it, can only ever be too small to withstand its abuse by others. When the description of god is up for grabs, it is not bound to any single person's idea of it. By objectifying and reifying her experience, Chittister leaves her idea of god vulnerable to the definitions of those whose understandings she might deny. Her god remains tethered to the descriptions she recounts and rejects simply because she still calls it "God." It is too easy for Chittister's god to be taken over by her opponents. If we all named our dogs "Dog," they would all come running at the sound of their name—gentle, tail-wagging ones; big, playful ones; and yes, dangerous, snarly ones. Indistinguishable as it is from other similarly named deities like those vying for anything that will hasten Armageddon, for instance, or the execution of homosexuals, or the shrouding of women, your god is suddenly in the newspaper, cheering for the other team. A god that can be lassoed with so little effort is a weak god indeed. Worthy though Chittister's experience is, she has bound it with a fickle name.

Throughout *God at 2000* the authors, each working to describe very personal yet accessible understandings of the concept of god, find themselves bound to the terminology of classical theology. The unfortunate effect is to render some of the articles almost meaningless to any who are not conversant in some strain of traditional Christianity. While seeking to escape a conservative theology, these incredibly creative thinkers find themselves trussed by the language of an equally unhelpful liberal one.

It was with further disappointment that I read Chittister's 2009 book, *The Breath of the Soul: Reflections on Prayer*, and noted that despite her desire to write god large in her life, that supernatural *source*, *agent*, and *promise* that upholds all the fundamentalist prayers (the one that looks an awful lot like that straw man god) is persistent in its presence here too. She leans upon it for support. It makes challenges bearable, she writes, and will bring needed insights. I have no doubt she experiences a sense of calm and peace from these images of God—many would. But it is her interpretation of what is happening in her life that brings her that comfort. Rather than moving us forward with the feisty, big understanding of god she'd offered at the turn of the millennium, she seems to have been paralyzed by the topic of prayer and held in a place she had tried to argue herself out of some years before.

## STILL HEARING VOICES? PINCH YOURSELF

The United Church of Christ in the United States launched a marketing and branding campaign in 2002 to raise awareness of its identity and theology. Known as the Stillspeaking Initiative, the campaign was built on a quote by comedian Gracie Allen: "Never place a period where God has placed a comma." When the first advertisement—a red-and-black poster with an oversized comma—was distributed to UCC congregations across the country, the campaign went viral.[10] Not only did it captivate those in the church looking for new ways to connect with a less-than-interested public, but it also held them firmly to the denomination's ongoing theological understandings, keeping faith with its pilgrim ancestors. In 1620, Pastor John Robinson (no, not the Honest to God John A.T. Robinson) reassured the church's forebears with a strikingly similar sentiment: "God still has more truth and light to break forth from God's Holy Word."[11]

The savvy campaign is now easily recognized both within and outside the denomination and even the country. While it might make us feel better, in truth it's essentially an empty statement. No one in the United Church of Christ can prove that God still speaks, or that, in fact, it ever did. If God still speaks, how on earth did the UCC make those decisions about supporting, nurturing, and recognizing church leaders who are female or self-declared homosexual and transgender individuals when God has clearly been heard telling other denominations to do exactly the opposite? What you're hearing, Richard Holloway, retired bishop of Edinburgh, reminds us, is nothing other than the voice of consciousness, the voice in the head, "projected not only inwards onto the soul, but outwards onto an independent objective reality."[12] It makes life rather difficult, he notes. "How can you negotiate the intricacies of living alongside people who are programmed by an invisible, inaudible voice? And the voice is still at work."[13]

Articulate, creative, and brilliant liberal theologians often speak in metaphor to talk about god. The word "god" is claimed to refer to some undefined and indefinable thing. Although metaphorical, the language they use remains highly descriptive and it fills out the picture. They speak of the "ground of all being" or "love" or "holy mystery" as the source of all goodness, as acting in our best interests and being true to the promise of salvation (or if that's too laden a term, at least to the absence of unnecessary pain or the fortitude to endure it). It is an ineffable god, they say. But an ineffable god cannot be known, so we can't claim it speaks one way or another. An ineffable god can't come down on the side of good. An ineffable god can't be argued to be loving, compassionate, attentive, or otherwise. If you believe in a god beyond description, I'm fine with that, but I'm with Steven Law when it comes to filling in all the blanks that ineffability necessarily leaves. You can't do it. When theologians try, Law charges them with "effing the ineffable." If whatever it is that "god" has come to mean in the liberal church is still able to speak, to pronounce on moral issues, to offer guidance and comfort, then it has to give up its silky, ethereal garments and be identified for what it really is: classical theism. You can't haul out the ineffability of god as a way to neutralize any argument that points to the horrific suffering in the world as proof there is no loving god, and then turn around and make your ineffable god the purveyor of all that is good when lovely things happen.[14] If it's ineffable, leave it ineffable. You can't have it both ways. Stop trying to eff it.

If we hold a theologically non-realist view, and are working to be honest and clear about what we are saying, if we want to move forward with integrity and the honesty that is essential to it, we have to stop acting and speaking as though we are in conversation with God. Either that or call out "Let's play pretend" clearly enough that others know that's what we're doing. It's not just others we seem to be trying to fool. Perhaps we have most desperately been trying to fool ourselves. But even very small children know when playing pretend is no longer fun. While the UCC's marketing campaign has cachet, it's really not worth the paper it's printed on.[15] The important conversation is not the one some believe takes place between humanity and God. The important conversation is the one we must enter into with ourselves and with one another, pushing ourselves beyond our former boundaries, climbing over and across what we have known to open ourselves to what we have not been willing to see, and in conversation, seeking the wisdom needed to address the complex problems we face.

A glimpse at the resources offered on denominational websites confirms the ongoing use of directly theistic language (or metaphors that veil it, but only thinly). Combine these prayers and hymns with the privileged position of the Bible, read each week as the sacred text in every church in Christendom, and it's easy to see how difficult it is for the average churchgoer to find alternative understandings of god, let alone ideas about religious non-realism. A preacher's theology may lean all the way to "I don't have a theology," but it's likely that people who sit in the pews in front of her don't get to hear about it. The songs, prayers, invocations, and absolutions—straight up or delivered with a metaphorical twist—all seem to posit that there is a real god out there about to do something, either because the preacher asked it to or because it has some kind of a plan. You might like to think it's a straw man, but I'd recommend an arm wrestle first. It's a precautious way to find out what you're really up against before you risk getting your butt kicked.

## BUT IT WORKS, DOESN'T IT?

My sister once had a large, unruly dog, Phoebe, who went blind. Once she did, unsure of what was around her, she became a dangerous behaviour problem. To train her, Rebecca was taught to use a clicker. If Phoebe did something right, she would hear a click and get a treat.

We know that rewarding good behaviour brings about positive results far more quickly than punishing bad behaviour. Long before we knew the mechanics of it, we established religious systems built on that very idea. A single incident that could be defined as the deity looking out for our tribe or a prayer being answered has, for the religious devotee and many a sceptic alike, often outweighed the voluminous evidence to the contrary. One good click and we're happy to give Pavlov—and God—all the compliance he wants.

It makes perfect sense, of course. In the natural world, where animals are governed primarily by their experiences of satiety and hunger, reward is a powerful instrument. What we have perhaps missed is this tie to our religious behaviours and the manner in which they reinforce the same system of reward and punishment. If we behave appropriately, even though our experience of hardship or pain does not change, we are eager to believe that positive results are forthcoming. We have interpreted, no matter how inconsistently, what has happened around us or to us as a divine click.

Many religious worldviews thrive on the simple click/reward system, holding believers in the hunger/satiety dichotomy that is the life of most sentient beings: something promises "food"—understood here as personal comfort, salvation, God's favour—and we are drawn toward it; something is neutral and we turn away from it; something suggests that *we* might be the food source—that we might lose something important to us—and we run away from it. Such religious worldviews keep us sandwiched between the possibility of comfort, well-being, and security and the possibility of discomfort, fear, and eternal death. We react to stimuli with the same sensitivity as a wild pig snuffling for truffles, ever searching for some morsel of infinite bliss, yet alert to anything that might intrude upon our comfort zone. Like a person with obsessive–compulsive disorder, the pig believes that if it does this one thing—this turning toward the smell of food—it will feel better soon. Truffles keep the pig's nose to the ground; religion keeps our eyes turned to the heavens.

Prayer has been our best-selling clicker. Whether we believe our prayers to have been answered or not, every time we have entered into the ritual that is prayer, we have reinforced the possibility that there are truffles coming our way, that we will feel better soon. And we've reinforced the reinforcement with a collective "Truffles this way!" whenever something "interesting" has happened, thus attributing to God, the universe, a cosmic force, or [fill in the blank] events that natural, sequential, logical systems and processes have caused. In our hunger for satiety, security, and safety, we tell ourselves these are "signs."

## YOU CAN'T GET THERE FROM HERE

The efficacy of prayer—proof that it works—has often been tied to the results we can get from the transcendent realm. But we often reassure ourselves that we have been rewarded for "laying siege to heaven"[16] even when what happens is not what we were praying for. M. D. Faber, a psychoanalyst and professor emeritus at the University of Victoria in Canada, argues that as we engage with our world as infants, we develop a way to self-soothe that creates a positive feedback loop uncannily like what believers describe as answered prayer. It is the magical interactions between the dependent, developing infant and what child psychiatrist Donald Winnicott calls the "good enough" mother* (one who offers the child what it needs but doesn't prevent it from acting to fulfill what needs it can) that Faber argues set the course for supplicatory prayer and our belief that, whether or not we get what we want, our prayers have been answered.

Winnicott's explorations take us to the world of the very young child as it begins the process of balancing its desire for the primary care giver (PCG)* with the reality that he or she is not as present as was once the case. To survive the transition, Winnicott explains, the child creates and identifies transitional objects that are able to soothe in the manner his or her PCG once did. Blankies, teddy bears, dolls, soothers—all serve as transitional objects that permit the child to detach from the PCG and move into independence.

Dipping into the work of psychologist Bronislaw Malinowski, Faber finds a link to magical behaviour rooted in the actions of the child in relation to the transitional object. Malinowski identifies what he calls a "gap" in reality that, when it opens, triggers a magical response from us. When we find ourselves at an impasse, unable to achieve whatever

---

* The literature on this topic refers exclusively to the primary care giver as "mother." I am utterly aware of the mistake it is to do so and will use the non–gender specific "primary care-giver," PCG, wherever possible.

we are seeking—the favourite Chardonnay to accompany a romantic dinner is not in stock, the degree granted by a renowned institution is unattainable because of pressing health concerns, the peace and quiet of a waterfront retreat is shattered by others using it for very different purposes—we project the desired outcome and find it manifest in the realities all about us. Our ability to find peace within the realities that *are* available to us (realities we were not initially pursuing) can be experienced as the intervention of a supernatural being or entity intent on preserving our peace of mind, our best interests. "It was meant to be," we might say when we are forced to try a new, less expensive wine and find its quality exceeds that of the one we couldn't get. We end up falling in love with a medical practitioner and give no more thought at all to higher education, proving to ourselves that "everything happens for a reason." Or heading to the cottage down the way to complain about the noise, we find that the transgressors are long-lost friends from whom we have been estranged and we get to enjoy not only a reunion but reconciliation: "God knew what I needed better than I did."

When we pray for something to happen, we are, Faber argues, even more likely to make the leap to a positive outcome regardless of what happens, because as we grew, prayer became our transitional object, fulfilling our needs in exactly the same way childhood objects once did. We are primed through prayer to constantly look for proof it has worked. As I sat with a woman struggling through the final indignities of cancer, she shared with me her belief that her prayers had been answered. Cancer was the gift God had given her in response to a fervent prayer that she be reconciled with her only child. In her mind, it had worked. It is exceedingly difficult to uncurl fingers so tightly wrapped around a belief to let go of something that we have always assumed was true and that helped make sense of the experience of life.

Barbara Bradley Hagerty, an award-winning religion correspondent with National Public Radio in the United States, challenges us to take a second look at some of the benefits of the spiritual life. In her book, *Fingerprints of God: What Science Is Learning about the Brain and Spiritual Experience*, she gives us the permission to reach for those benefits with scientific hands. Born into a Christian Science family, Bradley Hagerty began to question her faith when she swallowed a little round pill. And like Neo in *The Matrix*, she began to see the world clearly for the first time as soon as the pill was down her throat.

True, the pill was just Tylenol, but as it began to relieve the debilitating effects of the flu that Bradley Hagerty had been trying to weather drug-free, it also worked to begin unravelling her faith. Christian Scientists believe that trust in the human body—created perfectly by God—is all that is needed to pull a person through any illness. Her mother, a Christian Science healer, prayed to create health in individuals, and Bradley Hagerty writes of her mother's experience of healing her own broken hand.[17]

Tired after three decades of what she calls the "tough sledding" of working to fix all her problems with prayer, Bradley Hagerty "chose the ease and reliability of Tylenol over the hard-won healings of Christian Science."[18] But she kept asking questions and held fast to the idea of God, remaining open to the possibility of something inexplicable or even supernatural at work. That perspective threatened to undermine some of her credibility as a journalist in a profession with the golden rule that "you take nothing on faith, that you back up every line of every story you write with hard evidence."[19] Her book is the result of both a personal journey and what might be described as a spiritual/scientific odyssey.

Bradley Hagerty explores the science that she ultimately admits can neither prove nor disprove there is a god. There is no doubt that the scientific inquiry she presents is intriguing. From the enhanced levels of immune-boosting CD4 cells in HIV positive patients who increase their levels of spirituality post-diagnosis to the ability of people with near-death experiences (NDEs) to alter their brain rhythms, there are mysteries that have yet to be explained. Even the staunchest materialists—scientists who believe all human behaviour and experience can be brought down to the level of chemical and physical reactions—are often left shrugging their shoulders. The evidence so far refuses to be piled up in one corner or another, but Bradley Hagerty believes this may be because science has refused to look in the right places. With the tools that are available, she believes more and more evidence will mount, shave the advantage off the confidence of those pushing the materialist paradigm, and finally challenge them, too, to look for what she would call a spiritual purpose or motivating force behind much of human experience.

When I began my university education, I was going to be a nuclear physicist. I loved mathematics but loved physics more. I yearned to know how the world worked. Really worked. On a subatomic level. I was fascinated by the forces that drew matter together and those that pushed it apart. I was captivated by the reality that there was so much we could barely see, and so much more beyond that, and by the somewhat disorienting realization that we really didn't know so much of what we thought we knew. Cool. I wanted to play around in that kind of stuff and maybe help figure some of it out. Long story short—it didn't happen.

I mention it just to note that I love a good scientific theory and I salivate at the thought that there is the possibility of it being experimentally proven. I'm totally open to the idea that there is a soul, and that scientific inquiry might find it one day. I think the theories of NDEs are fascinating, and I'd love to see the unravelled proof that finally captures the truth about them. I have known, from a very early age, that we cannot see or measure all that is, and I have discovered that we have to take much on faith. I know that we walk on the theories and beliefs laid out for us by others, and that without confidence in *those* ideas, we would be too afraid to leave our beds in the morning or close our eyes at night.

The spiritual quest that Bradley Hagerty chronicles in her book is one to which many will relate. They want to know there is something there. They want security. They want answers. But not just any answers. When science throws back at them results that do not give them the security they want, they keep looking, keep studying, keep speculating. Those who go looking for a spiritual connection between prayer and health—a "god" gene that pushes us to explore beyond the veil of reality, proof of life after death, or a fingerprint that tells us God was here—will not stop short of finding what fits the thing they seek.

## BUT IT FITS, DOESN'T IT?

We need to remember, however, that the sincerity of people's persistence doesn't mean that what they are looking for is out there; it just means they will not stop looking, regardless of the evidence presented to them, and will continue to interpret what they find to support their hypotheses. The question we must ask, when we are offered their proofs, is "Can we be sure we are looking at what we're being told we are looking at?" I'm not convinced that we can. Not at face value. Not yet. The power of our presuppositions, our deeply embedded assumptions about life and truth and ourselves, plus our own needs and desires, can lead to any number of interpretations of an event, an experience, or a piece of information. Like the Jesus Seminar scholars, who are reminded to question their impulses when they are drawn to argue for something that reinforces their own worldview, we must be sceptical when the evidence we see is too close to what we want to see.

I read *Cosmos and Psyche: Intimations of a New World View* by Richard Tarnas shortly after it was published in 2006.[20] His previous book, *The Passion of the Western Mind: Understanding the Ideas That Have Shaped Our*

*World View*, presented an eloquent and sensitive view of the side of history so often neglected—the development of our ideas and their effect upon society. A radio host remarked that books about astrology and the paranormal usually hit File 13, the garbage, as quickly as they are unwrapped, but he said that one about astrology by an author as respected as Richard Tarnas begged to be explored further. I was similarly intrigued. If Tarnas had found some kind of link between the constellations that swirl past us in the night sky and the kind of people we are—a link that would help us understand ourselves, help us determine and fulfill our destinies—wouldn't that be exciting?

In the first chapter or so, the promise of *Cosmos and Psyche* continued to hold. But as I read on, it became increasingly clear that the evidence Tarnas was presenting was not evidence at all. It was simply a collection of assorted facts placed by conjecture on the windowsill of hope and turned, twisted, rearranged until they caught the light Tarnas thought was best. Other, equally substantial facts, similarly displayed to another advantage, would utterly undermine the thesis Tarnas was attempting to prove. Wishful thinking, though long the impetus for experimentation and the gathering of evidence (remember Mita Giacomini's argument against the use of randomized controlled trials for prayer studies?), cannot argue an airtight case. It may be essential to us—what would life be without the promise of possibility?—but no more so than an attempt at a more objective exploration of the gathered evidence. Objectivity is, of course, also an interpretation. All we can do is acknowledge that we all have assumptions, and that we're probably not aware of all of them, and then attempt to suspend our judgment long enough to look at something from a different point of view. Without even a try at objectivity, we cannot be sure that what we have found is what we were seeking. We may be happy to believe it is, but then let's call it our belief, not a fact.

## BUT WE'VE ALWAYS DONE IT THIS WAY!

John Bishop, a professor of philosophy at the University of Auckland, wrestles with the work of Lloyd Geering in an essay in *A Religious Atheist? Critical Essays on the Work of Lloyd Geering*, a critique of the theologian's work.[21] Bishop presents a fairly classic liberal criticism of the non-realist perspective of a theistic god. Remember, the theologically non-realist position states that there is no "thing," "spirit," "dimension," or "ultimate," theist or otherwise. Bishop recognizes that what Geering proposes—that there is no "Perfect Being, who is omnipotent, omniscient, omnibenevolent and omnipresent" ("omniGod," as Bishop confesses to "somewhat irreverently call Him"[22])—fails Anselm's ontological argument, which demands that God exist outside of the mind. Bishop argues that even if there is no "mind-independently existing" being, that doesn't mean there isn't *some* kind of god. In fact, he suggests that if there weren't, we would have difficulty finding anything worthy of our authentic worship.[23]

Well, yes, I guess that is so. But we should bring on the questions when we hear something like that. If we've arrived at the conclusion that there is no supernatural theist god, God, and it's *that* god who demanded the worship in the first place, then why are we out shopping for a new god? Just so we can keep the worship? If we've boiled water for potatoes and then find we have none, do we have to find something else to throw in the pot or can we just turn off the stove? We were boiling the water to cook the potatoes, but my guess is that wasn't the ultimate goal. We were boiling the water to cook potatoes so that we would have something to eat. If we can find something else to prepare by boiling it in the water, then by all means, let's toss it in. But if we can't, or there is something else at hand that would fill the void just as well or better—a garden full of zucchinis and tomatoes, perhaps—then we can flick the switch, turn off the gas, walk away from the stove, and make our way outside. There is no longer a mandate for us to stand and stir the water.

Similarly, if we have been praying to God because God was to be prayed to, and then we find that God—to whom we were offering praise, from whom we were seeking forgiveness, to whom we were giving thanks and making supplication—did not exist, do we still assume the stance or do we get up and try something different? What were we doing when we knelt in the first place? Why did we pick up the prayer beads? We did it to pray, but once again, the prayer was not the ultimate goal. We knelt down to pray because we wanted to feed our souls, because we entered that sacred space of discovery and hope, because we were afraid and looking for solace, because we realized we were alone and we didn't like the feeling, because it was what we were told would create harmony and peace in our world. We did it because we yearned for connection, affirmation, edification, and a sense of mission. It *was* the right thing to do.

Rather than assuming the stance and running through the same routine simply for the sake of assuming the stance and running through the same routine, we're ready for a way that doesn't require that theistic, supernatural, interventionist, triumphalistic, whatever-John-Bishop-called-it god. Bishop is holding a pot full of boiling water and he doesn't know what to do because he is convinced that boiling the water is the point. It never was. Personal spiritual development was the point. Community cohesion was the point. Recognizing our place in the universe was the point. Engaging our passions was the point. Recognizing our beauty was the point. Owning our complicity was the point. Religion was just the pot we cooked all that in. And prayer is the tool we grabbed most often to stir it with.

# 7

## MOVING ON WITH THE VALUES

I love the late Church of England bishop John A. T. Robinson. In his book, *Honest to God*, he offered the church a beautiful clarion call to drop the word "God" for at least a generation. It was inspirational. People across the church and far outside its doors were inspired by it. They are still inspired by it. I read all the time about how inspired they are.

But it was two generations ago! Most who admire and applaud Robinson's idea still don't ever come close to living it out. I understand that context has the ability to significantly mitigate one's passion for this work, but context is not concrete. It can change. I have heard too many colleagues speak of themselves as being too close to retirement to risk their positions. "I'll leave it for the next person to do that stuff," they say, saddling the "next person" with challenges that, if they are too great a risk for someone almost out of the pulpit, will surely prove to be too great for someone just into it.

And so I honour those who are doing this work, difficult though their task is. Nancy Steeves and Christopher New in Edmonton—they are among the very few courageous clergy scattered throughout the world who continue to do this work in a traditional denomination. Rex Hunt was doing it in Canberra before he retired a couple of years ago. Ian Lawton at C3Exchange in Michigan risks the ire of his more traditional colleagues as he moves his church in completely new directions, and Muzi Cindi in South Africa is working to create a progressive community of faith within a context that is decidedly hostile to his work. Fred Plumer in Washington State pushes the envelope within the progressive community in the States. There must be others, perhaps many others, but I don't know of them. If you do, email me. It's not only liberals who are "reclaiming" the word "god," mind you; theologically non-realist progressives are risking preaching *beyond* the word "god." Make sure that they don't mind being outed as progressives, though; it's still a crazy world out there, and backlash can be ugly.

Speaking of which, I know people will be angry with me for the brevity of that list. They will imagine that they belong on it because they understand contemporary scholarship. But that's not what I'm talking about here. I'm talking about taking John Robinson up on his challenge and dropping the word "god." Lots of people call themselves progressives but remain firmly rooted in and unwilling to move from a classically liberal theological perspective—theistic god and all (terms of non–gender specific endearment notwithstanding).

Robinson was never suggesting that people stop believing in God. He just wanted them to stop using the word. He wanted questions about the meaning of life to get out from under the heavy answers that had dulled them, stretch their legs a bit, cover a little more ground, find some new territory or some old hidden gardens out back that people had forgotten for generations, get over the idea that the essence of life has to look a certain way, love a certain way, bleed a certain way. He wanted us to engage in the conversation. I admire that.

Instead of setting out on that creative hike, however, most theologians and clergy have chosen, in the face of the big questions about the nature of god, to become more vague, to ply more metaphors, to avoid more questions. Robinson's simple suggestion, which I know is really not that simple, has been overlooked.

I agree with the assertion made by author Tony Windross in his book, *The Thoughtful Guide to Faith*: using the image of god as anything other than a tool makes it an idol. I've heard dozens of iterations of the "it's not the signpost—it's where the post is pointing" spirituality offered up by various spiritual teachers to try to keep us from thinking we've nailed down what god is (even though, for the greater masses of Christians and non-Christians, we have actually pretty much nailed it down). It's important that the signpost not be the "*thing*." But when Windross then goes on to say that "we [must] work at re-imagining and re-creating the idea of God . . . so that it really *does* speak to the spiritual needs of our time,"[1] I no longer know what he's talking about. A god that speaks is more than a tool. It's a guide. An authority. A lawmaker. A provider. Why, it's a god, damn it. Even the most progressive thinkers I read seem to feel that if their ideas or practices aren't anchored in some version of god or a biblical story, they are somehow unsound.[2]

Australian theologian Nigel Leaves speaks of our need to save religion from its overly defined "domesticated God" and "its 'self-proclamation' as the only way."[3] I'm with him on that, but I doubt that stretching our understanding of god wide enough to include all people, the religious and the non-religious, is the answer. It would mean elevating the word "god" to a universal position that covers everyone's idea of the ultimate. Too many times, I've seen that idea morph into paternalistic imperialism. It shows up in interfaith materials, magazine articles, and grand gestures made by those who are trying to be polite without having to acknowledge how inappropriate their gestures can really be. Protesters at the Occupy Toronto site were visibly impressed when clergy offered to risk arrest by remaining in the tent-spattered park after an eviction notice had been presented, but breaking off chunks of bread from a loaf and sharing them informally with the crowd throughout the evening seemed a much more natural and meaningful interaction between people than did the formal communion service held by robed church officials on the cathedral steps that evening. If there is a meta-ultimate under which we might all be grouped, you can be sure it isn't the Christian idea of god. No buts. I don't care how refined you might argue it to be. I agree that "our continued existence may depend on getting it right"[4] this time, but when we call it ineffable and load it up with the attributes of a loving, interventionist, supernatural being . . . well, it's just not good enough anymore. It still smells like the old God rotting away in Philip Pullman's His Dark Materials trilogy.

Does getting it right really have to include the word "god"? Isn't there a level higher than that? Or a ground beneath us that is more firm, more foundational? This persistent need to connect with the concept of god, be justified by it and justify it, as if nothing has happened since we first came up with the idea, has dogged us through the past two millennia and threatens to overshadow our ability to see clearly in this one. Perhaps we fear that we haven't found anything else to be an equally sufficient anchor—if one is needed at all, beyond the prizing of love in our lives. A colleague recently challenged me to consider that perhaps our problems are grounded in the fact that we don't take the Bible seriously enough. When I asked what that would look like, she pointedly announced that we would be feeding the poor. But do we really need the Bible to know that we should feed the poor? Can't we figure that out on our own? And even if we did learn to feed the poor through those ancient stories, does that mean that we must eternally refer back to them to justify our choice to act justly? Does not love, lived out in acts of justice and compassion, stand quite well on its own? Does it not stand even better on its own, unattached to any specific religious or philosophical group or tradition, to any doctrine about God? Leaves is bang on: we do have to get it right. But I'm convinced that doing so takes us far away from the poisoned word that "god" has become to so many [It is time to move beyond the problems created by the word and concept of god and turn our minds to that which truly unites us all—life—while urging allegiance to that which brings well-being to all—love. Keep your god in your private devotional life if you want to; no one will mind. But couldn't the church, especially the liberal church—with its heritage of critical scholarship and passion for social justice—strike out boldly and proclaim that life is real and love is good and everything else is just stuff we've created to help us deal with life lovingly?

IF ONLY...

I'm not afraid of the word "love" and all the eye-rolling that goes on when people read it. It is not a simple concept when fused to the concept of justice, as it has been throughout much of the history of Christianity. Religion scholar John Dominic Crossan speaks of love and justice in the image of body and soul. Without one, you can't have the other. "Justice without love becomes brutal," he says, "and love without justice becomes banal."⁵ Let's wed those two things to the vision we have of the future and work together to make it so. But Crossan didn't need the hundred or more pages of digging into the Lord's Prayer that preceded his image to convince me it was a good one. It stands on its own. With or without the Bible. With or without God.

## CONFRONTING THE CHALLENGE OF LANGUAGE

For those raised within the embrace of the church, the nostalgic pull of its safe and secure worldview may still drive a desire to pray. If, however, someone arrived from another planet while you were praying and asked what you were doing, you might not find it all that easy to come up with an answer, particularly if you're from a mainline or liberal denomination. And if you've thought yourself beyond images of a supernatural deity who will do anything and everything for you if you get your prayer right, it's going to be even harder to explain.

Finding himself in exactly that theological "wasteland" after reading John A. T. Robinson's *Honest to God*, a correspondent wrote the following to the author: "I have a deep inner desire to return to church, which I find I can satisfy by attending church services abroad where I can understand nothing of the message, yet can be reminded by the environment and by the deeply reverent attitudes of the worshippers, as well as by the magnificent music and the religious pictures, of the intention behind the ritual, and of the deep religious experiences I used to feel as a boy."[6]

Fighting the chronic pain of religious disintegration, the writer offers us a glimpse of the problem we have been staring at for decades: for too many, our language is a barrier to whatever good might come of religious activity. Make the language incomprehensible, and the rituals, the music, and the experience may still have meaning. Having grown beyond the beliefs embedded in a magical understanding of the universe, many are no longer soothed or engaged by invitations to sit with the mysteries of the universe when those invitations come couched in those same magical terms. In our eagerness to hold on to what we thought religion provided, we interrupted the development of the language of faith in its adolescence and refused to let it mature along with the understandings of those it sought to serve. Frozen in the images and symbols of a former worldview, the language can no longer do for many seekers what it was originally imagined to do.

We cannot know what the "intention behind the ritual," as it is called by Robinson's correspondent, was, save perhaps some desire to be safe, to find security in a chaotic world, to achieve "salvation," if you will. But many no longer think of salvation as eternal life in the bosom of the Lord. We think of it as being lifted out of the muck and mire of everyday existence to an awareness of interconnectedness and the wonder of that. We preach about it as that, using metaphor hidden behind old words and symbols. The "intention behind the ritual" may yet have merit, but it is locked in rooms accessible only to those with theological decoder keys who can explain what salvation might mean in a postmodern, post-magical world—they and those who still believe in the magic and aren't looking for a decoder.

Perhaps we could create a new "intention behind the ritual." It could be to create and preserve space in our lives to honour and acknowledge the common human quest for meaning, the desire to find in this life something greater than the mechanics of reproduction and the labour of existence, a this-worldly salvation that might answer our growing existential angst (heck, that might have been the original intention anyway!). In times past, that quest was framed and enhanced by religious ceremony, by crafting a relationship with the spirits, the source, our gods. They knew what the meaning was and could guide us toward it. To honour them, we built cathedrals beautified with extraordinary art, windows, arches, and music, creating an environment in which we could contemplate the mysteries of the universe, of our own selves, of all that was unknown.

That is exactly what the Washington National Cathedral feels like a century after its cornerstone was laid: massive, awe-inspiring, beautiful. Boldly asserting its Christian witness, the cathedral was designed in medieval Gothic style to "evoke the sense of transcendent harmony and beauty of an earlier era and symbolizing in its grandeur the God of all nations."[7] It took eighty-three years to build.

Those eighty-three years were times of turbulent change in the world and in the church. Already feeling the cataclysmic blows of scientific pressure, Christianity would find the monolithic worldview it posited hammered by its exposure to other, equally passionate faiths, to horrors that living memory could not rouse nor intellectual minds justify, and to an explosion in secularism that offered myriad options for discerning meaning in life beyond religious belief. It was as though, with each chiselled blow that crafted the cathedral's stones, a chip flew also from the beautiful vision that had inspired it, until by 1990, when the edifice was finally complete, there was little left to the dream of a world made perfect through the triumphant realization of our Christian tale. And while I do not mourn the weakening of a belief system that has damaged and destroyed both whole cultures and intimate personal hopes, I do lament the loss of our communal recognition that there is more to life than fulfilling our personal desires as quickly as we are able.

We now build shopping malls and adorn them with Lalique crystal panels, water fountains, images of gods in the forms of women and men digitally enhanced to divine perfection. Burying our insecurities in material possessions and the quest for the "good life" is so cliché and yet it continues to exude its seductive appeal. Breaking free of the cycles of hungry consumption and its fleeting satisfaction seems to require oh so much energy. We have little of it left to engage in a detox program that will rid us of our feelings of inadequacy and insignificance. So we remain content to live anaesthetized against the perils that surround us, or we find ourselves facing the tragedies of our current reality (peak oil, the commoditization of water, etc.) with skill sets unmatched to the enormity of the task.

The language of prayer, as we have seen, is particularly frozen in time—and often damagingly so. While many in the church have shifted their *understanding* of words and practices still in use in order to become comfortable with them—that's exactly what you'll find in the Borg book *Speaking Christian*—those shifts only serve to further barricade the "intention behind the ritual" within strongholds of theological interpretation. The work has eroded universal access to the potential inherent in that time set aside by the church each week for contemplation, reflection, and reconnection with those things that are most important in life.

It is not that I think the work of reimaging and reinterpreting the language of prayer has been ill intentioned. It has unquestionably been immensely helpful to many people—comforting, affirming, encouraging—and so it binds them to the best the religion can be. But as the literacy rate within the church has risen with the teaching of contemporary scholarship and exposure to the metaphorical meaning of the Christian lexicon, those outside the church fall further and further behind. The chasm between the pulpit and the pew has been filled in by the increasing accessibility of contemporary scholarship. But have we filled the chasm up only to dig around the outside of the church a moat that will prevent anyone without the right language instruction from entering? Is that the future the church is choosing? To become increasingly irrelevant to the world outside its doors? The path of reinterpretation has brought the church to a place of inward-focused protectionism, a type of institutionalism where its energies predominantly serve only those who, no matter what, hold to the church's fundamental doctrines or who experience its theatre and pageantry as irretrievably intertwined with their sense of spirituality. I am sure this was not the intention behind the reclamation of Christian language, but it has become one of its detrimental effects and one that is seductively easy to snuggle into. I don't believe we can both snuggle in and engage the wider world, and so I call us to alter our course. The church has faltered; it is no longer as brave as it once was, but it must be.

## WHICH IS IT—NEW WINESKINS OR NEW WINE?

At another point in time, it seemed we were making progress in our understanding of things theological. Late in the nineteenth century, what was known as the New Theology sought to grapple with the challenges Christianity was experiencing as a result of the expansion of the scientific enterprise. John Burroughs, an American naturalist, essayist, and friend to many of the industrialists and thinkers of his time, expressed his disappointment. "I had hoped that the New

Theology, as it is called . . . had escaped from some of the trammels of the old, but, so far as I can see, its only escape is to substitute some softer literary phrases for the hard old dogmas. At bottom it seems to be about the same thing."[8] At the time, Burroughs was right. The church was trying to hold on to much of the same salvific, theistic, supernatural theology but cloak it in language that bred acceptability within a community grown increasingly critical. It was the same old wine fussed up in new wineskins. No threat of rupture, but as Burroughs had seen, nothing to get very excited about either.

We have a great deal more and better information at our fingertips now, and we have the knowledge and understanding that mean it's a whole new wine; it's not just the packaging that's changed this time. Since Burroughs' time, other gospels have been discovered, and new forms of criticism and clearer understandings of historical perspective have been brought to the task of interpreting Christianity. Many theologians have thought their way through to new interpretations that take contemporary historical, archaeological, literary, and other hermeneutical endeavours into consideration. But the church is still getting things twisted. New language, in Burroughs' time, simply covered the same old beliefs. Now, new beliefs—that is, understandings that challenged the old beliefs—are covered by the same old language.

Much that has been discovered about Christianity, and religion generally, over the past century has been woven by contemporary scholars into new worldviews that inform our cultural and social milieu. The church, in the more liberal denominations, has sought to honour the work of those scholars, including it in current curricula and ensuring that it is available to those being prepared for leadership.[9] But if the stand is taken that new ideas must be uttered in the same old images and metaphors, represented by the same old symbols, grounded in the same the same old story, and engaged with the same old rituals, the church will become eternally irrelevant to far too many. Those in the liberal church do what they have always done: stretch old language and metaphors over new understandings and ideas. But old wineskins aren't up to the pressure of new wine. It is a dangerous move on the part of mainline Christianity, which thinks it is making the safe choice. A long, slow leaking out of its richest wine—the worldviews envisioned by its brightest minds and by the generations most passionate about addressing contemporary issues—is already being seen as the result. Furthermore, the church's attempt to preserve itself in such a way ignores another rupture that already exists between the church and all those outside it—both those who have left the church of their youth and those who have never known it. Each of these demographics has had much to offer the conversation on right relationship, on life, on what is sacred, but neither has ever been recognized by the church as anything more than a mission field.

Christianity, which at its best provides a space to discover truths, create meanings, and contemplate mysteries, has grown too fond of the stuff with which it structures and fills that space—the language of the menacing dogma that undergirds everything it does, hidden though it is behind the heady haze of metaphor. The church has become more attached to its doctrine and the beliefs that protect and reinforce its identity than it is to the space those things were meant to create and hold for the sacred task of the contemplation of life, morality, and right relationship. The task of contemplating *church doctrine* has outranked the task of contemplating life itself.

## THE STAKES ARE TOO HIGH FOR STALLING

It is no longer healthy or safe for us to keep our eyes focused on anything but the realities of the world in which we live. A supernatural worldview, no matter how beautiful some may consider it, and the practices that reinforce it, anaesthetizes us to things we need to do if we are to create sustainability for our planet, our children, and their children. Stripped of a divine plan, we are challenged to be active participants who can mould the world around us rather than simply passive recipients who engage, now and again, in acts of devotion with the hope of altering the course of events.

We live in a matrix of incredibly complex natural systems, some of which we understand and many of which we don't. Without us, the world would still spin itself through eons of new life cycles and ages—continents continuing to shift, oceans rising and falling, stars coming into being and dying overhead. There is no good in that. There is no evil. There is only life unfolding into new life and into new life again. The scientific purists among us would call it energy, and truly, that is all it is. We have chosen to define its ebb and flow, and in so doing, we've attached meaning, blessing, curse to the experience of it. In the beginning—in our earliest moments of self-awareness, in *our* beginning—it was *not* God that created us. It was our ability to differentiate ourselves from the rest of the world through the use of language. It *was* "the word," although a very different understanding of it than that set out in John's Gospel. We used it to name ourselves, to define our surroundings, to categorize our world, to identify this as good and that as evil. Before the word, things just were. Since it, we have created heaven and hell. With it, we created God.

Without our interpretation of events and identification of objects and people, neither good nor evil exists. The naming of animals in the Genesis creation story witnesses to the power of the act of definition. As we define good and evil, we become the creators of good and evil. We are the source of all that is good. We are the source of all that is evil. So while we are part of the natural world, our ability to define what constitutes beauty and goodness, and to work toward creating it rather than toward what we define as repulsive and evil, gives us a different position and responsibility in relation to that world. We exist in a world that is not simply charming and lovely; one only has to view a few episodes of the BBC's popular *Planet Earth* series to get a really good idea of how gruesome it can be. But we, *Homo sapiens*, are able to transcend the base realities of the world, rise above a clicker mentality, and find our way forward to a life enhanced by purpose, beauty, and goodness. It is this unique perspective that allows us to rise above a survival mentality, one that we may honour as appropriate in the plant and animal world but that, in the realm of humanity, only ever desecrates us. We can because we are able to reflect upon past choices and extrapolate consequences from possible ones. It is what distinguishes but does not separate us from most of the other sentient beings on the planet.

In our distant past, the travesties we perpetrated were primarily against one another; many of them were in the name of religion, but many more were the result of our simple pursuit of security in an uncertain world. Over the centuries, the impetus for our actions—our quest for security—has not changed, but we have achieved the capacity to affect not only one another but also that entire matrix of complex natural systems. True, we have done much that is admirable, and that stands as testimony to what we are capable of doing. Taking measure on a planetary scale, however, the shadow we cast falls far and wide, deep and cold.

While there is much philosophical conversation on whether there is such a thing as goodness or evil, and if there is, what constitutes each of them, I'm going to take a stand on the issue. Outspoken atheist author Sam Harris risked the cold shoulders of his scientific community for doing the same in his remarkable book *The Moral Landscape*.[10] Writing from within the church, I have an easier time pronouncing on such things than someone whose colleagues veer away from subjects that are difficult to squeeze under a microscope. But we have little time to toy with philosophical or scientific arrogance when it comes to the life of our planet. Like prayer, philosophical exercises and scientific experiments that do not move toward or positively affect the experience of well-being by sentient life are just so much academic masturbation, and we have little time for that.[11] We need to develop solid definitions of good and solid definitions of evil, and then bring each of our decisions down squarely upon one or the other, the interpretation of each being influenced of course by the context in which it is unfolding.

Let good be our positive interaction with the planet's natural matrix; when we interact with the matrix of life with humility and respect, finding ways to live sustainably within it and building the potential for well-being across all species, let that be defined as good. And let evil be our negative interaction with the planet's natural matrix. When we desecrate the planet, use it for our own purposes, and act as monster gods indifferent to our impact on the fragile balance of life or the well-being of others who share it with us, let that be defined as evil. Moment by moment, day by day, generation by generation, we have made our choices, creating beauty, wholeness, and dignity in the lives of others and the planet but also desecrating them with discord, disharmony, and disruption. And our choices continue to be made, moment by moment, woven into a tapestry of terrible beauty by our own hands.

## FIRST WE HAVE TO LET GO

It is now devastatingly clear that if we hope to create any coherence between prayer and a theologically non-realist (TNR) world, there are going to be losses across the board. Removing the foundational understanding of a theistic all-seeing, all-knowing, all-everything god as source of all goodness has implications for hymnody, architecture, rituals, and language. Even if we choose not to eliminate the language that presupposes a supernatural deity and instead "fuzzy" our way through our liturgy, symbol, and god-language by calling it metaphor and myth, we can't fudge it when it comes to prayer. For all intents and purposes, traditional and much of liberal prayer posits a divine, supernatural, interventionist force—God, the universe, whatever. In a TNR world, there is no such supernatural being or force; like flat-earth geography, the concept is gone. The language of prayer is entirely interwoven with the idea of something beyond our natural ability to alter our own course, meet our own or others' needs, and change our own circumstances.

Of our losses regarding prayer as we move through this transition, three frame the most significant hole created by the shift: our *sense of the transcendent*; our *identity*, or the understanding we have of ourselves as Christians; and the response to our most primal need, the *comfort* we have known in the story of a world created and protected by a god we named God who loves us.

The absence of a supernatural YHWH (Yahweh)/God/Allah overseeing all life—no more master weaver ready to act in our lives upon request or promise that everything will work out—places the question of our salvation—our ability to find meaning and peace in the midst of the chaos that is life—before us. (We're really going to have to find a single word to replace "salvation"!) If the purpose of our prayer has been security and comfort, if we're looking for the clicker of positive reinforcement, with the loss of belief in an all-everything god, prayer too has lost its power. Our need for meaning and peace persists, however, along with our quest for comfort and satiety, and so we turn away and forage for truffles, for another source, feeling our way, finding the possible. This way. This way, our instincts tell us. Salvation—or whatever we might call it—is within us.

Beyond its impressive clicker power, prayer has been a vehicle for much that we need to take with us, the things that affect our attitudes, our feelings about ourselves, our openness to possibilities. Strength, comfort, peace, courage—these all remain as important as ever. They are also available in a multitude of ways, not at all exclusive to the practice of prayer. We have been learning to soothe ourselves, to care for one another, to find our own stability and strength. Like the Israelites in the desert—indeed like any displaced people forced to take only what they could carry—those who want to keep all the trappings of prayer will grumble and be cranky for a time as they are pushed to seek meaning beyond the answers that no longer work. Suffice it to say we know there will be upheaval. With the targets we have to meet, the slowing of global warming, the feeding and education of children, the reduction of maternal mortality, the elimination of interpersonal abuse, the preservation of threatened species—you know I could go on and on—we need to grab what we can, everything and anything that will call us to the deepest levels of compassion we can bear while moving us forward in the work of creating a sustainable future on this planet. Our interest in meeting those targets and our ability to do so will be driven by that same obsessive–compulsive urge we've always known: the desire for comfort, for security, for satiety.

As we consider prayer, its ability to help us deal with seemingly unbearable situations, and its offer of meaning at the end of a long corridor of pain and disillusionment, it is the loss of a loving being in whose presence we felt safe that rocks us most of all. Coming to terms with the impact of this loss has not gone well to date. We see despair and meaninglessness grow in proportion to our desire to be entertained, anaesthetized against what we perceive to be the too-hard realities of life. But this is the place from which we must start. This is the place where we must build that space into which all can be invited, so that we can talk about, meditate upon, hold sacred the struggle that is the human condition. We are back where we began: trying to find safety in an insecure world. This time, though, as we create, we can go straight to the facts of our existence, our dependence upon one another, and the fragile hope that is only and can only ever be in our own hands.

I'm urging us to head out beyond the persistence of language that ties us to a supernatural *source, agent,* and *promise* of goodness, the idea of a supernatural god that over-parented us and did not let us find our own way. I want nothing less than a language that honours the reality of the quest for security and doesn't cover it up with theological constructs that soothe our anxieties but do not call us to the greatness of our own humanity. Our language has folded us in half for most of our existence. We need language that will challenge us to get up from our knees, hand us back our dignity, ignite our compassion, and help us find all those crucial ways we need to live love into the world. Language that reinforces a system of belief that can drive someone back down to his knees, remove his dignity, hold him to a standard he can never meet, and silence his objection to the way things are with the promise of something no one has the right to promise unless she also has the power to bring it about is repugnant. It is especially so if we argue it's fine for us because we've revisioned it, reclaimed it, rebeautified it. Face it: if the language you use, whether in prayer, in song, or in simple conversation, is language that forces even one person to his knees, it is wrong. Hold out your hand. Help him up. And let's move on.

PART FOUR

# IN A WORLD BEYOND BELIEF

# 8

# (PRAYER) NATURALLY

There is no doubt that prayer has taken a "multiplicity of forms" over the ages, or that the list of those forms compiled in the early twentieth century by Friedrich Heiler is captivating and poetic. These are but a few of the broad continuums upon which, he notes, we have artfully stretched prayer:

> Prayer appears in history . . . as the calm collectedness of a devout individual soul, and as the ceremonial liturgy of a great congregation . . . as loud shouting and crying, and as still, silent absorption; as artistic poetry, and as stammering speech; as a childlike entreaty for life, health, and happiness, and as an earnest desire for power in the moral struggle of existence . . . as a selfish wish, and as an unselfish solicitude for a brother; as wild cursing and vengeful thirst, and as heroic intercession for personal enemies and persecutors; as a stormy clamour and demand, and as joyful renunciation and holy serenity.[1]

There are many more couplets in Heiler's list, and I'd highly recommend that you seek them out and enjoy them, but the ones above have been carefully extracted from it. Excluded are the pairs that were directly related to the idea of the supernatural *source*, *agent*, and *promise*. What remain are expressions of prayer that are beyond that construct and are significant elements of the human journey. Look at the list again. See yourself in the positions described. Note how they reflect the breadth of human experience. Prayer has, in addition to its entreaties to supernatural power, been significant in reminding us of the primal truths of our experience, both the best and the worst of who we can be.

Taking time out of our daily routines to get in touch with how we are feeling in the situations in which we find ourselves is something I think is extremely important. I don't do it enough, but I know it is important, and when I need to do it, it isn't a foreign concept. Is that because I'm familiar with the practice of prayer, the form used by many to do such reflection? Or is it because I have learned that my responses in situations are better when I have considered the matter from a variety of positions, including my emotional response to them? Remember that our major premise is that prayer must be significant because so many say they could not live without it, but also that it cannot be essential because so many others do live without it. So the answer to that question isn't clear. Those who have relied on prayer would take the former view; those who have not, the latter. Take the supernatural element out of prayer, however, and these very human elements—the ability to lament, to celebrate, to express fierce emotion, to concentrate, to struggle morally, and to live with care—are those that are perhaps the most important, despite what we have believed to be true. Prayer doesn't become nothing just because you take God out of it.

Elizabeth Roberts and Elias Amidon collected prayers from around the world and brought them together in a devotional volume called *Life Prayers*. In the introduction, they describe prayer as "offer[ing] a skilful means for marrying an inner sense of peace with the outer demands of

the world. . . . Prayer also gifts us with a deepening of our compassionate caring for the world."[2] Author Kathleen Norris touches on the same
quality in her book *Amazing Grace: A Vocabulary of Faith*, where she states
that prayer is "asking to be changed in ways you can't imagine."[3]

John Shelby Spong wrote about his daily practice of prayer, noting
that as his idea of god shifted so that he viewed god less as a personal
being and more as the source of life, so too did his understanding of
prayer. "Prayer became for me the way I lived, loved, and struggled,
the way I dared to be. Preparation for prayer was the time I spent . . .
recalling who I am. . . . Prayer for me is living."[4] His daily devotional
time is now *preparation* for prayer. Prayer is what happens once he gets
on with his day. Author Frederick Buechner would approve. He writes:

> Whatever else it may or may not be, prayer is at least talking
> to yourself, and that's in itself not always a bad idea. Talk to
> yourself about your own life, about what you've done and
> what you've failed to do, and about who you are and who
> you wish you were and who the people you love are and the
> people you don't love too. Talk to yourself about what mat-
> ters most to you, because if you don't you may forget what
> matters most to you.[5]

Obviously, not all ideas about prayer are grounded in the story of
a supernatural being who is waiting to hear our hearts turn toward
him so he can shower us with manifold blessings. For Norris, Spong,
and Buechner, the value of that story is questionable. For them, as
for many, that story no longer provides the same solidity it once did,
and it's no longer able to declare the same concepts to be truths. Like
these theologians, practitioners, and poets who have already walked
the edges of the definition of prayer, we too must be creative in our
response.

## OVER TO US—NATURALLY

I've been avoiding the acronym created when discussing the super-natural *source*, *agent*, and *promise*—SAP. Speaking about the god, God, as a supernatural SAP seemed irreverent even though I don't believe there is such a thing. But I want to use that acronym now as I shift our focus from the supernatural SAP to a natural one.

What is prayer without a supernatural *source*, *agent*, and *promise*? There are no easy answers, but I believe our genesis, the beginnings of our wondering, is also our greatest promise. We are human, called *Homo sapiens*. The beginning of who we are is wisdom (*sap* is the root element of the Latin verb for "to be wise"). It is not a supernatural SAP to which we look for our salvation, but to our own, human *sap* that we turn, our own wisdom, distilled through ages of history, lit by visions of possibility. It is only through our own wisdom that we will ever find our way to the creation of a world in which those difficult questions can be asked, wrestled with, and turned, through the labour of human hands, to hope. After all, prayer has never been more than a contract for hope. Perhaps, wisely offered, that is all it needs to be.

The motivation for action has always lain in our own broken hearts. Break our hearts with truth,[6] with the indifference of reality, with intimate knowledge of the lives of people on the next block or in another country or on the far side of the moon, and we'll do just about anything. Stretch our understanding beyond what we've relied upon to set the course for our decisions in the past, raise our consciousness about the condition of the world, and we will find ourselves acting in ways we never thought possible—sending money to strangers, open-ing our houses to traumatized animals, giving up eating meat several times a week if not forever, refusing to cave in to the latest fashion trends. As we are moved to respond, we become the agents for change, for goodness, for the relief of pain, for healing. It is not and has never been the supernatural god, God, who acted or who compelled us to act. We have compelled ourselves. We grow in wisdom as we open our hearts to truth. We grow in wisdom when we open our minds. We find that we, *Homo sapiens*, are the agents of change. We don't need to rely upon divine intervention. We no longer gaze into the heavens; we can rest our eyes upon those who share our journey with us, invite them to listen to what has been laid upon our hearts, and offer up the strength of our own hearts to listen to them.

We also realize that we are and always have been the source. What needs to happen comes from within our own midst. We find that the courage to stand up against injustice rises, bullet straight, from the anger that churns in our stomachs when we see it happening, particularly if it is to those we love. We find the strength to get out of bed, as Oriah Mountain Dreamer puts it in her evocative poem "The Invitation," "after the night of grief and despair, weary and bruised to the bone, and do what needs to be done to feed the children."[7] We find the will to dismantle walls built long ago, when, as children, we needed to create safe places for our hearts—walls that now, as adults, we find limit our ability to love and to be whole in relationship. We find the humour to laugh over memories of those we have loved when they are gone through the portal of death. We find the wisdom to stand still and strong and know who we are when what is happening to us or around us threatens to engulf us and imprint its own purpose on our souls. We find that we are the source of the gifts we need to deal with, respond to, engage, reject, embrace whatever we encounter. We are freed of the queue, released from waiting eternally for a divine source to mete out the things we need.

Despite the incredible resources we can find within ourselves, everything we need is not there. Despite what some positive-thinking gurus might claim, we cannot rely solely upon our own resources. We get trapped in boxes of our own making if we do, circumscribed by the extent of our own energies. We need what is outside of us—beyond us—too, intermingling it with what is within—a transimmanence that has been the source of all the good we have experienced, whether we've attributed it to something supernatural or simply the normal unfolding of life. The immanent, that which is within, instinctually reaches for those things we cannot achieve on our own. At the same time, the presence of resources we need to make the difference we see necessary—the transcendent—pulls us beyond our sense of self-sufficiency and presses us out into the open, where the new thing, whatever it is, can happen.

We need this transimmanence. If we don't get outside the shuttered rooms of our own viewpoints and prejudices periodically, we might forget that we are connected and connecting beings and come to see ourselves as islands with no need of empathy or compassion and no need to risk ourselves in love. It's not the same as a warm and fuzzy transcendent being who affirms your supremacy and perspective; it calls you past that self-centred comfort into a new understanding of yourself and the world around you. Nor is it the same as resting in the ignorance of your own existence, comfortable or otherwise; you are part of the matrix, and so are both responsible to and gifted by it.

Again, we are turned from the beseeching, heavenward gaze that characterizes belief in a theistic being toward meeting the eyes of those around us. Take a deep breath, stretch out your shoulders, and recognize that you are as big as you are and so no longer diminished in relation to a divine being who not only had it all together but also was the only way you were going to get it all together. You are capable of making your own way. It is true too, however, that there are those who, for many, many reasons, will never "get it all together." When we find them, we step up to the plate, take a swing at their demons for them,[8] and offer ourselves and our own strengths, as much as we are able, to carry them. No one left behind—remember that. Not because leaving someone behind would be a disgrace or a loss to God, as the creators of the No 1 Left Behind website may believe,[9] but because it would be an affront to our own humanity and to theirs.

## THAT WOULD BE US AGAIN, BUT . . .

What about that third aspect of the supernatural *source, agent,* and *promise* god? That aspect of God as the supernatural promise of goodness, the comforting assurance that God is in ultimate control, so all will be well, no matter how things look at the moment. It gets harder here. In the other two expectations we had of God—source and agent—the natural answer was that we are the source of goodness and we are the agents that bring it into being. However, giving up God as supernatural promise doesn't mean we, as natural agents in this world, can promise goodness. When it came to altering the other expectations we had of God we took on the role, we assumed responsibility—we would be source to ourselves and others; we would be the agents of change. But we are not the promise of peace. We are not the promise of justice. We are not the promise of goodness. We are not the promise of anything. We are fallible, imperfect, broken, limited, often mistaken, often wrapped up in ourselves. We are ordinary *natural* human beings, with no supernatural source or agency to back up any promises we might make.

We haven't lost the promise, though. We're not "giving up" something real. The truth is, there never was the promise of reconciliation or healing or peace or the end of suffering. Never. We wanted it; of course we did. We wanted it very badly, especially in the face of loss, hardships, disease, and destruction. We wanted life to make sense and we wanted a final answer, an ultimate guarantee of goodness. We projected it up onto the god-being and trusted that he or she meant it. But we certainly didn't see it consistently in our own lives. Oh, lots of things have worked out for us, and for some of us more than for others; but many things have not worked out at all, and some of those have been tragic. We haven't seen God bring comfort to the lives of millions around the world who suffer every day without promise of relief. Even when it comes to "afterlife"—we simply do not know anything about it, save the wishful thinking penned in ancient books. There is no guarantee there either. The loss of the supernatural god's promise of goodness is only the loss of an idea, not of a reality—an idea that brought comfort and assurance, but an idea nonetheless. So we look to whatever it is that we can provide that might naturally step into the empty space that the promise of goodness once filled. What is it we can offer that does not pretend something we cannot achieve? If we are not the *promise* of goodness, then what?

What we are is not the *promise* of but the *potential* for goodness.

Dictionaries tell us that potential means "having possibility, capability, or power." Yes, we have that. "The inherent ability or capacity for growth, development, or coming into being." Yes, that's us. "The work required to move an amount of mass from a reference point to a designated point in a gravitational field."[10] Well, actually, yes. Exactly.

Being agents of goodness, giving ourselves and receiving others as sources of goodness, often requires moving our mass against a strong pull in other directions. We're not promise, but we're the only answer we've got. We are natural potential, and that's the only potential there is. Our expectations are now of us. We are the source, we are the agents, and we are the potential for goodness. *Source, agent, potential.* Natural *sap. Homo sapiens.* Beings of wisdom.

What we are doing is exchanging supernatural assumptions for natural ones and supernatural agency for natural agency. The assumption that underlies the concept of prayer is no longer about a divine being but is about being itself. The foundation that underlies all of religion, in fact, is no longer a separate supreme person or entity; the foundation is life and love for ourselves, others, and the world. The losses are obvious and significant, and I'm not minimizing them. But I'm asking you to look at it not from a loss perspective but from what remains and what we gain. We still bring with us the kind of respect for life that prayer fostered within us and the commitment to justice and compassion that grew out of that. We recognize that it was our strength that got us through every situation in which prayer has failed us, a resilience that now grows out of the awareness of our own fallibility. When we, not a supernatural being, are responsible for results and are not able to accomplish what we have struggled toward, we are not destroyed; we can step back, grieve as we must, and begin building a new dream. When out of the midst of our deepest need, we shift our focus from the supernatural god, God, to the natural world, including all the things about it we cannot explain, we look to ourselves and one another for help, for meaning, for support, for relationship, and for that new dream. Much of the positive effect of prayer has been the result of our own strengths, intentions, and abilities, and we can celebrate that even as our reliance on old forms dissipates.

## ALTERED EXPERIENCE: NO SUPERNATURAL HIGH

When our expectations are supernatural, prayer brings us wonder and awe, a secure identity and sense of belonging, hope for change, and comfort and assurance for the future. What can we expect from a natural approach to life and a natural approach to the issue of prayer?

Does the loss of a personal god to relate to in prayer reduce you to a solely intellectual experience? Does "replacing" a personal god with a set of ideals leave you rather cold—ethical, but cold? Remember, we're not *giving up* a personal god. We were interpreting experience as related to and even caused by the god God, when in fact it was related to us. The answers we "got" from prayer were synchronicities we defined as being the result of prayer after the fact. The silences we experienced were not the shunning of an angry or absent god. They were the harsh realities with which we found, within us, the strength to cope. God seemed personal because we are personal, and so that is how we projected our earnest desires and needs. It is a huge credit to us that we are the multi-dimensional beings we are, and that we have been able to resource reality in the infinitely amazing ways we have. The richness is *in* us, not *beyond* us. When someone kneels in prayer, she has brought the best of her mind, emotion, will, choice, body, behaviour, wishes, dreams, and more. Fully engaged with life as natural, with ourselves and others as natural, we fire off in all dimensions. We think, critique, assess, challenge, and affirm. We feel joy, sadness, fear, compassion, anger, and more. We decide, choose, commit, persevere, and change. We act, we don't act; we do well, we stumble; we blow it, we start again; we live. Full engagement of all that we are is not the exclusive purview of those who pray. Those who have lived life fully without prayer have known this all along. Engage with all that life is. Engage and never stop. From "pray without ceasing" to "engage without ceasing." It seems a perfect match.

## Natural Wonder

While leading a workshop, I was asked by someone sceptical about the massive language challenge I was raising where wonder would go in the "God"-less world I described. "Would it be just [pause] science?"

We need to think hard before we put the word "just" in front of the word "science." Daily, those who are curious about our world and the many others that circle the sky day and night fling themselves against problems most of us will never even think about. When we do, there is so much to consider that we are often overwhelmed by the immensity of it. We can be utterly lost in wonder, awe, and amazement at what they touch, see, measure, question, peer into, and peel back. The beauty, diversity, intricacy, immensity, variety, majesty, fragility, and adaptability of the natural world is stunning. It is beyond us, all around us, within us, transcending our ability to understand, yet embracing us as part of the web, part of life, part of the wonder.

And that's just the stuff that doesn't talk. Think of human relationship and friendship, creativity and productivity, contemplation and imagination, artistry and poetry. We are humbled and amazed and grateful for the innumerable—utterly innumerable—human acts of courage, compassion, creativity, ability, perseverance, endurance, generosity, kindness, helpfulness, patience, loyalty, and justice. People transcend limits, go beyond the status quo, make a positive difference, and inspire others to do so as well. Contemplating these wonders over a lifetime is a rich experience indeed. We are transported again and again—sometimes as peak experiences of wonder and oneness, other times as heightened awareness of the deep dimensions of life beyond the superficiality of purely materialist living.

It is a wonderful world. But more, much more, than "just" wonderful.

## Natural Hope for Change

Embracing ourselves as the sole agents for change, we gain a heightened sense of the vast need and opportunity for doing good. This is both daunting and exciting. If we don't do it, it won't happen. Remember? No promise. Just potential. We experience an increased sense of the urgency, aware that no supernatural rescue will save us. The task is huge, the hour is late, and the need is real. As potential for goodness, we have it within ourselves to try to change situations for the better, to influence decisions that will affect people's lives, to communicate in ways that will build healthy relationships, to create beauty where none was before. We know we have limits, as others do and the world does, but we examine identified limits to see if they are real, adjust to them if they are, move through them if they are not.

## Natural Comfort

Through emerging technological advances, scientists are able to see and measure what is happening in our brains much more clearly than ever before. As studies progress, we learn more and more about our socialization, the importance of interactions that take place between our brains and the brains of those around us almost entirely beneath our awareness, the effects of prayer and meditation, and the contemplation of complex topics such as god.

Lionel Tiger and Michael McGuire—an anthropologist and a neuroscientist, respectively—put their individual passions together and push our understanding of what is significant in religious communities into the twenty-first century in their book *God's Brain*. Tiger and McGuire both saw the staying power of religion and wondered what made it so significant. With thousands of years of historical records, millions of religious sites around the world, billions of religious adherents, it's clear something significant has been happening and for some time. They recognized that the one underlying factor operating in every religious impulse is the human brain. In their words, "One brain, four thousand religions."[11]

Forcing into one room things that haven't normally been studied jointly—religion and the brain—Tiger and McGuire bagged the questions created by the worldviews of their two disciplines and their colliding ideas and used them to map out their study. The results of their work are fascinating.

In his neuroscience lab, McGuire watched what happened in the brains of male vervet monkeys as they exhibited certain behaviours, and he made a remarkable discovery: the monkeys who were in dominant positions had *double* the serotonin levels of those who were subordinate. Double is significant. Big-time significant in the scientific community.

Now, we're not talking about double the appetite or double the ability to stay awake. We are talking about serotonin, a neurotransmitter that is responsible for our feelings of well-being. It's the equivalent to a happy pill, and most of us make it all on our own. Finding out how to double your happy is a very significant event. Well, without drugs, I mean. Ecstasy and other MDMA drugs also produce extraordinary highs of serotonin, but over the long run, I think you'll find the delivery system Tiger and McGuire discovered far safer, if not as easily accessible.

The discovery led to a completely new understanding of how social relationships are created. The assumption had been that the primary factors in relationship were biological—our hormones pushed us toward relationship and community. These serotonin levels showed the opposite was true. What happens in community affects what happens in the body.[12]

When the status of the males was changed, their serotonin levels changed too, confirming that the amount of the chemical in the brain was the result of the communal relationships and not the other way around. It would seem that serotonin, the chemical that makes us feel good, oozes into our brains at a much higher rate when we experience displays of submissive behaviour that reinforce our status and importance. A smile, a handshake, your name mentioned positively, recognition by members of a group, etc.—all these serve as the crucial reinforcement we need. When we are acknowledged to be important, of value, loved, we get high on that affirmation.[13] It's that simple. Be around people who believe you're important and your serotonin fix for the day is delivered right where it's needed. With the added bonus that you don't need a dealer and you don't risk jail time.

George Clooney, as Ryan Bingham—a hired gun whose specialty is firing personnel for corporations that are downsizing—has the system down pat in *Up in the Air*, a 2009 Oscar contender. Enrolled in every prestigious frequent-flyer club possible, Bingham—who is against interpersonal commitment, arguing that the things that drag us down the most in our lives are our relationships—has created a "serotonin shake" upon which he appears to thrive. Each time an airline steward calls him by name, an employee who is about to be fired by him acknowledges his superiority, or a conference audience erupts in applause at the conclusion of his polished speech on travelling light, his brain shifts him into a serotonin high he can get nowhere else.

Unless he went to church, or synagogue, or temple, or mosque.*

### Religious Turn-on

Religion, it turns out, turns us on. And who wouldn't want that? Beyond the psychological well-being derived from a comforting belief in a supernatural deity, the social life of religious community can reproduce heightened feelings of happy like those McGuire saw in his lab. Tiger and McGuire argue that religion offers an anti-stress, "brain-soothing" experience worth the Sunday morning drive every time.

How does it do that?

What Tiger and McGuire put together in their study were the long-term effects on the brain of participating in religious activities. They identified three significant factors in the longevity and breadth of the religious pursuit—socialization, ritual, and beliefs. Each part of this triumvirate, as they call it, is pertinent to the study of prayer. Each of them, they argue, is a significant response to a frightening reality: the effects of stress on the body. Socialization, ritual, and belief all offer brain-soothing qualities that benefit first us and then, through us, the world around us. And they are all offered in the setting of the religious community.

---

* Okay, not *every* church, synagogue, temple, or mosque. Lots of them give new people the cold shoulder, and Bingham would likely have received more affirmation at the airport than he would in one of those. But a congregation well versed in welcoming and affirming visitors— that's the kind of place Bingham would need.

I know people often refer to churchgoers as sheep, but in this case think of them as McGuire's vervet monkeys. In religious gatherings, where there is little expectation of disruption (everyone knows the rules) and people are generally known (or are expected to be interested in becoming known), parishioners tend to be more willing to display behaviour that reinforces another's worth and identity as a member of the community. Each time that happens, a serotonin response is registered in the brain and the recipient is on his way to a feel-good high. (Kudos to my ninety-two-year-old friend Jeanne, who makes a point of smiling at everyone—and I mean *everyone*—not only in our church community but also on the street. And she'll keep on smiling every time she sees someone, even if it takes years for that someone to finally smile back. She is a walking serotonin factory for the community, helping to give people happy highs for free every single day.) Ironically, at the end of *Up in the Air*, church is exactly where Bingham finds out that the serotonin shake his airline points have earned him isn't working like it once did.

Serotonin responses triggered by friendly interactions combine with activity in the cortical region of the brain (this is the part devoted to recognizing faces),[14] the absence of abusive language,[15] and the acceptance of codes of dress, action, or behaviour that increase a sense of belonging and ratchet down anxiety[16] to create a very strong, very positive brain-soothing system, and because of that, a perfect environment for social cohesion and the staying power it offers. Religious communities are survivors for very good reasons.

Of course, there are still some things to discover about the complex serotonin fix. Introverts seem to need more positive recognition than extroverts to get the same boost, and the jury is still out on whether women need more than men. You may have noted that I've been singling out the guys in relation to the serotonin highs. More women use artificial serotonin boosters like Prozac, and studies have shown that they do not synthesize serotonin at nearly the same levels as men. Studies of primates suggest that females simply don't get as high on adulation as their male compatriots do.[17] (I'm being very careful not to comment on that.)

Furthermore, the reality is that a little squirt of serotonin once every so often is not going pull you out of the dumps as quickly as you might like it to. The effect on mood is not overwhelming, and it takes some time to experience an ongoing benefit. Those who participate regularly in church, often "in the building" or with other members of the congregation throughout the week, are much happier with their experience than those who attend irregularly. It's like any exercise. You have to do it regularly or it doesn't do you much good at all.[18]

Tiger and McGuire's research and analysis was supported when, in December 2010, sociologists Chaeyoon Lim and Robert Putnam published their findings that friendships and social networks in religious communities are significantly more closely linked to life satisfaction than beliefs. In fact, neither strength of religious faith nor certainty of belief made any difference. Those who "personally experience the presence of God" aren't any more satisfied with their lives than those who don't. Lim and Putnam's work virtually erased differences in private and subjective religiosity from the satisfaction quotients of participants.[19]

What Lim and Putnam found that mattered was regular attendance, the development of social networks within the religious community, and a clear sense of religious identity—that is, belonging. "Congregational social networks are distinct from other social networks only when they are accompanied by a strong sense of religious belonging," they wrote. "Conversely, a strong sense of identification enhances life satisfaction only when social networks in a congregation reinforce that identity."[20] In other words, it is "neither faith nor communities . . . that are important, but communities of faith."[21]

## Booster Power

All that is very interesting, but what does it say about our practice of prayer? Communal prayer in mainline congregations has always been led almost exclusively by the ministerial leader, the priest, or someone in a position of authority. And though there might be a great serotonin boost going on there for those persons—especially the males among them—it would seem logical to assume the opposite was happening in the pews. Congregants are often passive participants, asked to do nothing more than assume the position appropriate to the particular congregation's practices.

If you consider the roles played during prayer and Faber's argument that we return to the symbiotic relationship we experienced as very young children, it is possible that congregational members are, in fact, experiencing a serotonin boost. Given the fact that most people think they are speaking to God during prayer, it could be argued that believing God is attending to their concerns would result in a dramatic serotonin boost. That would be hugely more significant than whatever affirmation the priest or pastor was giving. I mean, if you've dialled up the Creator of the Known Universe and she takes your call, that's pretty impressive. And if you are offering prayers you are convinced God will always say yes to—a topic authors who write about prayer like to explore—your positive feedback loop could result in a very deep and lasting sense of well-being, well beyond anything you might otherwise get here on earth.

But what happens when that affirmation doesn't come? What about prayer requests God doesn't grant? Most people, I expect, are praying for results, and more often than not, those results just aren't that evident. Primates that are sent back down in the ranks lose their serotonin boost. Tiger and McGuire even suggest that the loss of regular affirmation may be the reason so many men die in the first year of their retirement.[22] Imagine believing you have God's undivided attention and then it seems he's not paying attention anymore. He's stopped caring. Life gives you a bad turn, and using the old paradigm you've been given, that means you're either bad, unworthy of notice, or inexplicably alone. A desperately sad teenager once sobbed from the heart to me, "There is no god and I'm so lonely!" At some point before that realization, he must have believed God was there with him, watching over him, caring for him. He saw himself as important in God's eyes, but at that particular moment in his life, when his emotional pain seemed unbearable, he wasn't able to replace the affirmation God had provided with anything or anyone else. It was a horrible moment. I couldn't give him back that god—he knew it and I knew it. Sometimes, when the crash has been that enormous, we don't seem to be enough. All I could do was give of myself. It's all we can ever do.*

The second and third elements of Tiger and McGuire's secular triumvirate—ritual and belief—also offer powerful brain-soothing effects. We participate in rituals because they are honoured as significant acts within a community and because they reinforce our beliefs. Rituals make us feel safe. They affirm our membership in a group. They help others recognize us as members who will provide for our safety. Not that mainline congregations are likely to turn to violence if someone doesn't know when to stand up or sit down, but think about the violence that has erupted throughout the annals of history for reasons that might seem now to be insignificant, or that continue to this day based on beliefs regarding appropriate dress or behaviour. It probably wouldn't take an anthropologist and a neuroscientist to draw the line between a violation of communal etiquette and risks to personal safety throughout history. Breaches of protocol are now mostly fodder

---

* Former evangelicals have also expressed the dreadful sense of loss they experience when they lose that very intimate connection they once had with God. They have no idea what they were connected to, but it provided them a sense of comfort, security, and importance that they have great difficulty replacing.

for newspaper sales and network ratings, especially when they involve photos of Michelle Obama placing her arm around Queen Elizabeth II during an official visit or of Prime Minister Stephen Harper stepping up to take the royal salute from the military on Canada Day 2009, an honour usually reserved for a representative of the monarchy. In less civil societies, we can imagine political breaches might have caused dangerous, life-threateningly severe repercussions.

Ritual doesn't need to be something wahoo, and I'm hoping that, by now, you'll know I wouldn't want it to be. It doesn't need to involve candles either, but it can. It doesn't need to involve water, but it can. It doesn't need to involve sand, or earth, or flowers, or fabric, or stones, or chips of sea glass, or whistles, or kites, or coins, or ribbons, or anything. But it can. Ritual is a symbolic act that is recognizable as something the community owns and knows is theirs. The way people gather when they arrive, the exchange of greeting, the opening words or actions, the closing elements, the way they take leave of one another. Do they pick up a stone on the way in and put it back when they leave? Do they sit in the same chair? Do they embrace one another or have a special way of shaking hands? One of our members introduced us to hugging with our faces going over the left shoulder instead of the habitual right so that our hearts meet as we embrace. And we often "watch each other away" as we leave, holding on to the idea that we offer ourselves to one another, and should anything happen between the good-bye we share and the next time we gather, that strength can be drawn on even in our absence. Ritual is tailored to the community and reflects its general style. But it can also begin to define the community as it appeals to certain personality types.

When we have it right, when we see that we are acting, speaking, dressing, responding in ways that are standard for the group we are in, we feel safe. There is incredible comfort in that experience of safety which lowers our levels of stress, that poisonous threat to our well-being.

We have created communities that have done this for millennia. Mostly, we've called them religions, but in truth, although belief may have been the impetus for our doing so, it was not nearly the greatest benefit.

What activities could we engage in if we wished to enter into these experiences? Could prayer be reconfigured so that it could still be useful? Would we have to call it prayer? I've stated throughout this book that while we want to lay to rest all that is not helpful, we also want to retain everything that is. I'm suggesting that the four elements of traditional prayer in mainline denominations, and in the personal prayer lives of many, reflect natural human needs and aspirations. They are not religious terms, although they've been used primarily in religious settings. I believe that this points to the real benefit we can derive from religion and traditional prayer. We no longer need the connection to supernatural ideas, but we don't want to lose the recognition of crucial human realities.

Author Karen Armstrong, through her explorations of world religions, has found her way toward compassion as a central theme around which all people of goodwill might gather. To help bring about such work, she created a Charter for Compassion.[23] There is no god identified in the charter. No "transcendent," no "sacred," no "ultimate"— words that may exclude someone who might passionately agree with the charter but reject or find no meaning in those concepts. Armstrong seems to have stepped beyond the divisive barriers of religion toward a place of non-exclusive ideals. These ideals, then, necessary as they are to the sustainability of our planet and the responsibility we have to honour the dignity in all living things, become accessible to everyone.

While Armstrong may still use the word "god" in her personal devotional life, she does not use it here but focuses instead on what John A.T. Robinson's correspondent identified as the "intention behind the ritual." To Armstrong, that intention is a crucial and ongoing conversation about compassion, so she creates a virtual space for that conversation to continue among all people into the twenty-first century. She recognizes, it would seem, that theistic language and the realist god it implies are impediments to the evolution of that conversation. I honour Armstrong for taking, as she once did from the cloistered traditions of the convent, that initial and freeing step beyond the cloistered language of our faith tradition.

## Bolte of Insight . . . Natural High

I know many would be happy to leave me to the world's wonders, but they might also argue that I too easily dismiss what they have experienced and describe as their encounters with the supernatural god or a divine energy. They will be inclined to set aside my perspective as that of someone who doesn't understand or has had no experience of the divine. I'm sure I haven't, but I'm not sure I haven't shared the same experiences. That's the thing. It's not the experience that sets us apart; it's the interpretation.

Ever since I was a young girl swinging back and forth on a hard wooden swing at my grandmother's cottage, deep in the self-absorption of adolescence, I have, on occasion, experienced what I would call an altered perception of reality. I see and sense things differently for a bit, becoming totally and utterly aware of my connection with what reality really is. I have described it as being interwoven with the rest of what is—the word "reality" doesn't quite seem to fit.

It wasn't until I was in my late thirties that I realized the same thing didn't happen to everyone. You might think that a bit peculiar. It's not. Remember, I grew up within a very liberal denomination and never had a foundation that would have suggested God was giving me a unique experience. I didn't gravitate toward a mystical explanation in the same way others, confident of the origins of such experiences, were wont to do. Even when I studied Christian mystics at theological college, I didn't identify my experiences with anything I read as those described as mystics often do. The framework into which the experiences of Christian mystics were embedded is simply of a different order than the natural physical reality from which I supposed my experiences to arise. It might help to note that I had failed to notice that other things I experienced weren't the same as those experienced by everyone else too. My headaches, for example, weren't diagnosed as migraines until I was in my forties, though I'd had them—often over a dozen a month—since I was eight. I had simply assumed they were ordinary headaches, and because I didn't have some of the classic symptoms, the right medical diagnosis wasn't made.

Since I made the connection between my experiences and those others have had, I've become increasingly uncomfortable with labelling them "mystical." I am loath to ground an experience in a religious or otherworldly reality that I otherwise reject simply because I do not understand what that experience is. It's too convenient—and too easily co-opted by others to suit their purposes. I think of it as connection, but within myself—as a step into a distilled reality that is, through the process of clarification, hyper-real, texturized, potent. Perhaps my migraines are part of what I experience, the blood vessels in a particular part of my brain dilating in ways that create a shift in perception. I simply don't know.

It was in March 2008 that neuroscientist Jill Bolte Taylor's lecture at a TED (Technology Entertainment and Design) convention was posted to the Internet. Shortly afterward, I watched, fascinated with her description of the stroke she had experienced years before, which had effectively taken her left hemisphere offline and rendered her riveted to the wonder of in-the-moment living that only the right hemisphere can offer. Without being grounded by the left hemisphere's incessant interpretation of everything, its cataloguing of information like numbers, letters, facts, and words, the world is experienced without boundaries. Everything is sensation and oneness and peace. No lists, no pressures, no place you need to be.

But it wasn't Bolte Taylor's description of the stroke that connected her experience to mine. I mean, she was having a stroke! I'd never had a stroke, so my first screening of the lecture, like my reading of the mystics at theological college, didn't twig anything. But when I returned to the lecture to review it for another purpose, it was as though I were watching with a different set of eyes. Her explanations of the brain and how each hemisphere worked helped ground my experience in the anatomical world of my own brain, which is where I had always assumed it was happening. And it met my experience in another profound way.

You see, when my experience of an altered reality is over, I am bereft. I am left with an intense feeling of separation that borders on despair, as well as a sadness that grows out of having experienced completion and then being denied it within the everyday routine I have to return to. Confined, as we all are, by our senses, our bodies, our contexts, our left hemispheres, I come away from such experiences feeling as though torn from a much greater reality, one in which everything is known, understood, accepted, and so filled with peace. Hungers are sated, angers dissipated, hatreds dissolved, distances erased. The mosaic of reality I experience brings this home to me each time I am cast into it; the illusion of space existing between me and other people, things, and life forms is completely obliterated and I want to stay there, to keep the experience of that. Losing it is just that—loss. Incredible loss. Bolte Taylor's descriptions of the experience of slipping away from the right brain overload and back into the hard-core reality that the left brain compulsively stamps all over everything was similar. Watching her talk, I knew the loss she was describing. It was the same loss. I knew, watching the lecture, that somehow my right brain occasionally goes on overdrive for brief periods of time—short, limited segments of my life that inform me of the vast unknowns beyond our normal sensory perception. Not otherworldly beyond. This-worldly beyond. This-worldly and absolutely amazing.

What took me back to the TED lecture, and so to the unravelling of the connection between it and my own experiences, was Paul. The first time I listened to Bolte Taylor talk, I knew that she was describing someone else: Paul. Paul-on-the-road-to-Damascus Paul. Paul-caught-up-into-the-third-heaven Paul.* And that, I thought, was cool.

As she lay in the hospital, experiencing the loss of separateness between her and the world around her, an intimate and complete oneness with the universe that she called nirvana, Bolte Taylor realized what a gift the experience was for her and could potentially be for the world. She speaks of her "stroke of insight" during those difficult days:

> [I]f I have found nirvana and I'm still alive then everyone who is alive can find nirvana and I pictured a world filled with beautiful, peaceful, compassionate people who knew that they could come to this space at any time and that they could purposely choose to step to the right of their left hemispheres and find this peace. . . . What a stroke of insight this could be to how we live our lives.[24]

While Paul lost his sight, not his speech, his dramatic conversion from a life spent hunting and persecuting Christians is something that, short of actually hearing a voice from the heavens, would take a significant event of some kind to accomplish. Jill Bolte Taylor's stroke of insight pushed her to realize the incredible connection we have—one to the other. Paul's conversion, previously argued by some to have been a stroke of another kind, may have been just such an experience and, with only first-century interpretations of the event available, easily processed as a divine intervention in his life. Indeed,

---

* Although Paul suggests that he is speaking about someone else when describing "being caught up into the third heaven" (2 Cor. 12:2–4), many scholars believe the description is autobiographical.

the fact that Paul appears to use his experience in different ways to affect different constituents suggests that it was not as cut and dried as many would like to believe. The outcome—that he found himself protecting and advancing the message of a community bound together by a belief that life was sacred—is entirely in keeping with the lived experience of someone who, like Bolte Taylor, had a powerful, life-altering, connection-making stroke of insight. He may have called it God, but now that we've looked closely, we can see that he was equally able to find his way toward just relationships without a supernatural god or divine energy guiding him.

We have wrapped ourselves in theological straitjackets that have, for thousands of years, prevented us grasping the truths about who we are and what is it we can do. If we were able to head back to our scriptural documents and read them without the interpretations affixed to them by the contexts out of which they grew—that is, if we could read about events such as Paul's experience on the road to Damascus and bring *only* twenty-first interpretations to them—what a different story of faith we would have! What a different understanding of ourselves we would have come to! If we free ourselves from the interpretations that could only ever have been as good as they could only ever have been, we can fast forward ourselves to this century, this world, this reality, and the challenges that are facing us now and actually sound like that's where we are.

# 9

# NATURAL ACTS

So what have I accomplished so far? Well, if you're still with me, looking around, you'll now see that everything that once stood tall and strong on the concept of a supernatural god as your source of goodness has now fallen with it, including the comforting idea that God answers prayers. And you've lost not only the kind of petitionary or confessional prayer that filled your sense of need and looked for a response, but also adoration, thanksgiving, and the opportunity to spill yourself out humbly and contritely. Who's left to listen? What's there to praise? How do you know what's right or wrong? Who names your guilt? How can you ever be forgiven? Who catches you when you fall and is strong enough to pull you back up?

Those questions are significant for all of us, not just those who are wondering what to do now that they don't pray anymore. Those who never did pray, or who stopped a long time ago, are also touched by these questions because they speak to the human condition. Is it important to have something that we hold in such high esteem we consider it worthy of our adoration? Are we diminished if we do or if we don't? How do we call ourselves and each another to account? Or do we have to bother? Can we be grateful without someone or something to be grateful to? And perhaps most challenging of all, what do we do with all the need, all the pain, all the lament, all the horrible situations existing in the world this second? Heaped one upon the other, our needs and desires may once have reached the highest heavens. Now they land in a heap on our own doorsteps. It might be the same pile, but our response has to be dramatically different.

The ACTS (adoration, confession, thanksgiving, and supplication) framework introduced the four general categories of prayer touched on in these questions. They each addressed something deeply important in the human experience—awe, guilt, gratitude, and need. As they helped us come to terms with the realities that a supernatural god set before us as the *source, agent,* and *promise* of all goodness, so too can they help us come to terms with the challenge we now realize as the natural source, agent, and potential for goodness in our lives, the lives of others, and the world.

## Language, Naturally

These terms—adoration, confession, thanksgiving, and supplication—have been applied to prayer and, as a result, are closely aligned with the idea of the supernatural god, God. Perhaps too closely. Before you head out on this next part of the journey, consider some other options for the concept of prayer that might break those hardened links. Meditation. Reflection. Focused thought. Deliberation. New words for what you do can open up new ways of thinking about what you're doing: adoration becomes awe and wonder; confession becomes reflecting on your place in the world and how you live within your relationships; thanksgiving is the simplicity of living with gratitude; and supplication can get to the root of your true needs and seek out possibilities that are helpful.

Prayer, or focused thought, can affirm that we are the only natural source of goodness, agent of goodness, and potential for goodness. It can remind us of both our opportunity and our responsibility. It can keep refocusing us toward more effective use of our time and energy as active, engaged people. And it can hold before us for our response the urgency in the world.

Prayer, or deliberation, can be seen as attentiveness. Attentiveness to our thoughts, feelings, desires, fears, drives, worries, and delights. Attentiveness to all those things as they are experienced by others. And attentiveness to the local, global, human, and non-human world and its needs and opportunities.

Prayer, or meditation, can be seen as reaching. Reaching in to identify our needs and reaching beyond to what we can do to try to meet them. Reaching out to others' strengths to ask for help and to others' wisdom to ask for guidance, and then reaching beyond our present state of understanding and motivation. Reaching out to touch the needs and dreams of others and, with them, reaching beyond to meet needs and fulfill dreams as we can.

Prayer, or centring, can use a language of reverence for life, for self, for others, for nature. A language of wonder, awe, and amazement. A language of appreciation and gratitude. Of self-reflection, honesty, and commitment to growth. Of care and concern for others—those we know and those we will never know, but who are affected by our way of life.

Call it meditation, call it intentional thought, call it focus or centring or altered state of consciousness, or call it prayer. I'm just urging that we engage in it. I think naturalist John Burroughs, naturally, would have liked it.

## ADORATION

*Amorphous, the morning,*
*coalescing dawn into day's full light.*
*Ebullient the songbird's*

*dulcet lullaby on the breeze.*
*Myriad wonders unfold,*
*epiphanies each,*
*nebulous in form,*
*resplendent in possibility.*
*Serenity.*
*Sublime.*
*Tranquillity.*
*May it be so.*[1]

It quickly became obvious to me that I wasn't going to be able to work "tessellated" into the "focused moment" I was preparing for Sunday's service. I'd set the challenge—to use all the beautiful words on a lengthy online list of them—too high, and I was going to have to back off it a bit. In fact, as the brevity of the final product, above, proves, I backed off considerably.

"Tessellated" is a lovely word, though. It means a checkerboard pattern made up of regular shapes repeated throughout a surface. Its most sublime forms adorn Turkish palaces and intricate artwork. Its most mundane are perhaps the thousands of miles of suburban driveways now covered with hexagonal pavers. Perhaps you can see why it wouldn't squeeze itself into that particular piece of focused moment writing.

Canadian gardening maestro Marjorie Harris drew wide-eyed stares and bewilderment from neighbours and contractors when she managed to squeeze "tessellated" into her Toronto backyard, though. Tearing out all the sod, she laid square patio stones in a checkerboard pattern throughout the length and breadth of the narrow space. A few seasons later, her garden blossomed full and with extraordinary beauty, filling in over the garish stones, softening their edges, juxtaposing brave, bold colours with more delicate hues, and creating a four-season oasis for contemplation and delight.[2] Tessellated, when it comes to gardens, may not be everyone's choice, but it proved to be the perfect design for Harris' inimitable spirit.

The words on the list are beautiful—there is no doubt about that. If they aren't there purely for the way they flow over our palate and ripple past our lips, they made the list because they conjure images of softness and light, clarity and loveliness. Each, on its own, is a perfect jewel that, placed in the middle of a sentence, enhances everything that comes before and after with its unique cadence or grace.

But none of these beautiful words is able to accomplish what the highly symbolic words of faith do, particularly those that are conjured in the opening moments of religious services, words that move us to the adoration of what we have lifted before us for our edification and admonishment. They are the names for complex concepts that have been personified by those who would follow them: God, Allah, Christ, YHWH, Holy Spirit, Jehovah, Lord. Words that are exclusive to the symbolic life of a religious group can instil a deep sense of awe in those who use them for that purpose. The language of faith has been the portal through which believers moved into the stance of humble adoration. For many, it remains so. A few minutes in a contemporary Christian concert brings home the incredible power such words still hold for evangelical Christians. The beatific faces of young people lost in the wonder of a love they feel very deeply are powerfully beautiful.

Interestingly, words like "God" or "Allah" or "Jehovah" may also contribute to an important aspect of brain health. In *How God Changes Your Brain*, the bi-disciplinary team of Andrew Newberg and Mark Robert Waldman—Newberg is a neuroscientist and Waldman a psychologist—grapples with new scientific discoveries, exploring how they apply to aspects of our lives that usually fall under the heading "spiritual." While assessing the results of an online survey on spirituality and the more than one thousand references to god made there, Newberg and Waldman found that 99 percent of respondents used the term in a highly abstract way.[3] That, they argue, is one of the many benefits the idea of god has had for our brains. When we think of concepts like "god"—focusing particularly on how they feel to us or what they look like—the activity in our brains can be very high and is not limited to one place. True, a single synapse might fire off an answer to the question "What does God look like?" but it's likely to be attached to an image you had as a young child, when your brain first sought out concrete connections.[4] Over time, though, if you've thought about the concept of god further, you've engaged many more images and ideas, and the connections in your brain related to the idea have grown considerably. Thinking about a concept like god is a great brain workout, as long as you let your brain off its leash a bit and continue to move beyond prescriptive, and therefore restrictive, images. Perhaps the intense brain activity is connected to the powerful experience of awe and the expressions of rapt wonder.

For those of us who have stretched our heads around the concept of god more than a few times, the benefits should be clear. We probably realized a tremendous boost in connections in the synapses of our brains as we worked our way toward new understandings, and we could very well be better off for it. But what happens when we stop using the term "god" to describe or explore ideas that are beyond simple answers? What happens when we stop running through the ninety-nine names for Allah? Do those parts of our brains end up in stasis or, worse, atrophy? When we walk away from adoration of our all-knowing, all-loving, all-everywhere deity, do we end up with nothing that might pull praise from our lips? We too need words that "bring on the magic," that cast us into that place of humble adoration. Beyond belief in the mystery of the supernatural—that which is clearly beyond our understanding—is there anything left to captivate us, or is the mystery lost in a universe that can now be scientifically measured and micro- and telescopically explored?

We haven't to look far, I don't think, to find words laden with similar mystery. There are many, many words for abstract concepts that defy definition: love, kindness, courage, life, death. Like the names of deities and concepts as big as god, they send our brains skipping through fields of inexpressible intrigue. In fact, those who have spent the past few decades reclaiming the image of God for a non-theistic audience will find that most of the concepts they have grasped to do the job are similarly abstract. Many of them will be exactly the concepts raised in the list of Allah's names, the whole collection a vast web of conjured images and so exactly the kind of mind stretch that does us incredible good, even when it is separated from the idea of a divine being whose image is composed of them.

Rather than conjuring a particular thing, abstract ideas like love leave us working to find the explanation that fits the particular circumstances in which we happen to find ourselves. Shift those circumstances to another place, another group, another time, and the definition shifts too. Our minds whirl around such words, seeking definition, lighting on a multitude of images, ideas, and wisps of meaning that elude definition. How many verses, songs, tributes, and epitaphs has love been carved into, each its own peculiar rendering of what was meant by its use? Words like "love" virtually incite mystery. As far as exercising our brains goes, explaining love could be just as fulfilling as considering god.

And what of the values that complement love: truth, beauty, goodness, compassion? Each of these has a remarkable capacity for interpretation. We sheltered ourselves underneath such giant concepts when we attributed them to God. Can they not now stand on their own, to the same effect and with the same power? Are we not able to offer up something akin to humble adoration in response to them?

Like the idea of god, values—both good and bad—are abstract concepts that do not exist independent of the human mind. We created them. Humane ideals (justice, beauty, truth, goodness) and inhumane ones (injustice, tyranny, hatred, evil) are a human response to life. None of them have substance beyond what we give them, and we have the responsibility to choose which become dominant in our lives. That's why any suggestion that we follow or adhere to values must be qualified. There are a lot of self-serving, misery-creating values out there, and many who live their lives in accord with them. Choose wisely and stay focused.

Our values become real and are recognized only when they are lived out within the context of relationship or are defined by a community and projected as ideals. Any of the humane values we would live by—goodness, beauty, and truth—might be pulled out of any ugliness, any challenge, any grief, any hunger, any hurt. They are as omnipresent as God ever was. At our bidding, they seep through the mundane, the practical, the prosaic—and yes, even the horrific—to be centred within our field of vision. Give any one of them an inch, in fact, and it will take over any vista—physical, geographical, intellectual, emotional. We see what we prime ourselves to see. If we look for justice, we will see justice. If we look for injustice, we will see injustice.

Our world is full of mysteries, but many of them, given scientific inquiry and rational exploration, will become the stuff of everyday knowledge as we learn more and can more accurately pinpoint our whereabouts in relation to the rest of the universe. The claim that a supernatural god is the source of all we know and acts as the agent of justice and good in the world operated, until very recently, in that peculiar realm of mystery, sheltered by mystery's diaphanous veil. Whenever two plus two didn't add up to God, it was simply "a mystery," and people of faith were expected to accept that they could not possibly know what God knew.

The fatal flaw in the claim that God acted within the world, bringing about good and meting out justice, was the claim itself. Once scientific inquiry edged its way into the examination of such claims, God had nowhere to hide, for the realm of inquiry that lies within the purview of science—the natural world—is exactly the one God was claimed to affect. The truth is, we lost faith in that authoritative deity because we gave him too much power. It was the classic Peter Principle in action: we promoted God to the level of his incompetency, and in accordance with the principle, failure was the only possible outcome.

With the concept of a supernatural god deposed from the position of "higher authority," and with it the role of moral compass, to what do we look for guidance, and should we even be doing so? Lionel Tiger and Mark McGuire argue that shared belief in a common higher authority is crucial for religious entities and has made religion an important factor in the evolutionary development of the brain and in the positive influence that religious systems can have in society. In religious ritual, the shared belief that there is a higher authority from which group members take their cues is an important part of the process. In the most cohesive religious groups, everyone acknowledges that authority, and everyone agrees to follow its direction and live according to its laws. But while Tiger and McGuire are certainly referring to gods or universal forces, they are also referring to what they call "beliefs," and beliefs don't have to be about supernatural entities. In fact, they don't need to be about entities at all.

Noting that Buddhism does not have a god but still displays the same benefits as other religions, Tiger and McGuire looked to the formal practices and ritualized elements within the Buddhist path and found that these stood in as the higher authority to which Buddhists adhered. Ritual was another element the team had identified as an important factor in religious community. But in the community within which I serve, the idea of god differs from one person to the next, and there is no highly ritualized anything that identifies members and binds them to a discipline. We do share something in common, though, and I believe that is the "higher authority" that fills the need Tiger and McGuire articulated: *that higher authority is a common set of humane values, chosen by the community and vulnerable to the community's continuing interpretation.*

For instance, say we decide that a particular value—compassion, perhaps—is one we choose to live by, one of our guiding principles. When a situation arises, we review it with that principle in mind. We get as much information about the situation as we can. We assess what other values we've chosen that will be impacted if we choose to live as compassionately as possible. We review the situation again. We consult. We discuss. We struggle our way through all the competing values the situation evokes. And then we make our choice, recognizing even as we do that it will more than likely fall short of one or another of the other ideals we'd set for ourselves. We lament that shortfall. We lament our inability to be perfect. And we commit to hold on to compassion as a value by which we want to live, even though we fall short of its heights; we still hold that it is essential to being human and providing for the world as we want it to be. We still believe in it.

It is important to note that the vulnerability of this "higher authority" is not the same as that which felled the supernatural god, God. We make no claim that the values are invulnerable. We make no claim that the values themselves placed in such a position have any ability to affect change in the physical realm. Yes, they influence humans to act in ways that change their environment, but they do not affect it without that assistance; they are not the source of what is good—we are. They are not the agents of that good—we are. This is close to what liberal Christians mean when they speak of themselves being the hands of God. Although it is rarely acknowledged, even in liberal Christian circles, the implication, and it's a correct one, is that without human hands, God is impotent; any concept is. The vulnerability such values have is our own continued interpretation and evaluation of them, our ongoing discernment of what it is we, as a human community, now need. Context changes; realities demand different responses; the values that guide us need to be responsive to emergent needs. We choose what to keep and what to set aside as the principles by which we will live.

There will be those who will point to other attempts to set particular principles as masters of human community and argue that these failed either for want of a deity or because of the corruption of human vice: socialism extrapolated into an enforced dehumanization of diversity and giftedness; capitalism to the devaluation of human life to its monetary productivity. Rather than being failures of the values themselves, both are examples of the failure of human community to review, revise, and revoke the supremacy of particular principles when their power became absolute and destructive. Humanity without any guiding principles, I believe, can only ever be less than it could be with them, and I believe we must try—harder, perhaps, but try nonetheless.

There will also be those who argue that we don't need anything called religion, and I'm sympathetic to the challenge. I believe, however, that those things identified by Tiger and McGuire as significant for the religious mind are also things that are crucial for human community. We thrive when we have clarity around how we are to be with one another. Without such guiding principles, we tend to devolve into cantankerous, self-centred brats. With so many fingers on the triggers of so many nuclear bombs, we can't afford just to let things happen the way they happen. We need to set the values by which the course forward can be charted.

The word "reverence" captures the profound awe that can be experienced in the face of love. Reverence is a position we take in relation to those great things that inspire, edify, challenge, condemn, and rearrange our worldviews. It's what my Gulf of Mexico morning pulled out of me. It's what describes the space in which I do the work that has been called prayer. It's something we need, something crucial to the well-being of this planet—reverence for life, for love, for beauty.

Each Sunday as we begin our service at West Hill, we pay homage to the values by which we choose to live. In place of the adoration we might once have given to an almighty god, we now take a few moments to identify the values we choose to hold as sacred in our community and in our lives. By "sacred," I remind those gathered, we mean those things that are too important to risk getting lost, undermined, ignored, and destroyed in our world—things we want the next generation's next generation to still know and cherish. And then I list a few of them, such as dignity, forgiveness, beauty—whatever happens to be at the forefront of my own mind that day. The community then folds itself into a reverent silence in which each person is able to recall what is important, on that day, to him or her. We bring that collective moment to a close with one of a number of songs that draw our attention even more closely to those things that earn our devotion, our adoration, if you will. Through the opening moments of the service, we set our values before us that we might be reminded of them and edified in our pursuit of them throughout our time together.

> Our thoughts we now centre on all that is good,
> on all that we know is worthy,
> so we may focus attention on the richness of truth
> restoring our souls for the journey.
>
> To all that is worthy,
> to all we believe is true,
> to all we deeply value,
> we commit ourselves anew.[5]

Humans have bowed their heads before a higher authority since the first religious impulse suggested that to do so might make life better. We have followed paths set out for us by those who claimed to have inside knowledge, and many of those paths have been decidedly narrow. We know now that many of the paths charted by religious traditions do not lead to the lands promised, and they can no longer offer the consolation or comfort they once did.

We find ourselves in a tessellated garden. There is no path, only stepping stones that barely touch at their outermost points. The quest here is not for a particular place; there is no particular place, no destination. The quest is for beauty, for what inspires and uplifts, for what makes our hearts swell, for what makes us feel as big as we really are— and we are really big. We are drawn forward by the gifts we find along the way, the unexpected delights, the fellow travellers we meet, the blessings we offer one another. The ideals and values that lead us forward from this place and this point in time are peculiar to this time and place. Another point along the way will demand a new perspective, new interpretations, perhaps new ideals and principles. It must— it will have different parameters, different realities to be taken into account. But here, in this tessellated place, if we walk—directed only by our carefully balanced quest for well-being for ourselves, others, all life on the planet and the planet itself—we stand the chance of dwelling in this garden in a peace we have not yet known. Here, outside of the prescribed corridors and narrow gateways of faith, many find that peace.

## CONFESSION

*We shelter ourselves with images of who we think we are—*
*intelligent and well-informed;*
*compassionate and well-intentioned—*

*until those wrenching, wild, chaotic moments*
*when we learn otherwise,*
*when life exposes us to glimpses of our otherselves—*
*intelligent but ill-informed;*
*compassionate but causing harm—*
*and we wish we could flee from the complicities of our lives.*
*Into the lives of others, we are bound to be woven.*
*Into the eyes of others, we are compelled to look.*
*So it is we pray we may be*
*in the realities of others,*
*a gentle presence*
*that when we stand before them,*
*in utter, full disclosure of who we truly are,*
*we will not shy from the reflection in their eyes—*
*not the eyes of our children,*
*not the eyes of our partners,*
*not the eyes of our companions on the journey,*
*not the eyes of those we may never know.*
*As travellers who would see with a clear and honest vision,*
*we pray.*
*Amen.*

*Turn, Turn, Turn . . .*

I recall participating in a confessional prayer exercise in which, standing with one arm outstretched before me, my finger pointing to the distant horizon, I turned slowly until I had drawn a circle entirely around me. The meditation that went along with it suggested that I focus on the image of God entirely encompassing me. With its all-knowing presence surrounding me, so it went, there was no place to hide, no reason to dissemble, no purpose in obfuscation. I was already nailed. Might as well, then, be open and honest in my prayer.

I got it. Prayer needed to be utterly, viscerally honest if it was going to be anything. If I hid something from God, I hid it from myself too. And if I wasn't going to be honest with myself, there was little prayer would ever do for me.

The underlying premise to this kind of meditative prayer is that the practitioner is the one responsible for doing the work. It's a liberal conception of god that understands it not as a divine being from whom forgiveness is sought but rather as a foil against which one's own shortcomings can be seen. It's the impetus for one's own work toward whole-i-ness. Confession is made to oneself or to a community, and once truths are heard, acknowledged, and brought into the circle of awareness, the work of healing and forgiveness can begin. Restoration and reconciliation become possible.

Confession is identified as a crucial element of psychological and spiritual health by Paul Olson, author of *The Reconciled Life: A Critical Theory of Counseling*. Within the theological realm, where Olson locates the discussion of meaning, values, and relationships, he finds the term "reconciliation" particularly apt, recognizing that it is used to highlight the "crucial importance of relationships." When we describe reconciliation—being at one with, coming to terms with, being at peace with, etc.—the word "with" is always present. Reconciliation, Olson notes, is always relational.[6]

Olson credits Jewish philosopher Martin Buber with the concept of the fundamental nature of relation. In *I and Thou*, Buber explored the two primary relationships we can have: an I-Thou or an I-It. The former—I-Thou—demands that we engage with our whole being, recognizing the inherent worth and value of the person, thing, or idea. We treat the other with reverence. The latter—I-It—allows us to operate in relationships that are disengaged from the person, thing, or idea. We do not see the other as being worth anything beyond what they are worth to us as a commodity. There is no reverence in such relationships.[7]

The predominant relationships to which we are exposed and into which we are encouraged—in almost all media advertising; in much, if not most, of our varied forms of entertainment; in our workplaces; and increasingly, in the corridors of our learning institutions—are I-It relationships. What can I acquire and use to my best advantage? How can I beat someone or how can we beat some other team? What course of study will provide the most lucrative position for me? While these relationships might make the world go around, they do not make it a better place. We make it a better place only when we build I-Thou relationships.

Our relationships abound, many of them with people, places, and things we wouldn't normally think of in a relational way. The I-Thou relationship means we make each of our connections sacred. What exists between you and me, what lies between me and my family or me and the people who farm my food or sew my clothes in some foreign land, what is between me and the rhinos in South Africa or the books and ornaments on my shelves—all these must be made sacred. This is the human task. There is no greater or more important undertaking than this. And there is none more difficult.

In *The Restaurant at the End of the Universe*,[8] the second book in Douglas Adams' five-book trilogy known as *The Hitchhiker's Guide to the Galaxy*, we are introduced to the Total Perspective Vortex. It is ostensibly the worst torture device known to sentient beings. Its horror? Clarification of one's exact position in respect to everything else in the universe. Constantly harassed by a wife who argued he never had perspective, Trin Tragula created the Vortex and let her try it out first. Unfortunately, the experience killed her brain, a price Tragula felt was worth paying for the proof that he was right.

Standing in the face of a higher authority composed of our most transcendent values is not unlike climbing into the Total Perspective Vortex. Like my encircling prayer, with God recognized as omniscient, the Vortex is no place to hide. The Total Perspective Vortex takes the place of that omniscience but gives us the responsibility for operating it. We see only what we are ready to see. We expose ourselves only to what we can survive. In truth, our perspective can never be total; Adams knew the fate of Tragula's wife's—madness—would also be ours if it were. And because we cannot experience perspective's total effect, we are protected in a way and as much as we want to be.

When we open ourselves to seeing connections, however, to finding our place in relation to the people and issues in our relationships, something happens to us. We are changed by what we allow ourselves to see. It is bowing our heads, figuratively, to those ideals, those values we have named as crucial to human community, then measuring our shortcomings and acknowledging the sometimes selfish choices that have thwarted our efforts, challenges that have kept us from our goals. We see we are not perfect, but we are not destroyed by that fact. Rather, we are strengthened by the recognition that it's the goodness in us that condemns our actions. We are able to forgive ourselves, and then find our way toward making a new commitment to try again. Emerging from the Vortex, from reflective consideration of our relationships, we see the world differently and know the complicity of our place in it. Being in community, involved in a ritual that places us all in the same position in relation to the higher authority of our ideals, is deeply moving.

When we begin to see with I-Thou and I-It eyes, we become adept at identifying where we have faltered, where we have failed to live up to our humane-ity, and how we can make reparations. No, we cannot live up to all the ideals we set for ourselves. No, we will not create only I-Thou relationships in our lives. Yes, there are limits to what we can do. But we can and must see how we are in the world, and when we do, we can make an informed choice. Circumstances, contexts, challenges—all filter their own light on the options before us and we can choose only in the light of our own lives.

We can also see when others have placed us in I-Thou or I-It relationships with them, and we can feel the difference their choices make. It is difficult to hold someone to I-Thou when they have no interest in building a bond with you that honours the humanity of you both. It is difficult to watch when I-It relationships to others, to things, to places are chosen; we are all diminished. While on vacation, I found myself on a tour boat standing behind a man whose T-shirt read "All God's creatures have a place in the world. Right next to the potatoes and vegetables." Below was a picture of a plate with leftover bones and gravy on it. We have much to learn about I-Thou and how to live it out on a planet grown increasingly small and fragile.

## The Weight of Naughty, Naughty

I have no intention of confessing all my sins to you, instructional though that might be, but I do want to bring you one small story from my childhood. Each year, in preparation for Christmas, my mother would bring out all the cards received from friends and relatives the previous year. She'd go through them one by one and compose her card list for that season, changing addresses, removing those who had died during the year, and adding a few from the previous year's pile of greetings. When she was done, my sisters and I were given the cards so we could create tags for our Christmas presents from the colourful pictures on the front. It was a favourite family tradition.

In the midst of one of our recycling sessions, my elder sister and I began to fight. I have no idea what we argued about, but I have a stark slow-motion image of what I did. Reaching for a tag she had made, one we'd both admired and celebrated as perfect, I deliberately picked it up and tore it in two.

Now, you might think this a paltry little "sin" to confess, and as sins go, it may appear so. It shocked me at the time and lived with me for many years, however, because it had the same impetus as sins considered far more heinous: the intent to do harm, the choice to desecrate rather than make sacred. As I tore the tag in two, it wasn't my sister's angry scream that startled me most—it was the realization that I could and would act in such an intentionally hurtful way. I had *deliberately* set out to hurt my sister and was startled at my desire to do so. The incident might seem trivial to an outsider, just one of many arguments and wrestling matches of childhood; perhaps it is even long forgotten by my sister. But it had a lasting impact on me. I had become aware of my capacity to choose harm (evil?), and it both humbled and frightened me.

## The Clarity of a Third-Party Definition

There is something to the argument that if you don't know that what you're doing is bad or don't realize the harm that will come of your action, it isn't a sin. In that light, however, much of what we may come to regret in our lives is not nearly as "evil" as my prepubescent tag-tearing Christmas meltdown. Although many of our actions, duly considered, cause harm to ourselves, others, or the planet, we rarely make a deliberate choice to inflict that harm, and in many cases, we cannot predict the harm that will come.

We don't, for example, move house so that our children will lose all their friends and become depressed, though that might be a result of our choice. When we're on our way to the annual back-to-school sales to get bargains on our children's new gym shoes and geometry sets, we don't consider the children who will never be educated or receive appropriate medical attention because of a global trade market that keeps them caught in a vortex of extreme poverty. We don't drive hours to work and back so that our grandchildren will not have any fossil fuels. We don't fall in love with abusive partners because we want to get hurt. We simply walk into walls, veer off into the bracken and stinging nettle, jump off cliffs, bump into people, and run over others as we attempt to get our needs and wants met. We damage things, break things, hurt ourselves and others. Not because we set out to do so. We do it as part of our living, eating, finding and maintaining shelter. Living, when we stare at it full on, is a consumptive and violent reality, and as we breathe, we are complicit in it. Sometimes it is only through the kind of rigorous hindsight we might engage in through hours of therapy that we are able to understand how we came to hurt another person, ourselves, or the fragile planet upon which we live; how we can refrain from doing so again in the future; and how we can live with ourselves when the damage we wreak is beyond our efforts to control or repair.

Without the theistic god, God, informing our assessment of ourselves, however, our task is much cleaner. We eliminate a significant but external source of shame. With no god before whom our sins have to be acknowledged, that source of shame simply dissolves. There is no perfect being against whom we are measured. There is no all-seeing god who watches our every move. There is no all-knowing deity who has a wire on our most personal thoughts. There is no damnation in our bodily functions, needs, and desires. We are not inherently sinful, because there is no "inherently sinful" to be. An intentional review of the damage we have done and the relationships we have dishonoured will be about stuff we have the power to change. It will be about guilt, not shame, and so related to our actions, not our essence. The shame we experience will be like that brought on by my tag-tearing episode, and it will come about because we violate our own sense of ethics, our values. It too will be a result we can work with, grow through, and change. Actions that once caused deep shame can become opportunities for communal and personal healing, because the responsibility for them resides in human hands and hearts. With no deity involved, we are able to own our responsibilities.

## *Ecnagorra: Confession's Essential Element*

In her very personal reflection on depression as it is manifest in the experience of acedia—a state of apathy and disinterest—author Kathleen Norris struggles with our distaste for the idea of sin and our attempts to clean it up and remove it from our sight. She invites us to consider the wisdom of doing away altogether with confession, whether within the context of congregational gatherings or undertaken privately, and asks if there isn't value in reflecting on our complicity in systems of injustice, oppression, intolerance, and greed. Is there not some value in recognizing when we have been part of the reason our relationships have failed, our children are angry, our physical bodies are letting us down? Norris' impulse toward self-reflection and judgment is a good one.

There is, nestled within the folds of confessional prayer, an element that is crucial to our spiritual health: humility. Unlike shame, which undermines our sense of self-worth, humility allows us to view our imperfection as something natural and true, and with which we must wrestle, often on a daily basis. Humility confronts our arrogance, our pretensions to grandeur and perfection, our belief that we deserve the best of the best of the best. Tracking its etymological roots back through "humble" to "humus," we find it growing out of the same compost that gave us the word "human." Connecting us to the earth, humility brings us back down to our primordial beginnings and reminds us that we are not gods. Our perspective, however enlightened, is tied to our basest truths. We mess up, we make mistakes, we are fallible—deeply and sometimes irreversibly, lamentably so. Humility affirms that reality as normative. We are not aberrant when we mess up. We are human.

That doesn't mean that we don't need to care about what we do and what we don't. The United Church of Canada's Song of Faith convicts us with the words "selfishness, cowardice, or apathy." We don't get a pass on bad behaviour or habitually poor or self-centred choices simply because we are human. We don't get a pass just because we couldn't bother to get involved. We shouldn't let it pass when someone shrugs his shoulders at a mess he's made that has had deeply hurtful results and dismisses it with the phrase "I'm only human." We should be especially unimpressed if that individual is actually a national, corporate, institutional, or community leader, someone in whom the public has placed great trust, or a corporation's shareholders, who in the pursuit of profits are protected by limited liability laws and turn a blind eye to the irreversible desecration of natural habitats and the destruction of local market economies. Acknowledging human frailty is just the first step in a long process toward healing and restoration. Opening our eyes to I-It relationships can provide shocking revelations.

Psychiatrist Karl Menninger reflected on the complexities inherent in understanding the sin in which we are involved but from which we do not extricate ourselves. He challenged us to see the wrong in it, regardless of how reasoned may be our ongoing participation in it—we have to move house to accept a new job; we need to save money; we wish to give our children a rich learning environment with as many options as possible; we need to live in an affordable community and commute to work; we need to feel we are loved. Each impetus is valid and reasonable, yet each can lead to deeply harmful, even tragic consequences, as noted above.

When we look at the broader, deeper picture, however, we get a sense of the connection between our actions and the harm we inflict upon those around us and the world. Wilfully ignoring that connection or hiding it does not absolve us from our complicity in the wrongdoing. Ignorance of the truth, Menninger posited, should not spare us our guilt any more than ignorance of the law should spare us from punishment for our crimes.

Our prayers of confession have helped us sit with those complicities. Communally or on our own, we have seen ourselves before one we believed knew everything and who we feared would hold us accountable. It has been deeply important that we do this and face the truths of our lives, deeply important that we have had this image in place of a judge who has checked our anger and bracketed our impulses, holding us within the acceptable parameters of community as he did so.

Religious conservatives are often quick to point out the moral turpitude of those who have no fear of such a god. They enjoy naming fascists and despots, arguing that because these individuals did not believe in or fear God, they carried out horrific acts. What they often neglect to realize, however, is that it was not the religion, or lack of it, that permitted their actions; it was their own values that informed the choices they made. After all, innumerable heinous acts have been committed in the name of religion too. In *How God Changes Your Brain*, Andrew Newberg and Mark Waldman point out with breathtaking clarity that neither religion nor the lack of it has anything to do with the acts of despots. "The enemy is not religion; the enemy is anger, hostility, intolerance, separatism, extreme idealism, and prejudicial fear—be it secular, religious, or political."[9] I would add that the remedy is not religion either. The remedy is honest self-examination, humility, and commitment to wholeness and peace, to the creation of I-Thou relationships.

In *Harry Potter and the Philosopher's Stone*, Harry finds himself in front of the Mirror of Erised. The inscription on the mirror—"*Erised stra ehru oyt ube cafru oyt on wohsi*"—is not in some strange wizard language but is written in reverse: "I show not your face but your heart[']s desire." "Erised" is "desire" spelled backwards.

I like the technique Rowling has used. Rather than giving the mirror a name with some esoteric meaning or linking it to another character in an already complex storyline, she reminds us of the mirror's function while simultaneously underscoring the importance of it. We think about those things that might be seen glazed before us were we to stand in front of such a magical object. Could we withstand the visual, the truth of what our hearts really yearn for? Interesting thought . . .

The technique invites us to consider an alternative to the traditional concept of confession—creating a word or a phrase (as Rowling has done) that, by its very nature, helps us recognize the importance of what we're doing. In so doing, we open up the possibility of confession in a religiously non-realist context that can provide some of the benefits of confessional prayer without encasing it in the detrimental theological burdens traditional confessions relayed.

Ecnagorra. It spells "arrogance" backwards. In our non-realist context, it reminds us that arrogance gets in the way of our ability to find the right path, the right response, the options that will be the most loving. It is a time for humility, the opposite of arrogance. It creates space for I-Thou to grow. It stands firm in the face of I-It relationships and so protects our humanity. If we are to move forward in our understanding of ourselves, others, and the world around us, we need, before anything else, to set aside our arrogance, to sit humbly and truthfully before the highest ideals and principles we've named for ourselves, and to assess our actions in relation to them. We do not bow before the face of God and repent. We sit in the circle with those with whom we share this planet; we sit in circle with the "we" of our own potentials; we sit in circle with the awe-full silence of the world's beauty. The way we want to live, the way we have *chosen* to live is at the centre, and we, along with those with whom we sit, reflect upon how well or how poorly we have been able to live up to those ideals. Ecnagorra. A time of humble reflection. Ecnagorra, the opportunity to recommit, no matter how far we've missed the mark.

It is crucial to human relationship and well-being that we see as much as we can see of ourselves and our impact on all our relationships. We do not need a supernatural arbiter of justice to connect the dots between our choices and their implications. We do not need a divine being to point out our I-It moments and condemn us for them. We do not need an all-knowing god. Stand in a circle with your arm outstretched and your finger pointing to the far horizon. Turn, turn, turn and encompass yourself with *our* all-knowingness. *We know.* The wholeness that is us—the collective wisdom that is humanity on the planet—*knows.* You are part of that knowing. You know what you need to know to create I-Thou, to live I-Thou relationships with the people, the things, the places in your world. You know. You do. Accept that you do.

## THANKSGIVING

*It fills my deepest need,*
*this peace, this space,*
*this empty plain of afternoon*
*laid out before me.*
*The squirrel who arrives as I type the word,*
*-close-*
*-at my feet-*
*neither of us sure whose the greater alarm*
*but safe, slow, measured*
*as we take each other in.*
*The wings of birds thrumming and beating against*
*an invisible gift of sky,*
*lacing the blue together*
*as they cross and cross and recross its expanse,*
*writing thanksgiving upon it*
*with their filmy, shadowed wings.*
*They do that for me.*
*I asked them to.*

*The sunlight,*
*sifted through a mess of leaves*
*soon to repose upon a waiting earth,*
*warms my heart as much or more*
*than the air through which it makes its way*
*to my scrap of waiting afternoon.*
*I breathe the sunshine in,*
*into my need, my peace, my space.*
*I am bathed in beauty.*
*I am humbled.*
*I am refreshed.*
*I am ready, once again.*

*May it be so.*
*May it ever be so.*

There are some old hymns that seem to fill you to capacity and, when that's not enough, get hold of your sternum and just open you up. They are called "chestnuts" by some, particularly those who have moved on to more contemporary styles of music, but they continue to capture the hearts and souls of believers and beyond believers around the world. In early 2011, Carrie Underwood, a country singer best known for a song about carving her name into the leather seats of a cheating boyfriend's four-wheel drive and knocking out its headlights with a Louisville Slugger, pulled an entire audience of peers to a standing ovation when she belted out "How Great Thou Art" (based on a Swedish poem by Carl Gustav Boberg and translated by British missionary Stuart K. Hine).

The words to the first couple of verses of the hymn are grand and sweeping.

Oh Lord my God,
When I in awesome wonder,
Consider all the worlds
Thy hands have made,
I see the stars,
I hear the rolling thunder,
Thy power throughout
The universe displayed!

Then sings my soul,
My Savior, God, to Thee:
How great thou art!
How great thou art!

Noticeably absent from Underwood's rendition were lines commonly included as the third verse. And no wonder. Added to the original piece by a Christian evangelist, these are the lines that offend the sensibilities of many:

And when I think that God, his Son not sparing,
Sent him to die, I scarce can take it in
That on the cross, my burden gladly bearing,
He bled and died to take away my sin.

It's the kind of thanksgiving that has poured forth from Christianity for most of its history. But it's not the only kind, and just because we walk away from the supernatural god, God, from whom all blessings—including the idea of atonement—were thought to flow, that doesn't mean we walk away from thanksgiving.

Living in a spirit of gratitude is what the first two verses of "How Great Thou Art" are all about. Forest glades, rolling thunder, stars

. . . it's all good. I can belt them out with the best of them, lustily, just as Charles Wesley admonished us to do. That we have directed our thanks toward a heavenly Father is not a bad thing either. It is just something from a previous worldview. So where do we direct our thanks when we no longer believe in a god that is the source of everything, the means by which good things make their way to us (and the bad too, remember), and the assurance that all will work out well in the end, whenever that end might be?

In a children's book called *Grandad's Prayers of the Earth*,[10] Douglas Wood describes thanksgiving as a way of being in the world, of walking through the day with a sense of gratitude that is not directed toward anything other than the object for which you're thankful—trees, rocks, water. That would extend, of course, to the people with whom we share our lives. In a sense, he's weaving the "I-Thou" relationship into the everyday experiences of a child, inviting him to reverence the things around him and to live with them with respect.

Extending gratitude for little things has the power to wedge its way in between me and my frustration at all those things that never really come together the way I'd planned them. Big thanksgivings don't seem to do that as well. They sometimes just exacerbate our irritability. Few are those who can really celebrate another's success, really get into deep thanksgiving for something that happened to someone else. She slam-dunks a promotion three weeks after returning from mat leave. He wrangles a real estate deal that gets him a house in the country and a condo in town. An old friend melts away those extra pounds and wears her grade eight graduation dress to your junior school reunion. The narrowed eyes, the feigned smiles, the slight step backwards—these things give it away. We want to be standing in the centre of the benevolence beam ourselves. Someone else's limelight . . . well, that kind of light tends to cast shadows, and lots of us don't look or feel all that great in the shadows. We want to be gracious, we really do, but big thanksgivings are hard. Damned hard.

Those little ones, though—the little thanksgivings—they're like wedges. And wedges spread things open, make room, let stuff in. Little thanksgivings have a lot to teach us about big thanksgivings. By taking a child by the hand and showing her there is much to be grateful for, we gain the opportunity to look around and see that we are *in relation* with everything about us. The process of acknowledging each person, object, place, idea with which we are in relation and finding a way to reverence everything squeezes that little thanksgiving wedge in a bit further. It creates a practice that can provide perspective on just about anything.

Scott and I are in the middle of a move. Well, I'm really hoping we're way past the middle, since we've been moving for seven months now. It's been one unbelievable disaster after another. From undisclosed highway constructions, camouflaged foundational water issues, and mice infestations to moving trucks that were too small and a flooring contractor who broke in through the window when he lost the keys and then poured mortar down our drains when we asked him not to dump it on the lawn again—we've seen it all. We are living with emptied cardboard boxes laid out as flooring, bathrooms with sinks that are standing only on the pipes that hold them, a kitchen that has no sink or countertop but does sport an amazing non-functioning dishwasher, and now we're facing a seasonal clothing change without any idea where the boxes containing our sweaters are. Believe me, there have been lots of times I could have screamed, but because of the little thanksgivings we've been reckoning each day, we've kept our sense of humour. As night falls, the stillness settles, and the day's clamour fades, we take stock of our immense fortune. The challenges we've encountered are, as a dear friend would say, first-world problems, and the reality is that we are privileged to have been able to bring them on ourselves. We didn't have to move; we had the *option* to move. We didn't have to tear out the kitchen; we had the *option* to tear out the kitchen. We didn't have to remove the decrepit bathroom vanities; we had the *option* to remove the bathroom vanities. We *chose* everything, and while the implementation of our choices hasn't been smooth by any stretch of the imagination, acknowledging the reality of our situation—the real reality, that is—helps us to see more appreciatively, by that very interesting light, the gifts we do have. In the middle of the storm that whirls around us, we open our door and listen to crickets; we have been welcomed into the yard by cardinals and chickadees, woodpeckers and nuthatches; we take shelter under towering trees that line the walkway behind our home; we engage in delightful conversation with new neighbours; we walk down the lane and stand in the opening we call the "big sky" place while children swing in the park beside us. These are not extraordinary pleasures, but they are *our* pleasures, and as we share our little thanksgivings with each other, they brighten our lives, our relationship, our world. Rather than being pulled away from each other as we contend with multiple challenges, we have felt the little thanksgivings pressing us together as they wedge their way into our every day. Sometimes, they are our only defence.

And we need defences. Without them, our cynicism would mount sky-high. In its first year on Canadian airwaves, the Sun TV network, a Fox-style news channel, interviewed Canadian interpretive dancer Margie Gillis after seeing a performance in which she stated that she believed the world was becoming less compassionate. The interviewer, Krista Erickson, attacked Gillis, an icon in the dance industry, arguing that the government grants she and her company had received over the past thirteen years were evidence of an overwhelming generosity on the part of the Canadian people. She misconstrued Gillis' interpretive dance to suit her own purposes, placing the dancer in an "I-It" relationship, all to score broadcast points and much-coveted industry notoriety. Gillis, for her part, exuded grace and calm throughout the ambush, responding with a strength few of us could have mustered in similar circumstances. Although commentators from the news channel later argued that the much-maligned Erickson had "merely" asked a question and was not deserving of the forty-five hundred complaints that went to the Canadian Broadcast Standards Council, it was clear to most who watched that she was an artful choreographer herself, whirling Gillis indelicately through a single-issue interview that, while high on "information," was low on appreciation of what that information really meant.

Every moment that Erickson spoke reinforced Gillis' contention: we are witnessing less and less compassion in our world, on our streets, in our lives. American economist Jeremy Rifkin, author of *The Empathic Civilization: The Race to Global Consciousness in a World in Crisis*, believes we are moving toward the realization of an empathic civilization—and the science might support his theory—but most of us feel that on a personal level, in our workplaces and our schools, on our TV screens and in political arenas, we are witnessing a diminishment of compassion. It results, I believe, from an unchecked growth in cynicism, which has long travelled with us but has in recent years become a persistent, unruly companion. It ridicules efforts to celebrate beauty, to speak gently, to offer assistance, to work for peaceful change in the world. It bullies the wedges of gratitude and strikes fear into many who might have otherwise slipped them into place. Cynicism robs us of our humanity, takes away our dignity, and sits on the sidelines pointing fingers and smirking. It offers no constructive effort but merely does its best to undermine any positive endeavours others might undertake. It is a cold world that nurtures this unlovely guest, and ours is becoming increasingly so.

It is into this world, and into Rifkin's hope, that I believe our little thanksgivings must wedge themselves. Turn off Fox News and talk radio and turn on the music. Turn away from the incessant reports of gang violence and increasing security threats and turn toward the task of creating supportive, nurturing communities that raise kids within a safe environment. Turn off your air conditioning and open your windows, tuning your ear to the sounds of your neighbourhood. Turn aside from the gossip magazines that line the grocery checkout counters and log on to *Ode Magazine*'s online portal for "intelligent optimists." Turn toward the smartass in the office and question her interpretation of events, not to diminish her but to raise up what might be helpful, inspiring, worthy—the things that mightn't stand a chance amid cynicism's wreckage. Get to know your neighbours; build community; close your umbrella and drench yourself in the rain; wear clothes that feel good; listen to spoken-word poetry; count the stars; read to children; draw your finger along the lines that rim the eyes of someone you love; rustle the leaves as (to paraphrase the second verse of How Great Thou Art") "through the woods and forest glades [you] wander, and hear the birds sing sweetly in the trees; When [you] look down from lofty mountain grandeur and hear the brook and feel the gentle breeze." Let your soul sing.

Wedge your thanksgivings in, bit by little bit, until the benevolence beam you once wished would shine *on* you instead shines *from* you and everything around you glows in its remarkable light.

## SUPPLICATION

*Ah.*
*Now I know.*
*This is that "weight of the world" of which so many speak.*
*This tremor in my knees,*
*this hollow liquid that once was just my heart,*
*this feeling that I can't—*
*I can't—*
*I can't get enough air.*
*This is that weight.*
*Would that I could lift it clear and shift it somewhere else—*
*somewhere far away.*

*Another world.*
*Not yours.*
*Not mine.*
*Not ours.*
*Or better still*
*transform it*
*to gift,*
*to possibility,*
*to endless fields of all we ever needed.*
*Together we might do that.*
*Together we might carry this weight—*
*own it full out—*
*launder it with our tears, our anger, our frustration,*
*then rinse it with our labour*
*and, in so doing,*
*make it new—*
*make it something beautiful,*
*something good,*
*so that as we carry it together,*
*we sing.*
*We all sing.*
*Together we might make it so.*
*Amen.*

Who doesn't love a good oxymoron?

Theologically non-realist prayers of supplication. It's a stretch. With the phrase "theologically non-realist" meaning there's nothing out there either listening to or answering us, and prayers of supplication deeply rooted in the idea of the supernatural, the whole thing gets a little weird. Prayers of supplication work well with the idea of a supernatural god—that is, a god that's the *source* of everything good, the *agent* who can bring about that good, and the one who *promises* that all will be well—looking out for our best interests. We ask, it responds. Except, of course, when it doesn't. Which is, with no offence meant to those who still believe, all the time.

A supernatural *source, agent,* and *promise* god is not what we need anyway. Not now. The *sap* that is the beginning of wisdom, *sapientiam,* is the root of who we are—*Homo sapiens*—and that is our answer. We have known for a long, long time that it was wisdom we needed, and we have sought it wherever we thought it might be found, including the heavens. To access the wisdom we thought was there, we threw ourselves prostrate on the ground, fell down on our knees, bowed our heads, or simply closed our eyes. But it wasn't there. It is here, within us and around us. So we continue to strain our way forward, peering into an uncertain future and seeking wisdom in *this* world. Perhaps it has taken us to this point in our history to be able, through technology and empathy, to connect well enough that we can really forge and make accessible the wisdom we need—a global wisdom that might be our only hope.

## THE PRAYER FIX

Because of the kind of work I do, people often ask who my community prays to. We don't pray "to" anything. I speak about what we do as praying "into" community. Some in the congregation say, when they are asked, "We don't pray 'to.' We pray 'for.'" Still others wouldn't use the word "pray" to describe what we do at all; they'd say we share concerns and celebrations with one another. Having read *God's Brain,* I can now understand some of the reason that works so well. It's important to remember that West Hill is a community with history. It's changed, but change is a process. We still use the word "pray" in our services, though what we do looks very different. My expectation is that what we do will continue to change.

The portion of the service we have traditionally called community prayer has shifted and changed over the years. Once, members of the community wrote prayers out and placed them in a box or stood just prior to the prayer time and told the leader what they wanted to have offered on their behalf. Those prayers would then be reiterated by the leader, and each followed with a response. The leader would say, "For this, O Gracious One," and the congregation would reply, "We give you thanks." Or if it had been a prayer of lament, the leader would open the responsive verse with "O God, in your mercy," and the people would say, "Hear our prayer." These statements have been replaced with non-theistic, non-supernatural, and non-exclusive ones. For celebratory prayers, the leader says, "In this abundant blessing," and the congregation replies, "We share the joy." When lament is offered, the leader says, "In this, our time of need," and the congregation completes the phrase with "May love abound." These lines now punctuate emails I receive with pastoral concerns from members. They are an important part of the fabric of our community.

But a more significant change, I believe, is related to who offers the prayer. What was once handed to the "minister" is now offered into the congregation by its participants. Of course, a box remains for those who do not wish to speak publicly, but for the most part, individuals, even those who may be in the community for the first time, recognize the acceptance and intimacy created through the time of prayer and participate in it. Prayer is engaged by the whole community. The leader stands in the middle of the aisle, "in" the community, literally. Microphones are available for use by participants. Prayer is offered by the leader and by others. At the end of any particular offering—lament or celebration—we say the responsive piece before moving on to the next person. That little piece creates an immediate affirmative response for the individual, telling him that what he's raised is of value to the community because he is valued by the community. It is personal and communal.

When participation involves sharing on an intimate level with a group, which praying aloud with others does, and affirmation is received from fellow participants and those in leadership positions, serotonin levels are very likely boosted considerably as the individual is recognized and affirmed as important to the group. Follow-up by other members at the conclusion of the service and throughout the week reinforces the importance of the person within the community. The affirmation individuals receive by way of hugs, nods, handshakes, and phone calls comes with its own complimentary serotonin fix attached. The healing begins as people pray into the community, for one another; they are literally healing their own hearts, their disappointments, and their lives, boosting chemicals in their brains that help them cope with incredibly difficult situations. And often, connection is made, something is offered that is crucial to the situation the individual is facing—legal connections, medical advice, anecdotal suggestions, books, items . . . in a word, help. It's the best impact I've ever witnessed prayer having.

## LOOK UP. LOOK WA-A-A-A-A-Y UP

Set as our ideals, the values by which we live hold us to standards that few of us—in all honesty, none of us—are able to meet. Values are not perfect beings, superhumans against whom we measure ourselves. They do not hold us in a place of imperfection, measured against a perfect incarnation who has already walked the earth before us, a role the legend of Jesus as the divine and guiltless son of God has cast us into. Living with these values as our higher authority requires that we be in relationship, that we get them dirty, that we plaster them, over and over, against the realities of our lives and so press our lives into the possibility that they are. We live them into reality. In our hands, they lose their ideal status, and so when we gather, we falteringly lift them up together and press them back up into that hole, that place

God once lived, into the position of honour, of authority, where they belong. Lived through us as they are, they can never be tyrants in our lives. Only aspirations. Only inspiration.

## Ignore the Man behind the Curtain

Remember that curtain in Frank Baum's *The Wizard of Oz*? From the moment she awoke in the magical, enchanted world of Oz, Dorothy was trying to make her way home. She was told her only hope was the magic of the wizard, and so she followed the yellow brick road that would lead her to him. But once there, she found that he wasn't a wizard at all. He was only a wizened old man who lived behind the curtain and created the fantastic effects that had led the Munchkins to believe in his supernatural power.[*]

But Dorothy still got home. It didn't matter that there was no wizard to help her. The story reminds us that like Dorothy, we need to make it work ourselves. She was open to what might happen, sought the best suggestions possible, and found herself finally pulled from her dream by Auntie Em, safely back in Kansas. As for the Cowardly Lion, the Scarecrow, and the Tin Man, all it took for them to realize their dreams was the touch of an ordinary person—no wizard, no magic, simply something entirely beyond their immediate capabilities. Something they couldn't have expected or made happen. A moment that pulled them completely beyond the definitions and limitations each had previously felt, pulling them out from beneath the tragedy of their own perceptions. A moment of transcendence.

Beyond the magical thinking that convinced us prayer was working—the self-soothing loop we learned as infants—we have some accounting to do. The magic curtain has been worked so well by some

---

[*] It is no surprise to learn that Frank Baum was the son-in-law of Matilda Jocelyn Gage, one of the strongest feminists ever to walk the planet. She convinced him to publish his stories, and she influenced the strongly feminist vision of utopia we find in the land of Oz.

people that they seem to have created an entirely magical world over-seen by an entirely benevolent god who, though not very good at full disclosure, promised abundance somewhere down the line. Even those of us not so convinced have seen connections, have been emboldened by things we have labelled results, or have at least wondered, as I did when my son, Izaak, became suddenly well again.

## Situationally Transcendent Resources

The religious naturalist Jerome Stone calls the seemingly miraculous events that occur in our lives "situationally transcendent resources of renewal."[11] When we hit the limit of our capacity to influence or improve our circumstances and then something happens that manages to surpass our boundaries, he calls it the manifestation of a "transcendent" resource. That's because Stone considers anything transcendent if it comes to us from beyond what we could have managed or even imagined on our own—it comes from *beyond* our own capabilities at the time. Its causes fall entirely within the natural realm of things, however, despite the fact that we could not have expected them or made them happen ourselves; they transcended our own realm of possibilities.

There is no denying that "Impossible things are happening every day!" as Cinderella's Fairy Godmother once sang encouragingly to both Leslie Ann Warren and me. Though you're not likely to be driven around in a pumpkin coach any time soon, we experience those impossible things ourselves or hear stories of them all the time: someone gets better when they weren't expected to; a child's goldfish comes back to life; the tree falls on the empty side of the driveway. I listened recently to a news report on our national broadcasting net-work that went on and on about how horrific a traffic accident *might* have been had the tractor-trailer involved slid in a different direction. The reporter was absolutely captivated by the miraculous save the trucker had managed. It happened. It really happened, we call out to one another.

Every such experience we've had seems to have come about in a miraculous, magical way. Not in Faber's magical way, through which we self-soothe with less than what we really wanted, but in startling, life-changing ways that we really did want but hadn't been able to realize on our own. In unravelling the tangle of what really happened (were we able to sort it all out), we could claim only the causes we'd be able to prove—the very real, very accessible, very non-supernatural happenings that made the story's punchline possible. That we don't know all the complex happenings, that we can't draw a line between cause and effect, doesn't mean that we are forced to fall back on supernatural explanations as though there are no natural ones. We have no authority to argue that there is such a link, regardless of what we may "believe" we are seeing. We simply don't know what all the contributing factors are, and the truth is we may never know. But natural explanations, every time we have ultimately found them, have been reproducible, measurable, and very real. Supernatural explanations, every time we've sought to grasp them, have eluded and made fools of us.

The only thing supernatural about a supernatural explanation is the explanation itself. Just because we don't understand something doesn't mean we couldn't ever understand it, given the ability to decipher it (the knowledge we need to trace the nerve responses, read the synaptic development of our brains, see the space between things instead of assuming it is filled with nothing and waving our hands at whatever else is there—waves, strings, frequencies, whatever). People get better for no apparent reason; trucks veer out of the way, air brakes screeching, at the excruciatingly last minute; ladybugs land on our arms when we least expect it; people open the doors of our lives and walk in, unannounced. We don't need to resort to supernatural explanations to accept, with joy and thanksgiving, the wonder that happens. What one may call a miracle, another may simply accept as the mysterious unfolding of life, and another still might work to unravel, charting the chemical, physical, emotional, and contextual realities that made it happen. We call it as we see it.

Stone challenges us to drop the supernatural origins of the wonders that surround us and accept them as gifts, situationally transcendent gifts that we experience because we allow ourselves to see the wonder within them. Living with a reverence for life and the inexplicable ways in which it unfolds around and within us is a very important aspect of the religious life that we cannot afford to lose, even as we stand in the crater left by the deconstruction of its central assumptions. In fact, a reverence for life fills that crater exquisitely well.

Seeing events as situational and their origins as natural also clears up a very big problem that divine origin brings to the question of cause and effect. Bruce Wilkinson, the author of *The Prayer of Jabez*, tells the story of being late for a plane he was trying to catch. On the way to the airport, he prayed for the flight to be delayed, and lo and behold, it was. Now, if God really did stuff like that, those who pray for planes to be delayed have a lot to answer for: the missed connecting flights, the angry spouses, the lost sales, the broken appointments, the empty seat at the last performance of the grade eight musical. Split-second shifts in lives can make huge differences. Put hundreds of people off their schedules for several hours for your own convenience and there's something to be said for the dignity inherent in just missing the flight. We can only hope that as Wilkinson arrived at his gate, he fell to his knees and apologized to everyone. It would have been the least he could do.

Recognizing that transcendent events are situational allows them to bear us goodness, even as we realize that they may not be good for someone else. In an episode of *Grey's Anatomy*, we were exposed to the very real horror of what yearning after good can mean. A young boy awaiting a heart transplant discloses his disgust with his mother's practice of praying every day that he'd get a heart. As far as he could tell, she was praying that someone else's child would die so he could live, and the concept was repulsive to him.[12] Yet we wait for miracles like these in our lives, and we are right to celebrate them when they occur. Released from the image of a deity that would reward some by the devastation of others, however, we can open ourselves to a gift borne by whatever circumstances bring it to us. The plane we are late for is itself late. What a stroke of luck! An accident victim had completed her organ donor card. How beautifully generous! Jerome Stone and his situationally transcendent resources of renewal allow us to be open to the possibility of such gift happening, to the hope, and the prayer even, and they allow us to do it with dignity and a natural humility.

## Stop Motivating Me!

The loss of the supernatural omnigod we constructed also takes away much of the motivation for doing good and refraining from evil that has kept much of humanity on the straight and narrow. The distinction between what we do because we have to and what we do because we're moved to is highlighted by Lance Secretan in his book *Inspire!* Secretan, who would likely be offended if we called him a motivational speaker, actually points to the difference between motivation, which is reward- and fear-based, and inspiration, which is values-based. The supernatural *source, agent,* and *promise* God was entirely reward- and fear-based. The rewards for performance were always tinged with the repercussions of bad or non-performance. Motivation thrives on that same idea. Secretan argues that when the system of reward and punishment is replaced with a values-based system that inspires people to be the best they can be and to offer their best potential to any situation, the benefits to everyone increase exponentially.[13] People start choosing to behave in ways that are consistent with the values they are inspired to hold.

If the idea of human potential is values-based, however, we need to recognize the reality of self-centred, destructive values. Of course we have the potential to do evil. At a very young age, we can choose to hurt. But at an even younger, pre-verbal age, we empathize, crying when other babies cry; offering what soothes us—our own precious transitional objects—to others to soothe them too; kissing and hugging our primary caregivers when we see they are sad. We are hardwired to empathize, and proper nurture in those early years reinforces that wiring. We can, if we are attentive to the work of child-rearing, actually raise our capacity for empathy and so reduce our capacity to do harm. As highly empathic individuals, we simply couldn't stand the pain *we* would experience were we to inflict harm on others. To understand how important that job of child-rearing really is, we need to look again at the brain.

Our amygdalae—two almond-shaped masses wrapped up in our limbic system—have been part of our brains for a long, long time. They are linked to our emotions, particularly fear, and the processes that can mitigate the impact of whatever threat we encounter. They are central to the familiar "fight, flight, or freeze" responses that our brains generate when we are exposed to stressful situations. We could expect to find that those who had excellent "fight, flight, or freeze" responses were the ones who survived within a species.

It's the newer parts of our brains that are interesting, though, especially when it comes to things religious. Our heads aren't shaped like crocodile heads; we have frontal lobes. They give us that nice high brow, a place where we can pull up to our mental conference table and think our way through to the best course of action, rather than simply firing off the most expeditious reaction. In other words, it's where we do our most "human" and "humane" thinking.

## Decision Switching

Work on pair bonding by anthropologists Robin Dunbar and Susanne Shultz explains why humans have this enormous—in comparison to other primates—frontal lobe in which all that thinking and consideration takes place. Pairing for life is something that few animals do, and those of us who have attempted it several times know why. It requires incredible coordination of activity and the ability to anticipate the implications of choosing one's potential partner, weighing carefully his or her abilities as they are able to complement yours in the work of survival. You don't want to get caught pairing up for life with a partner who will not assist with rearing offspring or is unable to forage for the food required to feed a growing family. (There is, actually, a much longer list of other things you also don't want to get stuck with. If you're unsure, txt me . . .)

Because of the higher cognitive abilities needed to pair bond, animals that select and maintain partners for life have, not surprisingly, a larger neocortex, which is where complex and abstract thought takes place. And of course, an increased capacity for problem-solving, planning, and the anticipation of results follows with the increased size of the neocortex. But humans have also been able to transfer the capacity to pair bond to others than those with whom they are in a reproductive relationship. They, and very few other species, are able to develop intense, life-long relationships with other members of their social group. And *that* is the most significant thing about this pair-bond stuff. Because we have been able to develop feelings of consideration and empathy for larger numbers of people, we have developed a brain that can think the way ours can. It is our ability to be social, *not* our ability to protect and serve merely our own interests, that has made us who we are today. It's our ability to *empathize with* others, not our ability to *capitalize on* them, that has saved us, thus far, from extinction.[14]

Contrary to those who, like laissez-faire economics guru Milton

Friedman, argue we are better to cast our future on the whims and will of the market and free ourselves of our concern for others outside our circle of influence, Dunbar and Shultz demonstrate that our interdependence is an evolutionary benefit, not a hindrance. "Strong social bonds, high levels of intelligence, intense parenting, and long periods of learning are among factors used by higher primates to depress environmentally induced mortality."[15]

Scholars are recognizing that our quest for survival and our need to reproduce isn't sufficient to fuel the expansive reality of human community. Searching for what might have driven the development of increasingly complex and interconnected community, they are exploring the possibility that we are an "affectionate species that continuously seeks to broaden and deepen our relationships and connections to others."[16] We reach out in order to transcend ourselves. The connections we make provide us the opportunity to continue the process.

Lodged in the crevice between the amygdalae of the ancient limbic system and the newer frontal lobe is the anterior cingulate. When compared with the amygdalae, it's a baby. In addition to helping us create social bonds, the anterior cingulate steers our decision making toward either our frontal lobes or our amygdalae. In other words, it is our decision switching station. If it steers a train of thought toward the amygdalae, we're going to react with fight, flight, or freeze; if it steers that train of thought toward the frontal lobe, it is going to carry us right to the place where we've set up that conference table, which is where we do our rational thinking.

The development of the switching station determines which track we'll run the train on. If the switches are weak and undeveloped, our limbic brain gets the switch and we're into an emotional response. If they are strong and healthy, we take a breath, consider the options and their potential effects on ourselves, others, and the world around us, and make a more considered, more empathic response. Mirror neurons, those that create a mirror response in us when we see an action in another (think of a baby sticking its tongue out at you when you stick your tongue out at it), seem to be located primarily in the neocortex when they are related to action. When they are related to emotion, however, they appear to fire off in the anterior cingulate, right where this switching station has evolved. When we see someone cry, we have a harder time keeping it together ourselves. When we see someone smile, we feel better. Our brains are interconnected in ways we are just discovering.

That difference between routing our train of thought to our limbic system or our frontal lobes is roughly the difference between our old tribal religions—filled as they are with angry, judgmental gods—and the newer more ecologically and justice-oriented expressions of the liberal church—which are less focused on a theistic being and more geared toward considering what is good for everyone. It's another premise Newberg and Waldman put forward in *How God Changes Your Brain*, and its clarity is stunning. Our brains have, very literally, evolved our idea of god. As the anterior cingulate developed and offered us options, our frontal lobes grew better able to make choices. Our brains, in fact, gave us choices.

Waldman and Newberg also note that participating in prayer— or its sister act, meditation—may have been a significant part of that evolution. In participants from every religious system, the health of the brain is improved whenever a concept such as god has been considered, in part because of the vast brain territory such a concept engages. The part of our brain most affected by prayer and meditation is that crucial anterior cingulate, the decision switching station. Its spindle-shaped cells, known as von Economo neurons (VENs), are central to "intelligent behaviour, that is, emotional self-control, focused problem solving, error recognition, and adaptive response to changing conditions."[17] As these cells grow stronger—and prayer and meditation help enormously in that area—the probability increases that our thought train is going to end up in the frontal lobes, where the experiences and interests of others will be taken into account.

Of course, the VENs need to be present in order to be strengthened, right? But we aren't born with a full set of them, just as we aren't born with a full set of teeth. In fact, we have only about 15 percent of an average load of VENs when we are born. That could be similar to the percentage of hair follicles we have at birth too, but hair follicles are likely to develop on their own, because our genetic makeup is predisposed to provide them. Von Economo neurons, however, are . . . well, neurons; they need a stimulating environment in which to develop, and it is too tragically true that such an environment is not always available. VENs develop within the first eight months of life and seemingly only in an empathically rich environment.[18] Only with one of child psychologist Donald Winnicott's "good-enough" primary caregivers. Only when a child's physical and emotional needs are being met. They take several years to come to maturity, and studies are suggesting that their survival may be "enhanced or reduced by environmental conditions of enrichment or stress, thus potentially influencing adult competence or dysfunction in emotional self-control and problem-solving capacity."[19] If we want an empathic civilization, we need to start creating one in the first moment of every child's life.[20]

If, we might ask, we no longer have the foundational premise upon which most religions are built—that is, supernatural *source, agent,* and *promise* gods or another world that exists beneath or behind our experience of reality—and we reduce or remove the fundamental vehicle through which we approached that god or otherworldly reality (prayer or meditation), will we not be placing both our capacity for empathy and our future evolution at risk? Apparently not. We may want to keep the prayer and meditation practices, but according to Newberg and Waldman, we can heave the supernatural element of it and not look back.

While researching the improvements to memory and empathy—the functions of the anterior cingulate—caused by prayer or meditation, Waldman and Newberg included individuals who did not use *any* image or concept of god while they did the exercises provided. Results showed that the brain function of these participants improved in the same measure as that of those using God as an image while they prayed or meditated.[21] Prayer with *or without* God provided equally positive results within eight weeks of twelve minutes of meditation per day. The significant factor seemed to be not God, not an alternative reality, but the intentional focus on breathing and a desire for improvement in a particular area. God provided a powerful placebo. But we do not need the placebo. We can create positive results ourselves.

### Practicalities

It isn't just strengthening our brains, or at least the anterior cingulate part of them, that we've been after when we've bowed our heads in supplication, though. We've been after results. When we turn to non-supernaturally focused prayer within community, it is possible to see positive results almost immediately. At West Hill, participants rise and invite the community to share their celebrations and their sorrows, and the community's response is immediate. Sometimes laughter breaks out, sometimes tears. Always a response.

A key element in creating the space within which a healing intimacy can be realized is the introduction offered by the facilitator, minister, or leader. Because prayer is such a highly symbolic act, what is happening can be interpreted by participants in widely diverse ways—especially if it looks, smells, and wags its tail like all the prayer participants have ever experienced. I believe it is important to be clear that whatever may be happening, it's not something any particular crowd or leader has its finger on. I can tell you what I *don't* think is happening, but I can't tell you what will happen. I don't know. You don't know.

Being honest about that is part of the non-exclusive element toward which you want to be heading. There is incredible power in the spoken word when it is offered into a room of empathically charged people. That power can do amazing things. Let it operate on its own and don't try to manipulate or control it. If you are a leader, think of yourself as a midwife. If you are a participant, simply be open to what you might have to offer—spiritually, in the sense of strength, humour, understanding; and physically, in the sense of physical objects or personal skills—in the moment or later, at some other time or other place.

Perhaps words such as these can be used to invite a group into a time of deep sharing: "As a community, we have the privilege of offering our truths to one another, of sharing our burdens, laments, and sorrows, as well as our delights, celebrations, and joys. Offering our sadness or anger into community provides us respite, and as others share its burden, we are en-coeur-aged—we feel their hearts wrap around us and know strength. Bringing our happiness invites others, whose hearts may also be laden, to be lifted with us. Through community, we are enriched. May this be a time in which we offer hope, encouragement, and love." If you wish to speak specifically of prayer, I find it helpful to come right out and say, "We neither claim prayer works nor declare we understand its effects, but we know that when we open ourselves fully to ourselves and one another, we can be changed. May this be a place where and a time when we can do such work surrounded with love and care." Or speak of the transimmanence of what prayer has been and continues to provide. "Try as we might, we cannot always meet our own expectations, cannot bring good out of bad situations, cannot reach far enough to stave off the pain we feel or know another feels. Here, now, we find ourselves in community. Here, now, let the depths of our hearts speak to the richness that is present in this community, and wherever possible, may we find resources that transcend our personal abilities."

If you are not in a community that is willing to explore beyond the boundaries of traditional prayer because you can't find one, keep looking. Use the power of the Internet to connect with others who are similarly isolated. Connect and connect and connect, and as you do, open yourself and those with you to the "miracle" that community offers by way of situationally transcendent resources. What you say triggers something in someone else's brain. What someone else feels triggers something in yours. Back and forth, your brains are firing off, influencing one another, and making a difference. Sometimes an imperceptible difference at the time, but over the course of a deepening relationship and coming to know one another better, possibilities expand exponentially and impossible things start happening. I'm not talking miracles. Don't get me wrong. I'm talking about empathic responses that people have to one another's needs, and the lengths they will go to in order to help make a situation better. Grow that community in any way you can find it.

If you are not in a community that is willing to explore beyond the boundaries of traditional prayer because you don't want to be in such a community, read the above paragraph again. You *need* community. It's what makes you human.

## What's Bigger than Big?

When I consider the things people pray for most fervently, it's a difficult list, and for the most part, we're not going to be able to bring about the results people are looking for, try as we might. We can't cure fourth-stage ovarian cancer or child-onset diabetes. We can't turn clocks back the one second that would make all the difference in the world. We can't bring people back to life or hold them tightly enough so they don't slip away from us. We can't pray our way to the money we need to get ourselves out of debt or free a loved one from addiction or get the abuse to stop. We can't bring about world peace—not two of us with our heads bowed and our hands clasped, and not four hundred thousand spread across the churches, mosques, synagogues, sweat lodges, and temples of the nation. We can't stop global warming or pollution, or bring back the untold thousands of species that have or will become extinct because of our lifestyles and greed. Not with our heads bowed anyway.

What we can do is what we've always been able to do. Find out about things. Share what you know. Ask questions about what you don't. Commit yourself to work for change that is so positive it lets people live with dignity, change that includes recognizing the dignity inherent in the other sentient beings with whom we share this planet, change that is likely going to cost you but is going to make a real difference. What we can do is get educated and spread education. What we can do is take care of our own health, making sure we're dealing with real health issues and not the ones pharmaceutical companies keep making up for a wealthy, pampered clientele. That means we'll have more resources to help take care of the health of those who don't have access to what we have. What we can do is fund more than just research for a cure; we can fund research that's looking for a cause or a way to prevent disease in the first place. What we can do is live more in tune with the balance of the earth, and where that is next to impossible, we can find ways to reduce our eco-footprint as much as we are able. We can invest in well-being. Yours. Mine. Ours. The big "ours"—as in, all life on this planet. And yes, that is going to cost you too.

When we enter into the introspective place that is prayer or the practice of meditation or a focused few moments before the elevator door opens or the peaceful process of tea-making that fills the last half hour before the children come bursting through the door, we engage in the essential work of opening ourselves to the situationally transcendent resources around us and to re-creating ourselves as those resources for others. We let dissonant thoughts coalesce into insight; our minds meander to places of illumination and possibility, and we connect. Whether you argue that the connection is with something other than yourself, or that it is simply of a line of dots you hadn't seen before is of little consequence to me or anyone. What is of consequence is that you do it; that you listen to what goes on in your brain, in your heart, in your world; and that you enter into that conversation fully and reverentially. This is the essence of practice—call it what you will—that is essential. The essential essence of what we're talking about. If "prayer" is nothing more than being present, it is much and it is important. Being present: it takes work, attention, energy, and humility to be present—especially to yourself.

Beyond the supernatural promise of an incredibly bright by and by is the human *potential* that can offer an even brighter future in the here and now. When we are brutally honest with ourselves, we see that the promises we looked to God to fulfill were never realized in any accountable way. I, for one, am not prepared to bet our lives and the future of this planet on such inconsistent results. But I am prepared to put my best effort into creating the potential for good to develop and grow in the world. We are all *able* to do that. If we consistently *choose* to do that, we can make an incredible difference.

PART FIVE

# IN A WORLD IN NEED

# EMPACT

A couple of years ago, stimulated by a book studied even earlier, the community I serve began the process of exploring together the ethics of the food we eat. Peter Singer's *The Ethics of What We Eat: Why Our Food Choices Matter* had challenged the stomachs and the diets of many participants. Those who brought the issue to the congregation's board asked important questions: How can we say we strive "to live consciously and caringly, increasing our awareness of the consequences of our actions, advocating for rights, and making ethically responsible decisions," and not consider how doing so might impact our food choices? How can we be signatories to the Earth Charter and not think through its principles as a community?[1]

As a congregation that had grappled with extremely sensitive issues and lived to tell the tales, we expected that the conversation, although not an easy one, would be undertaken in the same manner as all our challenging interactions—with openness, honesty, empathy, and humility.

That never got to happen.

Even before the study process had been set up, news of it hit the pews like wildfire, raising the spectre of Inquisition-like church committees forcing their way into homes and sweeping through cupboards and freezers in search of contraband food products. Damage control became the order of the day, and the passions of those who had brought the issue to the table were set aside as the process of caring for the congregation became paramount.

It was clear that while we were terrific at addressing doctrinal and liturgical issues, those that touched us on a personal, everyday basis, were more difficult to address. Ethical issues dealt with on a communal level would have challenging implications for our members and adherents on a personal level, even if we tried to keep clear boundaries between the two. Any social-justice ministry will have confronted that fine line many times. The issue was dealt with by developing a policy that required vegetarian and vegan options to be included at each congregational event. It was a compromise and achieved the balance that so much progressive thought must work to achieve. But like it or not, it is an issue, like so many other issues, that we—that's the big "we," and it includes you—are going to have to deal with eventually. And very likely in a much more dramatic and challenging way. Because our world is getting smaller. As it does, our walls will do one of two things: they will get thinner or they will get thicker. They will not stay the same.

As we sit at our tables with a meal in front of us, we may be moved to give thanks for the food, for those who prepared it, for those who farmed it, and even, when appropriate, for the animals who died so that we could have it (often cloaked in language that suggests they "gave" their lives to us). We are comfortably situated in a room filled with others who also have food on their plates. But make the walls of those rooms transparent, make them magically allow you to see into other rooms, in other homes, in other parts of the city, the country, the world. What do you see now? Who do you see? If you are not prepared to see, then make your walls thick and protect them as long as you can. You will likely not live to see the consequences anyway. But if you are prepared to see, then line your room with the faces of those who have put that food on your plate and lift your fork humbly as they look on.

I line my dining room with the faces of children who will never have the opportunity to hope for what I have on my plate. It might just be a hangover from all the "starving children in China" so many of us heard about as children when we didn't like what was for supper, but I don't think so. I'm having to eat with an awareness of what is going on in the world that, a generation ago, most of us didn't have—about industrial farming and the ecological disaster and ethically repugnant reality it is; about the destruction of an ocean's worth of fish habitat, and the reckless annihilation of whole species to sate our palate; about the way sentient beings are genetically and chemically fattened up and ritually slaughtered, oftentimes brutally; about communities who seed their fields with carnations or chocolate instead of food they can eat so that multinational chains can have cheap impulse items at the check-out; about genetically altered food products that threaten the livelihoods of local farmers and promote a frenetic poisoning of the earth; about children with faces mangled by fungus and oozing sores caused by the pollution of their drinking water by the corporations that managed to move my raspberries from Chile to Canada in the middle of February; about Mexican labourers who are treated with contempt despite being desperately needed to do work no one else will do.

And that's just food. We haven't touched interpersonal, child, gender, and elder abuse; global warming; economics; corporatism; homo- and trans-phobia; workplace bullying; a litany of -isms. . . . There is no limit to the challenges we face, to the walls we need to bravely see beyond.

The liberal "Kingdom of God on earth" beliefs that I grew up with are not easy for me to give up. I'm not content with a ministry that deals with the few congregational skirmishes that rattle around behind closed doors or sweep through parking lots faster than dry leaves. I want to change the world. I'm impatient for the day I once thought of as the Day of the Lord, when suffering would end and all would know well-being and peace.[2] "It's not going to happen," the pragmatists say. "Stop talking," I respond, just before my eyes fill with tears.

What does it matter that we pray if our prayer will not bring about something akin to the Day of the Lord, the resolution of argument, the diminishment of arrogance, the celebration of beauty and laughter unbound from desperation? What does it matter what we call it if what it does is bring about this righting of relationship, this raising up of dignity? What does it matter if we neglect this vision and focus purely on our own spiritual integrity, our own spiritual highs?

I think it matters very much what we do and not so much what we call it. I think it matters very much if we make our walls thick or thin because we are so deeply enmeshed in the world around us that what we do within our own walls has an enormous impact beyond them. I think it matters very much what our choices are, because we are *Homo sapiens* and we must bring wisdom to them. Wisdom comes with a price and that price, most of the time, is our comfort. But we must take one more step out of our comfort zone, as eighty-four-year-old activist Dorli Rainey, who was pepper-sprayed at Occupy Seattle in November 2011, reminds us.[3] Only there will we ever be able to make the difference we may not want but desperately need to make.

Let us pray? No, it's not that easy. Let us get on with what we need to get on with. And that is going to be hard.

## FOUNDATION ISSUES

The assumption we can work with in order to do the work that needs to be done is no longer about a divine being who might assist us but about being itself—honouring it, developing it, celebrating it. The foundation is no longer a separate supreme person or entity; the foundation is life and love for ourselves, others, and the world. We choose this as our foundation, as a deep, immanent reality that also transcends us—it is within us and beyond us. And we also transcend ourselves as we stretch to live lovingly in spite of all that works against love. The foundation is deeply human and humanitarian. It is ages old, with an honourable heritage. If this does not seem as "firm a foundation" as a supernatural God, I haven't done a very good job so far.

If you're building a new wing to a hospital, or even a new addition to a small home, you can't just stretch the old foundation out so it will support new walls; it's already doing everything it was built to do, and it can't take anything more. You have to dig out a hole big enough to pour a whole new foundation. Unless, of course, you're building on solid rock.

The church has long used the image of the rock to imply the solidity of its religious foundations. But in response to contemporary knowledge and culture, that rock has fissured deeply. The very fact that evangelicals tell me the church is stronger than ever[4] and liberals tell me it's not is proof that something has gone seriously wrong with that rock-solid foundation.

During an evening discussion in Toronto, Diana Butler Bass shared anecdotes from her experiences with congregations across North America, noting that many serve as microcosms of what is happening in the world as people pull away from religious institutions and break the hold those institutions have had on spiritual and ethical matters. She then drew a line down the middle of a piece of paper and wrote a capital *S* on one side and a capital *R* on the other, inviting those gathered to call out the words they thought were relevant to spirituality and religion, respectively. Butler Bass was drawing out from the crowd the discrepancy between what they—a group of postmodern churchgoers in a liberal progressive denomination—connected with and what church is understood to be by the general public.

## SPLIT VISION

The lists held no surprises. Spirituality got words like "connection," "meaning," "wonder," "spirit," "mystery," and "awe." Religion got words like "doctrine," "dogma," "traditionalism," "rigid," "courts," and "rules." The line down the middle was crossed by the words "community" and "prayer." Still, it was interesting to see our assumptions written out in a graphic manner before us. The writing on the wall, so to speak.

As Western culture has become more affluent and dependence upon community has diminished, our identity as significant beings over and beyond the "tribe" has grown and our sense of personal worth and value has skyrocketed. In a consumer-driven capitalist society, individuals can, perhaps for the first time in history, measure their success by their ability to consume and the independence they perceive as a result. When we are strong, healthy, and wealthy, we have a heightened sense of self and personal entitlement. It is no surprise that as this shift toward individualism has taken place, the individualistic spiritualities—self-actualization or the attainment of altered states of consciousness through meditation—have grown in popularity. Signs of spiritual status, like the red-string bracelet worn by pop-recording star Madonna, a student of Kabbalistic Judaism, reinforce the prestige of the personal spiritual quest. The first person I ever knew to identify himself as a Buddhist was a self-made North American businessman who, having spent time in India learning from personal teachers, pursued his new spiritual path with the same dogged determination and disregard for those who might get in the way as he did his business goals. But he wore a red string tied around his neck as a symbol of the protection and continual embrace of his spiritual lama.

## BROADER VISTAS

Lillian Daniel, a United Church of Christ pastor, touched a nerve when, in a *Huffington Post* article that reads like it was originally typed in all caps,* she declared those who call themselves Spiritual But Not Religious (SBNR) boring.⁵ Stereotypically wrapping themselves in the glow of God-drenched sunsets and walks on the beach (Did I not mention the beach earlier? And a rainbow? Yikes!), they're simply avoiding the self-discipline that religious community demands, according to Daniel. She argues that SBNRs prefer the privilege of being self-centred to the challenge of having to hear something they don't like. There was a striking irony in Daniel's inability to open herself to the possibility that SBNRs—who, she reports, prefer the confines of air travel to disclose their SBNR-ishness to her—might have something to say that she should hear, even if it is something she doesn't like.

Daniel is perhaps too close to the religious culture she defends to see all the things people get to avoid if their spirituality can be nurtured outside the church. Doctrine, traditionalism, rules, courts, and so many other disparaged terms that ended up under the *R* column relate to the management of community. The regularized beliefs of doctrine helped define distinct communities of individuals who were dependent upon one another for their care and well-being; rules and courts stipulated how those individuals were to act within those communities; traditions reminded them of how specific beliefs, stories, promises, and rituals linked them to the ancestors who created and perpetuated them, and challenged them to keep their ways alive. Failure to uphold these traditions was understood to lead to grave individual and community consequences—sometimes even earth-shattering ones. As various forms of spirituality have captured the imaginations of those who hunger for a more individual sense of wellness and spiritual awareness, this stuff—all of it integral to the *communal* spiritual journey—is left in a heap. None of it is essential if your spiritual quest is wholly personal.

---

* All capital letters in an email or text message indicates the writer is screaming.

In fact, as the line down the middle of the Butler Bass flip chart indicates, the communal stuff of religion can become a hindrance to the personal quest. Who wants *rules* when they don't allow you to participate if you're not a member? And who wants to become a *member* if it means you have to sign a morality clause that discriminates against people for circumstances that are not choices (sexuality, sexual identity, race, origin, etc.)? Why reiterate and reinforce *tradition* if it perpetuates oppressive ideologies that were once crucial for our cultural survival but are now impediments to what might be considered basic morality? According to individualists, a communal set of beliefs and responsibilities only gets in the way of the personal spiritual pursuit. What was once necessary for social cohesion—the acceptance of shared beliefs and communal responsibilities—has become an encumbrance to personal spiritual growth. These absolutes no longer make sense to spiritual seekers.

The SBNRs who line up for hours to hear Deepak Chopra or tune in to Eckhart Tolle's dispassionate online video feeds are on personal trajectories that often have a common nemesis: organized religion. As the real world and our religious communities have rubbed up against each other, our belief systems have lost the power each held as a theoretical absolute. So too have they lost their idiosyncratic value as the beliefs and practices peculiar to each system became, for many, irrelevant in the heap of undermined promises, shattered worldviews, and outmoded regalia. Religion as it has currently evolved—the purveyor of absolutes and ethereal promises—can no longer answer the questions of twenty-first-century seekers after meaning.

What's more, as many SBNRs will point out, religion has become the problem in many ways precisely because of the values its more fundamentalist iterations project and reinforce. Those values often focus on an eternal afterlife and who gets to enjoy its benefits and rewards. That being the case, anything this side of the great abyss can rank only a distant second. Those who value things mired in the muck and guck of real life can be easily dismissed—or worse—in the pursuit of timeless recognition and eternal bliss. When scratched away, the veneer of spirituality on any of the great religious traditions exposes only the same problematic beliefs—there is a divine supernatural authority of some kind who will help only some of us, depending on what we do to earn that reward. Unfortunately, only those who are particularly well versed in the contemporary discussion of the tenets of their faith have the ability or predisposition to argue anything different. Adherents "on the street," so to speak, generally hold to the classically simple and straightforward understandings of their traditions, which profess to have a way to take care of the individual both in this life, here and now, and in the unknown and unknowable territory beyond death's portal.

Lillian Daniel was doing what we so often do when we're on the losing end of a playground rivalry—pointing her finger and yelling, "You're stupid!" Diana Butler Bass recognized the behaviour and responded with an article that invited the hurting religious side to open itself to what the SBNRs might reflect back to them. SBNR, she points out, is the fastest-growing alternative to mainline, evangelical, and Catholic denominations, and church decline is reflected in its growth. Her figures, gathered during the research for her book *Christianity After Religion*, due to be published in early 2012, show a steady increase in this newest category on the religious affiliation page. Butler Bass urges those in the church to "listen as non-defensively and fully as we possibly can, with wide-open hearts and nimble theological imaginations."[6]

The tendency to circle the wagons in situations where we are experiencing threat is understandable. In the church, whose social status has plummeted as precipitously as its membership numbers, the desire to do that is great. Indeed, thinking along Tiger and

McGuire's brain-soothing channels, it would make sense that we keep our behaviours, rituals, language, and symbols as distinct from the culture around us as we can. The more distinct we remain from the society around us, the more easily we will recognize each other and the likelier we are to survive. But this is precisely why those of us in the church need to take a serious look at what our foundations have been holding up and what we want them to do. If what we're building on will support the needs of only some of the population, then we're not building big enough or strong enough. We need to dig deeper and further if the positive influence that church might be is to be extended beyond "the frozen few." Of course, if we keep doing church the way many mainline congregations are doing it, it might be only you and Lillian Daniel left. But you'll be happy to know she'll let you hold her hand if it gets bouncy on the plane.

## SEEING BEYOND OURSELVES

There is another group, one we've alluded to peripherally, that wasn't necessary for the purposes of the exercise Diana Butler Bass led us through that evening, and so didn't show up on the lists: those who fit neither the "religious" nor the "spiritual" category. They may, at one time, have been connected with an organized religion, may have thought themselves spiritual if not religious, or may never have had significant experience with anything exclusive to either of those two columns. How they came to the position they are now in may vary, but to a person, they do not believe that religion or spirituality—anything supernatural—is necessary to a meaningful life. When we're making S/R lists, if we're operating with an "inside the church" perspective, we simply forget to put those people on the chart. They are invisible to us.

Under Daniel's tutelage, our S column has become the spiritual but not religious, SBNR. For the sake of clarity, let's just call this new column, with an apology for the negative-seeming tone, the *Neither* column.

But what words would have been jotted in the *Neither* column that evening in Toronto? With only 5 percent of the American population willing to identify themselves as not believing in God[7] (a number that soars to 23 percent north of the border[8]), we might expect to find a string of negatives dropping down from under the *Neither* header as those who believe in a divine being judge their neighbours who choose differently: selfish, argumentative, overconfident, heartless, intellectual (like that's a bad thing), anarchist, lacking respect for tradition, big-headed, Christless, etc., etc.

Of course, it's important to remember that the *SBNR/R* lists were created that evening by a group of people within the church who, as it turned out, like to describe themselves as spiritual but see themselves as part of a religious tradition it is their responsibility to change. Had the lists been prepared by those who identified themselves as neither religious nor spiritual, we might have seen dramatically different words included: superstitious, anti-intellectual, arrogant, self-centred, divisive, militant, fundamentalist, dangerous, etc., etc. Beauty, as we all know, is in the eye of the beholder.

While the two words that showed up on Diana Butler Bass' chart under both columns—"community" and "prayer"—are comfortable in either list, linking them and then tossing them into the *Neither* column would trigger an immediate allergic reaction. While community might be a commodity church provides that *Neithers* may wish to seek out, "prayer" simply does not belong. Someone with a perfume allergy can't just ignore the scented stuff and breathe in only the clean air—it's all contaminated. If *Neithers* are looking for community, they are not going to be interested in community that features traditional prayer.

Of all the words that appeared on Butler Bass' flip chart that night in Toronto, then, *only* the word "community" could safely be put under all three columns, had three columns appeared. If we are walking toward something radically non-exclusive but hoping to hold on to the function our religions and our spiritualities have offered—the brain-soothing, stress-relieving function—letting go of terms *and forms* that exclude is part of the process. According to the work of Lionel Tiger and Mark McGuire, supported by that of Chaeyoon Lim and Robert Putnam, there is real purpose in doing that.

Religious participation has, until recently, been a significant focus of time and energy within communities; in smaller rural areas, it's often the main source of social interaction next to the co-op. The results of both Tiger and McGuire's research and Lim and Putnam's research make perfect sense. They raise concerns, however, when we consider the dramatic drop in church attendance over the past two decades. With this kind of information about well-being and life satisfaction; their relationship to social networks, identity, and attendance at communities of faith; and the physiological link to serotonin production, we would want to ensure that strong, healthy religious communities continue. The trend in society, however, is toward the loss of religious community. It may be that a corresponding decline in well-being in our society will also result. Religious organizations that have social well-being at the forefront of their mandates—that is, liberal and mainline denominations—would do well to note the challenge and find ways to create communities of belonging that distil the elements essential to well-being out of the dogmatic concoction so many thinking people are so quick to avoid. Were these organizations able to do so, it might also be that some of the crankier atheists we hear from so much would do well to find a congregation and make a few friends.

## 5700 VARIETIES

We know what we can do. We can live in ways that create loving relationships—by which I mean just and compassionate ones—without the supernaturally infused belief systems we used to have. If there is any purpose at all to gathering people together so they can be supported in that work, our language, our forms, our symbols—all of it—will need to be clean of the detritus of that supernatural belief system. If there is any purpose to gathering people together so they may identify humane values by which they wish to live—to lift those values up into a position of chosen yet vulnerable authority, to use them to inspire each individual to live as closely aligned with those ideals as is possible and so influence the world in a positive way—we'll have to do it without anything that looks at all like traditional prayer. There will be many who will want to call such communities spiritual. I feel the draw toward that myself, because for me, the word "spiritual" means the challenge of living up to humane values that inspire me to live in right relationship with everything, including myself, and so describes what it is I think we need to do. But much as I might like to use the word, it's got problems too, and as many or more flavours as religion.

Compiling results of a survey on spiritual experiences, Newberg and Waldman found figures that would substantiate those Butler Bass has collected: while the interest in God's physical characteristics is falling for most people, the number of people interested in spirituality is on the rise.[9] But when the results of the survey were examined, the list of words used to describe spiritual experience ran to fifty-seven *hundred* words, most of which were used by less than 10 percent of the respondents. There was nothing to which the researchers could point that was common to the majority of spiritual experiences—not God (18 percent), not spirituality (17 percent), not even love (less than 10 percent).[10] If there is nothing we can point to in common, then calling a community "spiritual" might lead to some confusion about what the community offers. Better, I would think, to describe what it offers and invite those who are interested to participate.

The work undertaken by Lionel Tiger and Mark McGuire tells us that communities gathered around socialization, ritual, and belief are strong and have incredible brain-soothing effects on us—effects that can alleviate much of the brain-poisoning stress of our lives. That should be reason enough to gather people together and try to recreate those environments. Innovative communities that connect people intentionally (socialization), lift humane values into a position of chosen yet vulnerable authority (beliefs), and create stories, symbols, and actions (ritual) that remind each individual he or she is a beautiful part of a cohesive whole will accomplish the goal. Already, it is happening—sometimes in religious communities, sometimes in spiritual groups, sometimes outside either of those. Wherever it is already happening in a sustained and engaging way, people are being invited to grow. Let's keep doing that—either reworking existing communities or creating new ones—and then let's keep them as clean as we can.

## WE. ARE. FAMILY.

I have often spoken of our need to get beyond the divisive parameters of the religious groupings into which we have organized ourselves, because I find them dangerously myopic and self-interested. Jeremy Rifkin, however, points out in *The Empathic Civilization* that we have already gone beyond these parameters with results that were no less dangerous. Beyond religious groupings and their incumbent barriers, Rifkin argues we evolved nation-states, each with its own set of new barriers, behaviours, allegiances. They are relatively new in the history of humanity, but just as tribal as the communities of our prehistoric ancestors and rooted in the same anxiety-laden attempts to create security.[11]

When we are able to find our commonalities, whether they are physical attributes, group rituals and symbols, likes and dislikes, or national economic and political values, we are better able to see the other as "one of us," so to speak, and so to extend to that other the same privileges we enjoy ourselves. If we can do that better than we do now, we might forge a future in which we could triumph over our self-centred preferences and acknowledge that when we ensure basic needs and human rights are extended to all, we are not diminished; no one is. Tribalism, religion, and xenophobic nationalism grow out of a fear of lack, of not having enough, of being eradicated from the earth and so needing, desperately, to create identity, purpose, privilege. Knowing that it is the whole of humanity itself, not just a single tribe or sect, that may be eradicated can be a motivating factor in moving us toward greater cooperation.

The 1996 film *Independence Day*, with Will Smith as the protagonist, offers a glimpse of such possibility. Through evocative footage of communities around the world responding to an impending threat, the movie unites humanity in a common struggle against invading aliens. The effect is powerful but demonstrates a classic scapegoat archetype; we have to find the enemy before we can define the group and create the rules that will keep everyone in it safe. In stark contrast, Denis Villeneuve, in his film *Incendies*, based on the stage play by Wajdi Mouawad, painstakingly and repeatedly erases the distinctions we keep insisting upon in order to show us that drawing those very distinctions is what we should be afraid of.

Will it take a calamity of otherworldly scapegoat proportions to bring us together? Or can we learn from those who, like Villeneuve, remind us that we create our enemies, we draw the lines that divide us? While Rifkin pushes us forward in an attempt to find an affinity that will pull us together, he also pushes us backward to our evolutionary roots. In fact, *National Geographic*'s Genographic Project offers each of us an opportunity to get back to those roots, which are found in the genetic makeup of two individuals—one male and one female—whose DNA we all share.[12] For whatever reason, Mitochondrial Eve's DNA and Y-chromosomal Adam's DNA thrived and survived, and are replicated in the birth of every human on the planet. Technically that makes them parents of all of us, even though they never met.

Seeing us as the product of our DNA might seem to some to reduce us to less than we really are as humans, but Rifkin challenges us to find in that scientific fact a common tie that can bind us together. With that knowledge, Rifkin says, we should be able to stretch our understanding of group beyond nationality—as we have done by pulling ourselves beyond recognition of shared physical attributes and celebration of shared religious affiliation—to see ourselves as one human family. National allegiances are as dangerous as the divisive realities of religion, Rifkin warns, and so he digs back into our distant past to find the roots of a future empathic civilization. The People for Good movement placed across Canada billboards that say "Hug a stranger. If you go back far enough, we're all related." It's a simple concept, yet almost impossible to conceive.

Rifkin believes we are on the cusp of recognizing our interconnectedness through a mass expansion of empathy beyond any particular group to the whole of life on the planet. Grounding his argument in this common genetic signature we all share, Rifkin draws our bloodlines and shows they are all the same—we are one family, one pannational group, one unit that would, with Will Smith's intensity in *Independence Day*, defend each of its members to the death.[13]

Perhaps Rifkin is right. Or perhaps a combination of the scapegoat and the common genetics solutions to our divisive natures will pull us together, helping us find ourselves connected through a threat that doesn't distinguish a living enemy but rather identifies an economically, internationally, physically, and potentially life-as-we-know-it-threatening *issue*. That threat will help us see one another as family and push us toward the kind of empathic civilization Rifkin imagines. Perhaps something like climate change or peak oil or Earth's inability to provide for staggering population growth will be the key.

It is essential that we come to see ourselves as an interconnected whole, and Rifkin drives us toward that vision. Even as he does, however, he raises serious concerns. Civilization, an entity that appears to breed empathy, also consumes energy at an incredible and planet-threatening pace. It will be a race to reach the empathic civilization he envisions before the planet crumbles under the weight of our attempts to realize it. Erasing the lines between us and refusing to divide ourselves into fractious groups will be a difficult task as resources become scarce, populations are forced to migrate for climate and economic reasons, and the definition of comfort comes closer to survival than many in developed countries have had to consider in the last several hundred years. The commonality of our values and the language with which we describe them will be essential. It will be too easy to fracture community, drawing lines between those who are religious, spiritual, or neither; who are brown, white, or black; who are transgender, straight, or gay; who American, Eritrean, or Pakistani.

## BEYOND KUMBAYA

It is very likely clear to many people that "we" aren't all putting a concerted effort toward a shared vision of a sustainable future. At least not with common goals. It would be foolish to suggest that everyone was. Corporatist agendas continue to rape the earth, impoverish communities, and create sweat-countries out of which a minuscule percentage of the world's population can squeeze most of the planet's wealth.[14] As images of the latest corporately caused ecological disaster waft past us on our TV screens along with sound bites from executives seeking to mitigate the damage, it is easy to be cynical. Remarks made by Justice Rosalie Abella of the Supreme Court of Canada, during a speech in Toronto just prior to Hosni Mubarak's resignation as president of Egypt in February 2011, reflected on the ineffectiveness of the United Nations, particularly in response to critical situations like those that were unfolding in Egypt and had unfolded in Bosnia, Rwanda, the Congo, Sudan, Afghanistan, and so many other places where the UN had failed to bring about timely, peaceful solutions. She noted that we have come to "care more about the free flowing of goods than about human rights."[15] Political agendas, often hand in hand with corporatist ones, too readily pit interest groups against each other and deny "the people" the benefit of open dialogue and effective change. Religion continues, as it always has, to segregate communities, nations, continents. Suggesting we've arrived at a singular "we" in terms of our long-range interests could only be, at this point in time, a naive call, the sentimental singing of "Kumbaya" in the face of tragic realities.[16]

Nor do we want to arrive at that singular "we" if the vision is of one great homogenous blob where everyone thinks, believes, lives, and loves within the exact same frames of reference. Within any organization, diversity is crucial. It challenges the status quo and allows for innovation and creativity. It assures a future beyond the immediate realities the organization or organism faces. Diversity creates the energy that moves us forward. It is important that we remain diverse, but we must also find a way to work toward establishing what the base values are, what the long-range goal is, what sustainability looks and lives like. I know it sounds idealistic; however, driving ninety miles an hour down a dead-end street might be a ton of fun, but it's not going to last.

We already know that many of those delineations caused by corporatism, politics, religion, race, gender, sexuality, age—you name it—are, for the most part, unfruitful. They have the potential to fracture us along the lines of meaning and values. What is important to one isn't important to another, and what brings meaning and hope to a particular group denies the wisdom of the choices of another. We use the fault lines to make us feel special, better than someone else. They boost us just that tiny smidgen above everyone else, place us on the inside and others on the out, and in so doing, massage our fragile egos. Sure, we can set them aside for a time and cooperate on common goals, but as long as the differences between us are easily aggravated, the potential for them to destroy our chances of working toward a common goal are great.

## PANGAEA

It is generally accepted that our planet was once home to a single continent called Pangaea. Incredible forces broke it into huge land masses that, over the course of eons, drifted into the places they each now hold. We too were once a single people, and it was incredible forces that drove us apart as well, forces that pushed us away from one another as we each sought our survival. But our survival now lies in our recognition that we are one family—the people of Pangaea—in a quest for common ground and common values. Through that quest, regardless of where we place our own allegiances or self-definition, ideals, practices, and imperatives that are carefully chosen through open, civil discourse might then become part of a foundation for a cooperative future, inside or outside of religious traditions, with or without a sense of spiritual identity, whether one is religious, spiritual, or neither.

Most of us—in truth, probably all of us—have held only a core narrative that is incapable of aligning us with any but a small sliver of our planet's population. The dogma of our religious groups and the propaganda of our nationalistic ones have gone a long way toward fooling us into believing that we are safe only behind walls. We do not need to stand apart, to be estranged, to maintain humanly constructed divisions between us to find security. It is my hope that our need to end the damage these divisions perpetrate will be greater than our need to stay in our comfortable but defensive groups. Then we can open ourselves, more effectively than ever, to the dangerous and highly evolved act that, in so many iterations, was the foundational call of significant religious and secular movements: truly loving one another.

## BUT WHAT OF PRAYER?

The things that religious and spiritual progressives aspire to—right relationship, justice and equity, the celebration of beauty—are all things they might raise or consider in prayer. But prayer, we have seen, belongs exclusively to religious and spiritual communities, and it cannot transfer to a people as diverse and comprehensive as the only group capable of envisioning and creating a sustainable future: the people of Pangaea. Too many do not need religious or spiritual beliefs to thrive and find meaning; if creating communities in which these individuals can engage in the practice of finding and creating well-being is our future, then religious and spiritual words such as "prayer" will have no place there. There are elements of the practice of prayer, however, that can increase our propensity for good and strengthen our possibility of creating a sustainable future. It is not so important that we keep prayer as that we ensure those *elements* are present and available in a variety of ways acceptable to all, not just to those who identify with a particular religious group or those who see themselves as spiritual but not religious.

If you are a praying person who uses prayer as a spiritual tool without any idea of a theistic god or supernatural force to which you pray, think about what you get out of it. The kind of praying American philosopher Daniel Dennett described in *Breaking the Spell*, where prayer becomes little more than a diary entry, is what I mean.[17] What is it you are doing? And what is meaningful about it? Is it participating in a community ritual that fulfils you? Is it the twenty minutes of peace and quiet at the end of the day? Is it what brings you to attend to those things that are important in your life? Is it your commitment to your family, your community, yourself that you are focusing on, drawing yourself past the daily exhaustion, the resentment of those petty things that get you down, the anger at the impossibility of change in those places where it is so needed, the nonstop challenges of just keeping it together? Is it finding time in the midst of all that to orient yourself to the things that are important to you—not the latest crisis and your attempt to deal with it, but the long-standing values and beliefs that can keep you grounded in the middle of any crisis? Is that what prayer does for you? Great. Keep doing it. Call it prayer, even, if you like. But recognize that there will be many, including Dennett, who will not agree that praying is what you are doing.

So it is that as we begin to see ourselves more and more as the people of Pangaea, we will need to step away from the word "prayer" in the same way I have argued we will need to step away from the word "god"—at least in communal gatherings, where we might be misunderstood. Community is an integral part of human existence. It is the common element that links all three of the columns: spiritual, religious, and neither spiritual nor religious. If we can find common ground among these three, I believe we will be closer to finding common ground in other areas. Using these columns as guides, it is easy to see that any definition we might come up with for prayer would be only an imposition on one aspect of our larger group, which would then reject it. The only common ground we can find lies beyond the terrain of prayer, as integral to their lives as many find it. Any new understanding of prayer, its purpose and practice, speaks to only a slice of the human community, not all of it. I'm asking you to walk past those dividing lines to a place where *what we do* and *what we name it* are valid and meaningful and inspirational for all of us, not just the religious or spiritual among us. We've visited options already— focused thoughts, reflection, meditation, contemplation.

Leaving behind our old ideas about prayer is part of our work. Those old ideas don't belong in the world beyond the beliefs that divide. Prayer that is a personal ritual or practice that aids in compassionate thinking may always be part of spiritual practice—

even prayer that posits a supernatural source of benevolence. But prayer in a communal setting that makes the kinds of claims it has in the past is not and never has been helpful, and it is now not even desirable. Many of the benefits prayer has offered may be accessed in ways other than those traditionally understood to be encompassed by the word "prayer," just as many of the attributes of a loving and benevolent deity we called "God" could be celebrated elsewhere.

## EMPACT

Our evolution into an interconnected species within our environment has taken place over several million years, but in the past two centuries, we have drastically changed the environment within which we now evolve. The impact of those changes is yet to be seen. It appears, however, that whatever physical adaptations might prove helpful will have to be technologically provided—we simply cannot evolve our physical bodies quickly enough to make the rapid and complex changes that might be necessary. But if we survive, it will be because of what I'll call *empact*—the ability to empathically impact others, within and beyond our communities and the world around us. Unlike our ancestors, we do hold our future, and our ability to adapt to it, in our hands. Not folded hands but working hands, creative hands, hands reaching out to each other, hands that can learn how to love.

I like to think of the god we anthropomorphized and called God as a catalyst for this evolutionary step through which we become a species that empacts the world—that empathically impacts those around us, all life on the planet, and the very earth itself. A catalyst is the instigating factor in a chemical reaction that starts or speeds up a reaction without itself being consumed in the process. In our evolutionary process, God has been an important catalyst.

The consideration of religious concepts as complex as a god, as challenging as the god, God, as enormous as the multitude of interpretations can make it, has had an incredible effect on the physiological development of the human brain, on its evolution. The roots of many of our acts of justice and compassion have developed from our desire to live up to the expectations of ideals we carved into the image of God. Those desires have continually stretched our definition of who and what we consider worthy until now; we are beginning to see how small we are in consideration of the vast dignity that is life. As that consideration has grown, we have hallowed life more and more, raising our children with increasing love and attentiveness, building and strengthening the capacity of their brains to become instruments of empactful living. Since their brains develop differently because of our love, they too will be able to build the brains of their children for empactful living.

Like any catalyst and despite our greatest efforts, God has remained virtually unchanged throughout the process. While our highest ideals may be static, the way we have applied them within our contexts has shifted and changed over the course of our evolution as those contexts required deeper thinking, more complex answers. If God had simply been the list of ideals, unadulterated by a certain worldview, mirroring back to us their purity so that the ideals called us to account in meaningful ways, it might have continued to work for us. God might have stood a chance. But we chained the ideals with ancient worldviews that could not speak to new challenges, new horrors, new threats. In so doing, we ensured the list's eventual demise.

Deep, intentional, reflective prayer and its twin, meditation, have also been integral to the development of those portions of our brains that significantly enhance our ability to live empactful lives. The changes reflective prayer and meditation helped bring about in our brains and our lives remain integral to us. The outpouring of appreciation for all that surrounds and uplifts us, the expression of deepest remorse for our mistakes, the offering of sincerest gratitude for each gift that comes to us through sources that transcend our own limited abilities, and the acknowledgment and conveyance of our deepest desires to one another are the contemporary equivalents of what caused us to kneel in the past. Strengthening and exercising our ability to be empathic is something we *know* how to do now. We don't stumble upon it or happen into it. We can choose it because we know it is a possibility.

We are capable of building a deep and abiding awareness of who we are and how we are interconnected, interdependent, and inter-inspirational. We are capable of evolving empact as our response to people around us and our environment. It is that intentional reach into the depths of the heart/soul/mind that grounds us in the truths of those things and offers that process of evolution. We need it, call it what you will. If it is prayer, then so be it. If it is reflection, so be that too. Whatever it takes to remind us of our incredible beauty and to humble us in wonder before the exquisite diversity of life on this planet. Whatever it takes to turn us from our self-righteous arrogance to the humility of ecnagorra so that we can truly see one another. When prayer was at its best, this is what it did, pointing us, pulling us, cajoling us toward the balance between beauty and diversity, that we might find a sense of worth that honours life and us as some of its majestic offspring.

With the evolutionary process now able to sustain itself, the work well under way, we are in the position of being able to monitor, change, challenge, review, stabilize, and enhance those things needed to keep that evolutionary task on track. We can remove God from the reaction. The catalyst is no longer needed. We can do this on our own.

# EPILOGUE

If we could convince ourselves of a core narrative that offered us security in an insecure world, we might thrive in a way we could not without a narrative. So says Loyal Rue, professor of religion and philosophy at Luther College in Iowa, with his suggestion that we come up with a "noble lie" that will take us past the fear and rivet us to a confidence that will soothe our anxieties and make the world an easier place to live.[1] Rue looks to the fabrications of nature that help it create a better reality for itself—the moth that fakes the look of dried and cracked tree bark; the carnivorous flower that entices flying insects with its promise of nectar; the thrown chirrup of the ventriloquist cricket—and he argues not only that we could do the same but also that we already do. A noble lie, he says, will carry us beyond secular scepticism to a place of cohesive strength.

I'd argue that although our myths are developing at a fast and furious rate, they are not helping us at all. Our previous myth has allowed us to assume the right to a privileged station in the world, to consume Earth's resources at a ridiculous rate, and to presume a security that anaesthetized us to, and perhaps beyond, the moment of accountability into the age of comeuppance. Like our previous myths, our shiny new ones too often blind us to our responsibilities and hold up ideals that cost us rather than ennoble us—the myth that more will make us happy; that youth is more valuable than age; that we all "deserve" the best of everything; that if we improve it with technology, it will be better. The false security of our early myths gave us someone to say our prayers to before we climbed into bed and helped us sleep at night, but our new myths, wrapped as they are in the razor wire of an impossible dream, won't let us sleep at all. That is just as well. Sleeping will not solve our problems. It never has. *We* must solve our problems.

I believe instead that we must tell a noble truth, and that it could have the same effect as the noble lie with which Rue would have us save ourselves. The new story we tell must, I would argue, be one of utter truth. Rue calls on poets, novelists, and artists to write and create the noble lie, but I believe artists are engaged in speaking truth more surely than lies, and so I turn to them for inspiration.

A few years ago, I came across a photograph that touched a longing for connection that exists, ever watchful, within me. Not that I lack for connection. I have deep and meaningful relationships in my life that buoy my spirit and remind me of the precious and beautiful truths that can be found in the love known by two people, in the joys and tragedies shared among friends, in the courtesy and respect extended to strangers. Yet the connection that roots all of us to the rhythm of life itself, that connection is too easily lost or overlooked, even in the most meaningful relationships we know. We miss it. In the photograph, that yearning was displayed before me.

It captured a tall, featureless statue of a human figure standing on a rock promontory, staring out across a vast expanse of water. A hundred feet or so beyond it was another identical statue, and a hundred feet beyond that, yet another.

As it turned out, there were five eight-foot statues in all, bolted to the bare rock on the coast of Newfoundland, at the eastern edge of Canada. Unsigned, silent, the giant figures, created in the Prairies, hewn by a chainsaw from spruce and pine logs and blackened in a prairie fire, stared out over the North Atlantic for several months. A local woman named them *The Watchers*, but Peter von Tiesenhausen, the sculptor, had felt no need to identify the figures in any way. When asked what they represented, he'd simply said, "I want people to think deep thoughts. I want them to be aware of what's around. That place you live in is so friggin' magical, just like so many places in Canada."[2]

When I hunted down information on *The Watchers*, I was surprised to learn I could find cast-iron versions of the sculpture standing in a circle, facing out in five directions, in the centre of my city, Toronto. The original pieces had journeyed far elsewhere, their final resting place unknown to me. At the end of June 2001, von Tiesenhausen had returned to Newfoundland to retrieve the statues he'd fastened to the rock rising up over the coast and had taken them north, bolting them, this time, to the front of an icebreaker so they could make their way through the Northwest Passage and over to Tuktoyaktuk, a town some thirty miles from where I once lived. From there, they travelled across the ice road that weaves through the Mackenzie Delta, through the Yukon, to the Queen Charlotte Islands, and back to the Prairies.

The piece is now called *Full Circle*, in reference to the journey it took around Canada's perimeter, and the cast figures display each scar earned along the way—broken limbs bolted back in place, surfaces worn smooth or deeply gouged. I don't believe they ever should have been installed in a circle, though. Perhaps if there were a space inside the circle where children could crawl or a person could sit and feel the bulk of the figures' oversized protection, the power they exuded on that rocky promontory, the silent vigil that had captivated me first in a photograph, would still be felt. It is the protection they promised, the witness they made, that was their gift—staring, watching for their brothers and sisters on continents now lost to them, searching for the eyes of other children of Pangaea on distant shores. Perhaps that is what pulls at my heart—the sense of rupture and the longing for reunion.

Throughout human existence, we have prayed because prayer went out before us as a line of protection, a shield against the terrors and traumas of life. We have sheltered ourselves behind it, confident that it would hold off the greater sorrows, the ones we couldn't bear, and filter through to us only those our hearts could carry. We have wrapped our vulnerabilities with the image of a divine being whose outstretched arms made our way safe and, when the night came, curled around us and offered peace.

We know, you and I, that the image isn't the reality. We haven't known protection. We have had our hearts torn, our world ravaged. We know our children and our children's children can never be protected from pain or sorrow by prayers we utter or incantations we cast out to the universe. And yet there is this longing for that protection, and I am loath to tear that hope away. So I left this hardest part until the end, perhaps with the faint hope that as I wrote, I would find a thread that would weave itself into a tapestry I could throw over the horrid truth of our utter aloneness.

For me, there is no thread—only the yearning after one.

There is an inscription outside the library at Virginia Theological Seminary. It has wisdom to offer us as we head out for any day's undertaking, and most particularly for the work we do there—that of finding a noble truth that will guide us beyond the unknowns we fear and shelter us when we need it most. The inscription reads "Seek the truth, come whence it may, cost what it will."

The quote is attributed to William Sparrow, a mid-nineteenth-century dean of the seminary who, legend has it, ended each of his lectures with it. Directing me to Joseph Packard's 1902 *Recollections of a Long Life*, the seminary's librarian, Mitzi Budde, told me that there was more to the quote than managed to make its way into stone.[3] In between where truth comes from and what it will cost, Sparrow had interjected another challenge: "Lead where it will."

The best journeys are those we cannot predict, the ones we set out upon with eager anticipation, prepared for whatever might open up before us. We may think we know the destination as we set our foot upon the first step, but who we will be when we arrive, when our final step is done, is only ever unfathomable. Unimaginable beauty, incredible wonders, terrible dangers, delights, new faces, new understandings of ourselves, strange ideas—any or all of these things might lie before us. We can choose to shrink from them and return to the places we started from, or we can step into the fear and the unknown, risk the truths we find, and carry on. We know we will fall, and many times. We know we will fail, and many times. We know there will be deep sorrow, and we know there will be deep pain. It will be mixed in with the beauty and the goodness, the love and the awe, and so we will carry on. Like von Tiesenhausen's *Watchers*, wounded but forged with a remarkable new strength, we are never the same at the end of the journey, even if we have come full circle.

Author Dean Koontz has a profound love for animals, and for golden retrievers in particular. In his novel *Watchers*, he writes of an animal that has been scientifically bred to have the intelligence of a human being. It befriends and is befriended by Nora and Travis, two somewhat lost people who, through the dog's intervention, come to love themselves and each other. At one point, as the dog lies very ill and close to death, Nora pours out her heart to it. After listing the many ways the dog has changed her and Travis' lives, she continues,

> You did it because you love, and being loved in return was
> reward enough. And by just being what you are . . . you taught
> me a great lesson, a lesson I can't easily put into words. . .

> We have a responsibility to stand watch over one another, we
> are watchers, all of us, watchers, guarding against the dark-
> ness. You've taught me that we're all needed, even those who
> sometimes think we're worthless, plain, and dull. If we love
> and allow ourselves to be loved well, a person who loves is
> the most precious thing in the world, worth all the fortunes
> that ever were. That's what you've taught me . . . and because
> of you I'll never be the same.[4]

Perhaps Koontz had to use an animal to create a believable portrait
of what could be recognized as totally selfless giving. Perhaps it was
because he has felt the devotion of an animal—a being that doesn't
seek its own protection first, but puts itself forward to defend someone
it loves, no matter the cost. Perhaps that picture is too unblemished
for some, but I don't bring it forward as *the* truth; I bring it forward
as a *noble* truth, one to which we can aspire, one that calls us beyond
ourselves to something greater.

Through evolution, we have "risen above" our "baser" animal
instincts and can reflect on the moral implications of our decisions,
remembering the tragic outcomes of human choices and the dismal
responses to events beyond our control. We can imagine possibilities, both good and bad, and make our decisions with some expectation that we can control at least some aspects of our future. There
is writing on every wall on every side of us, and we can read most
of it clearly enough to know that we have not yet found our way to
fully living a noble truth that calls us to be watchers, guardians for
one another.

We have no prayer that can keep us safe. We have no prayer that
can intervene in the laws of the universe and keep away illness, evil,
calamity. We have no prayer that can heal a sick child or extend the
life of a loved one. We have no prayer that can change people's minds

and make them understand us, or that can turn their hearts and make them love us. We have no prayer that can move mountains. We have only ourselves. We have only ever had ourselves. But we have done all these things. And we can do more. Amen.

# ACKNOWLEDGMENTS

I'm not an author. If you've just finished reading this book, you might not believe me, but it's quite true. I'm not an author. I'm a writer. That's very different.

Writers look at the world around them and write about what they see from their peculiar perspective. The writing doesn't have to flow. It doesn't have to have a central meaning or purpose. One point doesn't have to lead to another and on to the next. Often, writers never really finish writing; their work just keeps on going over weeks, months, years, lifetimes. Stories, ideas, images, reflections, poetry, concepts, explanations, interpretations—anything can flow from the pen of a writer.

An author, on the other hand, is charged with creating a whole piece of work that makes sense, that has a central message and purpose. The work takes the reader on a journey from a beginning to a carefully considered end point. The ideas an author puts down on paper or posts into cyberspace have to flow, and all in the same direction, for the most part, with every idea building on the last and setting the stage for what comes next. An author presents a single "voice"—a recognizable quality to his or her writing that people can relate to, and that they come to know and learn to trust.

That the finished product of this writer meets the criteria of an author is the result of the efforts of many people who have been challenged enough by their belief that what I have to say merits an audience that they have blessed me with their ongoing support, encouragement, and confidence.

Bishop John Shelby Spong introduced me as a writer to David Kent, CEO of HarperCollins Canada, before I had written a word. Bishop Spong's unfailing support, along with the ever-encouraging messages from his partner, Christine, first pasted and then sewed on the wings with which I could make this journey. He now celebrates that I take flight on my own, often in skies he has not travelled, a rare gift from one's teacher and mentor.

Iris Tupholme and Jim Gifford of HarperCollins believed that I had more to say, even after the thousands of extra words it took me to say what I wanted to in my first book. Their faith allowed me to explore territory that lay exposed in the questions that followed the publication of *With or Without God*.

Nicole Langlois, challenged this time around with many more lives interwoven with her own, still found the time to weave my work into her spare moments, creating of it a seamless garment of which I could be proud. She is a wise and gifted woman who guides me with the stern but necessary beauty of the editor's pen.

Katharine Smithrim, whose generosity of spirit is matched only by her grace and beauty, crossed the country with the manuscript upon her lap and offered her wisdom to the task of finishing it as it needed to be finished, pushing me to help you, the reader, grapple with this piece of work. As the final weeks arrived, her gift of time and her eager willingness touched me deeply and allowed me to set aside my fear.

Moira French, Dana Wilson-Li, John DiPede, and Keith MacInnis— these leaders are magicians of a celebrated sort who conjured time when I believed none existed and gifted me with it so that, despite a challenging and vibrant ministry, I could find opportunity and the space I needed to write. For their amazing empathy and effort, I am deeply grateful. And as always, I thank the people of West Hill United and staff members Donna Lockhart and Babette Oliveira for extending support and patience with an absent-minded, if not totally absent, minister, so that together we could continue to explore community beyond the beliefs that divide.

Finally, Scott, my partner, without whom that which lies between the covers of this book would be just so many words. Looking into my heart, he sees what lies there and, with the raw material I am able to cast out into being, cuts and pastes, orders and rearranges until what I meant to say is suddenly there on the page in front of us both, clear, concise, and waiting to enter the hearts of those who open themselves to its offering. He has endured all that writing inflicts upon those who live with it and yet remains both before me and behind me as I need him, the source of my greatest strength and my truest effort. In so many ways, you are my roots. In so many others, you are my wings.

So it is that, as a writer, I am amazed, humbled, and deeply honoured by those who have laboured that I might offer this work as an author. May you each know the breadth of my unbounded gratitude.

# NOTES

Chapter 1: Prayer: Religion's Main Event

1. Ludwig Feuerbach, *The Essence of Christianity*, trans. George Eliot (1841; repr., Buffalo: Prometheus, 1989), 122.

2. Friedrich Heiler, *Prayer: A Study in the History and Psychology of Religion*, eds. Samuel McComb and John Edgar Park, trans. Samuel McComb (London: Oxford University Press, 1932), xiii.

3. Alfonso M. DiNola, *The Prayers of Man: From Primitive Peoples to Present Times* (Toronto: Heinemann, 1962), v.

4. St. John Climacus, "On Prayer," *The Ladder of Divine Ascent*, Step 28. www.orthodoxchristian. info/pages/Prayer.html.

5. Martin Luther, *A Simple Way to Pray*, www.hope-aurora.org/docs/ASimpleWaytoPray.pdf.

6. Heiler, *Prayer*, 90.

7. Paul Tillich, *Systematic Theology* I (Chicago: University of Chicago, 1951), 267.

8. Michael Morwood, *Praying the New Story* (Maryknoll, NY: Orbis, 2004), 7.

9. Timothy Jones, *The Art of Prayer* (Colorado Springs, CO: WaterBrook/Random House, 2005), 15.


Chapter 2: Stretching Beyond the Core Narrative

1. myth, *noun*. A traditional story, either wholly or partially fictitious, providing an explanation for or embodying a popular idea concerning some natural or social phenomenon or some religious belief or ritual. *Oxford English Dictionary*, 5th ed. (Oxford, UK: Oxford University Press, 2002), 1876.

2. John Dominic Crossan dissolves the comfortable distinction Christians often make when they differentiate the God of the Hebrew Scriptures from that of the Christian Scriptures by saying that the latter overcame the former's violent ways. Crossan identifies the Book of Revelation as the most violent in the entire Bible and notes that Christians are faced with the problematic question of how to bring about the kingdom of love they argue their religion is all about. "Is, then, God's nonviolent peace to be established by violent war?" Crossan asks. John Dominic Crossan, *The Greatest Prayer: Rediscovering the Revolutionary Message of the Lord's Prayer* (New York: HarperOne, 2010), 149–51.

3. A. J. Jacobs, *A Year of Living Biblically* (Toronto: Simon and Schuster, 2008).

4. James W. Fowler, *Stages of Faith: The Psychology of Human Development and the Quest for Meaning* (New York: HarperCollins, 1995). Fowler's book was originally published in 1981. A summary is available at faculty.plts.edu/gpence/html/fowler.htm.

5. Sam Harris, in *The Moral Landscape*, argues against the prevalent belief that there is no difference between well-being and the lack of well-being. He finds himself up against diverse groups of academics when he does so. Sam Harris, *The Moral Landscape: How Science Can Determine Human Values* (New York: Free Press, 2010), 15–22.

6. On International Women's Day 2009, the Vatican's semi-official newspaper, *l'Osservatore Romano*, published an editorial declaring the washing machine the technological development most responsible for the advancement of women. www.reuters.com/article/2009/03/09/us-vatican-washingmachine-idUSTRE5282ME20090309. It didn't go over particularly well. jezebel.com/5167410/vatican-washing-machine-has-done-more-to-liberate-women-than-pill-work.

7. The United Church of Canada, Statement of Faith of the Basis of Union, Article 19, reads, "We believe that there shall be a resurrection of the dead, both of the just and of the unjust, through the power of the Son of God, who shall come to judge the living and the dead; that the finally impenitent shall go away into eternal punishment and the righteous into life eternal." This is part of the document with which candidates for ordination must claim to be in essential agreement.

8. Three and four years after I started the process of radically altering the service, people would still confess to me that they'd never even thought to question the virgin birth or the bodily resurrection. They had believed those were things you just didn't question, and if you did . . . well, you quickly stopped. That was all.

9. Many of the stories I have been privileged to hear since the publication of *With or Without God*

were told to me by men and women who trained to be ministers, were ordained, and began parish ministry. Within the first few years, however, the stress of trying to share what they had learned was so great they were forced to leave the ministry altogether in order to remain healthy. Two clergy I knew had completely lost their ability to speak until after they left the church. Many more told of being on long-term disability or a hiatus from the ministry while they considered their options.

10. Marcus J. Borg, *Speaking Christian: Why Christian Words Have Lost Their Meaning and Power—And How They Can Be Restored* (New York: HarperOne, 2011), 18.

11. If we believed that real damage could be done to our congregants by withholding our knowledge—most critically, if withholding that knowledge would result in their spending eternity in a physical place known as hell—it would be imperative that we face the challenge and tell them what they need to know. But what liberal clergy know is that hell is only as likely to be real as any other fictional place. Although we may not be able to say *for certain* that the imagined events aren't going to happen, the likelihood of them happening is slim to none.

Here's an example to illustrate the point: I could tell a story about someone who comes through a door and is surprised to find that thirty of her closest friends are hiding behind the couch, waiting to wish her a happy birthday. That story might actually come true. But what if I said that in her surprise, the woman fell over the coffee table, breaking the crystal vase her grandmother gave her, and that as the vase shattered, the water in it spilled over her and she disappeared into thin air, only to return decades later with a tale about being in the lost city of Atlantis? Well, that would be a long, long shot. The existence of a hell in which eternal torment or perpetual punishment takes place is also a long, long shot. In other words, not telling parishioners about hell really *won't* hurt them. And most of the other details we leave out won't hurt them either.

12. Dozens of churches in Christchurch, New Zealand, were destroyed in the devastating 2011 earthquake and its aftershocks. Different denominations will need to share facilities in the future, as it's impractical to build new churches for every faith. We will watch and wait. Perhaps what rises from the rubble will be something truly remarkable. It depends on how much people need to take with them and how much they are able to leave behind.

13. John Wesley identified four things to use when thinking theologically—scripture, tradition, reason, and experience. The term "Wesleyan Quadrilateral" was coined by American philosopher

Albert Outler in 1964. He immediately regretted creating the term, as his intention was never to place all four on the same footing. Scripture was always the core element, to be illuminated through tradition, reason, and experience.

14. Plato's Cave is an allegory told as a dialogue between Socrates and Plato's brother, Glaucon. (Perhaps it should be called Socrates's Cave.) In it, Plato describes how the reality people experience is conditional upon what they are able to perceive. In the allegory, people who are chained to a wall in such a way that they can see only the shadows crossing it as the result of a fire behind them never come to understand what is really happening, what creates the shadows. Plato presents the philosopher as one who breaks free of the chains and is then able to describe reality in ways others cannot perceive on their own.

15. William R. Murry, *Reason and Reverence: Religious Humanism for the Twenty-first Century* (Boston: Skinner House Books, 2006), 97.

16. Diana Butler Bass, *A People's History of Christianity: The Other Side of the Story* (San Francisco: HarperOne, 2009), 57.

17. It is interesting that those who are often the most offended by the progressive perspective I present—and my hope is that it continues to evolve on a daily basis—are also the most adamant about identifying themselves as progressive. Progressives who are no longer moving are no longer progressives; they are liberals. If they don't watch out, they'll become fossilized. It's the way of the world.

18. Dr. Edward de Bono's "Six Thinking Hats" is a model for creative problem solving and discussion. De Bono's research into the brain's neural network as a self-organizing system convinced him that creative and constructive thinking is not just a natural gift but can be learned. Each coloured hat represents a different approach to thinking about an issue. As an individual works his or her way through the colours, more complete information is uncovered and better decisions can be made. Edward De Bono, *Six Thinking Hats* (New York: Back Bay, 1999).

19. TED is a non-profit organization with the aim of sharing ideas worth spreading. Lectures are available for viewing at www.ted.com.

20. J. R. Hinnells, ed., *A New Dictionary of Religions* (London: Penguin, 1995), 394

21. Immanuel Kant, preface to *Critique of Pure Reason*, 1st ed. (1781), trans. J. M. D. Meiklejohn. philosophy.eserver.org/kant/critique-of-pure-reason.txt.

22. Perhaps Tylor, too, was moved by Bertel Thorvaldson's haunting relief, *Night*, reproduced in

plaster and marble throughout the sculptor's lifetime and long after his death in 1844. A picture of it hangs in my living room. It depicts an angel in flight with two children in her arms. The angel is Night. The children are Sleep and Death.

23. Edward Burnett Tylor, quoted in L. L. Langness, *The Study of Culture*, rev. ed. (Novato, CA: Chandler & Sharp, 1987), 23.

24. Ibid., 27, 28.

25. Friedrich Heiler, *Das Gebet: Eine religionsgeschichtliche und religionspsychologische Untersuchung* (Munich: 1918).

26. Heiler, *Prayer*, i.

27. Ibid., 1.

28. Ibid., 296–300.

29. R. Scott Spurlock, Historian, University of Edinburgh, www.giffordlectures.org/Browse. asp?PubID=TPVORE&Cover=TRUE.

30. William James, *Varieties of Religious Experience: A Study in Human Nature* (London: Routledge, 2002), 375.

31. Ibid., 11.

32. Ibid., 402.

33. Marcel Mauss, *On Prayer*, ed. W. S. F. Pickering (New York: Berghahn, 2003).

34. Philip Zaleski and Carol Zaleski, *Prayer: A History* (New York: Houghton Mifflin, 2005), 3.

35. Rick Ostrander, *The Life of Prayer in a World of Science: Protestants, Prayer, and American Culture, 1870–1930* (New York: Oxford University Press, 2000), 13.

36. Harvey Hill, "History and Heresy: Religious Authority and the Trial of Charles Augustus Briggs," *U.S. Catholic Historian* 20, no. 3 (Summer 2002): 1–21.

37. Jennifer Michael Hecht, *Doubt: A History* (New York: HarperCollins, 2004).

38. I am indebted to Lloyd Geering for his book *Christian Faith at the Crossroads: A Map of Modern Religious History* (Santa Rosa, CA: Polebridge, 2001), which served to focus my thoughts and keep me on course in this expansive area of study.

39. Ibid., 184–92.

40. Don Cupitt, quoted in Nigel Leaves, *The God Problem: Alternatives to Fundamentalism* (Santa Rosa, CA: Polebridge, 2006), 75.

41. Former Arkansas governor Mike Huckabee, appearing at a Conservative Christian event called

"Rediscovering God in America," said, "There's no way in the world that there should have been Proposition 8, make it to the ballot, that was the first miracle, and then for it to pass and it happened because there were people like Lou [Engle, founder of "The Call" movement] and others on their faces before God who prayed." Commenting on the event, Pat Robertson said, "If the pastors will mobilize the churches and get them all fired up, they can win any initiative, they can win any election, but if they don't, then of course the secular forces will overwhelm them, and the church will be divided and impotent." blogs.cbn.com/thebrodyfile/archive/2009/06/08/huckabee-prop-8-passed-because-of-prayer.aspx.

42. It is often the case that when Christians come up against something they do not like, they attribute the work to Satan, maligning those who have been involved in the issue as they do. Bryan Fischer, a radio host for the American Family Association, did just that when he railed against those who were challenging Sarah Palin during her run for the vice-presidency. "The hatred directed at her is mindless, it is baseless, it is utterly irrational, and it is disturbing to an alarming degree. When we look into the face of the unvarnished and seething meanness focused on Ms. Palin, we are looking into the face of evil. We are looking into the face of Satan himself, who is the ultimate source of this vitriol and toxic hate." www.doubledutchpolitics.com/2011/01/afa-satan-is-making-people-criticize-sarah-palin/. Similar vitriolic language, such as that attributed to Palin herself, was blamed for normalizing violence in political discourse. "When someone like Sarah Palin posts a map with crosshairs centering on Democratic districts, when she favors a slogan such as 'Don't Retreat, Instead—RELOAD!' there are desperate people listening who are cleaning their weapons." Chris Hedges, *The Death of the Liberal Class* (Toronto: Alfred A. Knopf Canada, 2010), 22.

43. Every year, National Prayer Breakfasts are held in the United States and Canada. It has become increasingly important for political leaders to be seen at such events, and on February 3, 2011, President Barack Obama gave testimony, to a round of applause, of accepting Jesus Christ as his personal saviour. www.youtube.com/watch?v=Sjpyrfj4AWk. (Note: testimony appears at the five-minute mark.)

Chapter 3: Tracing the Influence of Core Assumptions

1. William James, *Varieties of Religious Experience: A Study in Human Nature* (London: Routledge, 2002), 524.

2. Not naive realists who are religious, though that is what is grammatically correct! It means a naive realist in his or her beliefs about all things religious.

3. *The Mouth of the Dragon*, a 1996 publication of the Women's Resource Centre in Aotearoa, New Zealand, is where I first met the non-realist approach. The authors, Susan Adams and John Salmon, submit that when naive realism dominates the church, it's a form of social control. As so often is the case with issues of power and control, the beliefs are "claimed to be embedded in some external reality and therefore validated by this external reality." The doctrine of revelation compounds this control, for it is treated as an unquestionable authority for identifying what is real and true. Religion's circular reasoning leaves a questioner unable to contradict the basis of the argument, unless he or she challenges the circularity itself. That is what religious non-realism does.

4. Ontario Consultants on Religious Tolerance, www.religioustolerance.org/curr_war.htm. The website religiouswar.org is only one page, on which is depicted symbols for each of the world's major religions. The caption below reads "Please kill each other soon, so we can have our planet back. Thanks." It is a striking indictment of religiously mandated divisions.

Chapter 4: In-Spired: Prayer in the Average Church

1. Joseph Jungmann, *Christian Prayer through the Centuries* (Toronto: Paulist, 1978), 8.

2. Everyone from the early church fathers through to modern-day preachers has considered the question of whether the Lord's Prayer is focused on acquiring the blessings of this world or those of the world to come. See Kenneth W. Stevenson, *The Lord's Prayer: A Text in Tradition* (Minneapolis: Fortress Press, 2004).

3. Jungmann, *Christian Prayer*, 20–21.

4. Ibid., 23.

5. Ibid., 34.

6. Ibid., 41–42.

7. Martin Brecht, *Martin Luther: His Road to Reformation, 1483–1521*, trans. James L. Schaaf (Minneapolis: Fortress Press, 1993), 180–82.

8. Catechism of the Catholic Church, part 4, section 1, article 2559. www.vatican.va/archive/ccc_css/archive/catechism/p4s1.htm.

9. Ibid., article 2560.

10. Ibid., article 2561.

11. Ibid., articles 2562, 2563.

12. Ibid., article 2565.

13. Although people have often argued with me that this is not the case, I know of two families whose children, originally baptized at United churches, were required to be rebaptized before they could enrol in Catholic schools. Because we do not use the official Trinitarian formula at West Hill United Church for baptism, a neighbouring jurisdiction introduced a resolution that no individuals from our congregation be transferred into good standing as members of any churches in that area. "[B]e it resolved that the General Council of The United Church of Canada identify those churches whose ordained leadership does not publicly advance the teachings of The United Church of Canada in the most fundamental parts including the reality of God as an independent being, and the meaning of the resurrected Jesus Christ as a historic person who is proclaimed as divine redeemer of humankind; and instruct that membership in such churches no longer authorizes transfer to membership in other United Church congregations; and that their trustees are no longer in possession of the church properties; and finally that it advise Revenue Canada that such congregations no longer meet the definition of charities which advance religion." Minutes of the 85th Annual Bay of Quinte Conference, the United Church of Canada, pp. 10–11. The motion failed to achieve the support required to transmit it to the General Council.

14. For more information about St. Mary's South Brisbane, visit their website at stmaryssouthbrisbane.com.

15. The Anglican Communion Covenant, www.anglicancommunion.org/commission/covenant/docs/The_Anglican_Covenant.pdf.

16. For more information on each of these types of prayer, see anglicancommunion.org/resources/acis/docs/cat1.cfm.

17. Michael Ingham, *Rites for a New Age: Understanding the Book of Alternative Services* (Toronto: Anglican Book Centre, 1986), 14.

18. Ibid., 20–21.

19. Ibid., 21.

20. Ibid., 21–22.

21. Ibid., 23.

22. www.united-church.ca/beliefs/statements/songfaith.

23. Mission Resourcing Network, Uniting Church of Australia, South Australia Synod, mrn. sa.uca.org.au/newsletters/prayer-letter.html.

24. Southern Baptist Convention Statement of Faith, www.sbc.net/bfm/bfm2000.asp.

25. Report of the Baptist Faith and Message Study Committee to the Southern Baptist Convention, adopted June 14, 2000. www.sbc.net/bfm/bfmpreamble.asp.

Chapter 5: Supernatural ACTS

1. The prayers that appear at the beginning of these ACTS sections were written by me for West Hill United Church. Each shows evidence of a persistent theism, which, over time, was relinquished.

2. James Tozer, "Is It a Sin? Christian Words Deleted from Oxford Dictionary." www.mailonsunday.co.uk/news/article-1092668/Is-sin-Christian-words-deleted-Oxford-dictionary.html.

3. The Hebrew Scriptures are those parts of the Christian Bible that precede the Gospels and Epistles of the overtly Christian texts. Although now recognized as complete in and of themselves, they continue to be referred to by many Christians as the Old Testament.

4. Lyn Bechtel, "Rethinking the Interpretation of Geneses 2:4B–3:24" in *A Feminist Companion to Genesis*, ed. Athalya Brenner (Sheffield, UK: Sheffield Academic Press, 1993), 77–117. fontes. lstc.edu/~rklein/Documents/bechtel.htm.

5. Marcus Borg, *Putting Away Childish Things: A Tale of Modern Faith* (New York: HarperOne, 2010), 160.

6. Matthew Fox, *Original Blessing* (New York: Tarcher, 2000).

7. Sharon Hymer, "Therapeutic and Redemptive Aspects of Religious Confession," *Journal of Religion and Health* 34, no. 1 (Spring 1995): 41–54.

8. Wainwright, William, "Jonathan Edwards," *The Stanford Encyclopedia of Philosophy*, ed. Edward N. Zalta, plato.stanford.edu/entries/edwards/.

9. In an effort to keep Edwards's evangelistic fervour alive, a website called Gospel GEMs (www. gospelgems.com) has made his sermon available in MP3 format online. Gospel GEMs provides solid biblical truth to Christians by offering Great Evangelical Messages (GEMs) from the past. Messages from such godly men as Charles Spurgeon, J. C. Ryle, Jonathan Edwards, George Whitefield, and John Bunyan are preached by Tony Capoccia (M.Div. 1983) and made available on regular audio CDs or as MP3 files.

10. H. Richard Niebuhr, *The Kingdom of God in America* (New York: Willet Clark, 1937), 193.

11. The Pew Forum on Religion and Public Life, "U.S. Religious Landscape Survey," religions. pewforum.org/reports#.

12. Brian Flemming, *The God Who Wasn't There* (Los Angeles: Beyond Belief Media, 2005).

13. Reuters, "Fed Report: Belief in Hell Boosts Economic Growth," www.usatoday.com/money/economy/fed/2004-07-27-fed-hell_x.htm.

14. World Bank, World Development Index, "Economy, 2007." siteresources.worldbank.org/DATASTATISTICS/Resources/wdi09introch4.pdf.

15. Stephen Pattison, Shame: Theory, Therapy, Theology (Cambridge, UK: Cambridge University Press, 2000), 226.

16. Ibid., 242.

17. Ibid.

18. Ibid.

19. The "mercy seat" is believed to have been a part of the top of the Ark of the Covenant, in which God was believed to reside—a portable tabernacle the Israelites moved from place to place with them. The mercy seat was a place of "wiping clean." In some evangelical churches, there is an opportunity for individuals to "come to the mercy seat" to be cleansed of sin and accepted into Jesus's forgiving embrace.

20. It is exactly this sort of attention to detail that allowed Robert Bentley to remark, shortly after his installation as the governor of Alabama, "Anybody here today who has not accepted Jesus Christ as their savior, I'm telling you, you're not my brother and you're not my sister, and I want to be your brother. . . . If the Holy Spirit lives in you that makes you my brothers and sisters. Anyone who has not accepted Jesus, I want to be your brothers and sisters [*sic*], too." Jay Reeves, "New Alabama Governor, Just Christians Are His Family," Associated Press, Yahoo News. news.yahoo.com/s/ap/20110119/ap_on_re_us/us_alabama_governor_christians_1.

21. Nadeem Aslam, *Wasted Vigil* (Toronto: Random House), 99.

22. David Willey, "Fewer Confessions and New Sins," BBC News, March 10, 2008. news.bbc.co.uk/2/hi/7287071.stm. While I am impressed by the Vatican's sensitivity to some of the ethical concerns reflected on the list (no, not the taking of drugs), it still seems like hubris on a very grand scale for an institution to make such pronouncements for all humanity. Indeed, one could argue that the church itself is guilty of one or two of the new deadly seven, particularly the violation of the fundamental rights of human nature. I'm not sure what the Vatican meant

by that, but I'd celebrate reading it as condemnation of any act that denied the inherent dignity and rights of lesbians, gays, and bisexual, transgender, and queer people.

23. Vatican Information Service News, "Publication of CDF Norms on Most Serious Crimes," Holy See Press Office, July 15, 2010. visnews-en.blogspot.com/2010/07/publication-of-cdf-norms-on-most.html.

24. There is much in the Roman Catholic ordinances regarding the priesthood that one might consider worthy of eternal damnation—like that rule of celibacy, which some argue is a significant factor in the lives of those who perpetrate sexual assaults upon children. It is easy to condemn the priests who prey upon children; however, while doing so, we must also condemn a system that has certainly sheltered them and may even, however unintentionally, have created the circumstances—high level of trust, implicit authority, celibacy, assumption of moral superiority of those who are celibate—in which they could act. Although data regarding rates of abuse by any group are unreliable because of the extreme traumatic nature of the event and the likelihood of it being underreported, controlling for other characteristics of abusers (intelligence, education, impaired cognitive abilities, etc.) may indicate a higher statistical likelihood of abuse among celibate clergy. Ryan C. W. Hall and Richard C. W. Hall, "A Profile of Pedophilia: Definition, Characteristics of Offenders, Recidivism, Treatment Outcomes, and Forensic Issues," *Mayo Clinic Proceedings* 82, no. 4 (April 2007): 457–71.

25. It was an honour to be included in a service led by the Roman Catholic Women Priest movement in 2007. The first such ordination to take place on land, and so within the boundaries of an ecclesial diocese, it was presided over by Bishop Patricia Fresen. The red cloth upon which the ordinands prostrated themselves—a powerful symbol, for me, of the leadership of women in any movement for positive change—was laid by me and Canadian author Irshad Manji.

26. The entire breakdown of the Psalms into categories, according to Jungmann, is as follows:

1. Penance: This purpose is served by the Seven Penitential Psalms, known as such from the days of Cassiodorus; 2. Spiritual joy: Psalms 16, 23, 53, 66, 69, 70, 85; 3. Praise and thanksgiving for God's benefits in the Old and New Testament: either the Alleluia Psalms or Psalms 71–73, 109–119, etc.; 4. In temptation and desolation: Psalms 21, 63, 67; 5. In times of boredom with life or of longing for Heaven: Psalms 41, 62, 83; 6. In distress: Psalms 12, 43, 50, 54, 70; 7. In good days: Psalms 33, 102, 103, 144, Canticum Benedicite; 8. On God's Law: Psalm 118; 9. On God's working for our salvation, beginning with the Prophets

up to the Lord's passion, resurrection, and ascension: with no reference (meaning the entire Psalter). Jungmann, *Christian Prayer*, 78.

27. www.cbc.ca/canada/toronto/story/2008/12/23/oakville-fire.html.

28. www.cbc.ca/canada/toronto/story/2008/12/24/molnar-improving.html.

29. Bertrand Russell, "A Free Man's Worship," in Christopher Morley, *Modern Essays* (New York: Harcourt Brace and Company, 1921), 263–77. Also available online at www.philosophicalsociety.com/Archives/A%20Free%20Man%27s%20Worship.htm.

30. Russell, "Free Man's Worship."

31. Supplicate, *verb. Shorter Oxford English Dictionary*, 5th ed. (New York: Oxford University Press, 2002), 3118.

32. Joel Osteen, *Your Best Life Now: 7 Steps for Living at Your Best Potential* (New York: Hachette, 2004).

33. www.joelosteen.com/HopeForToday/PrayTogether/Pages/PrayTogether.aspx.

34. Lauren Morello, "NOAA Makes It Official: 2011 Among Most Extreme Weather Years in History," *Scientific American*, June 17, 2011. www.scientificamerican.com/article.cfm?id=noaa-makes-2011-most-extreme-weather-year.

35. gamc.pcusa.org/ministries/pda/aid-begins-reach-flood-affected-families-pakistan/.

36. John Tyndall, "Reflections on Prayer and Natural Law," in *Fragments of Science*, vol. 2 (New York: Collier, 1905), 10. www.archive.org/stream/fragmenoscieno2tyndrich#page/10/mode/2up.

37. Tyndall, "The Belfast Address," in ibid., 156. www.archive.org/stream/fragmenoscieno2tyndrich#page/156/mode/2up.

38. James McCosh, quoted in John Tyndall, *The Prayer-Gauge Debate* (Boston: Congregational Publishing Society, 1876), 3. McCosh's article, along with Tyndall's original essay, was republished for Americans in *Littell's Living Age* 27 (1872), as found in Ostrander, *Prayer in a World of Science*, 21.

39. Ostrander, *Prayer in a World of Science*, 20, 21.

40. Tyndall, *Prayer-Gauge*, 114. www.archive.org/stream/prayergaugedebatootynd/prayergaugedebatootynd_djvu.txt.

41. Ostrander, *Prayer in a World of Science*, 23, 24.

42. Tyndall, *Prayer-Gauge*, 115.

43. George Muller, *The Life of Trust* (New York: Crowell, 1877), as found in Ostrander, *Prayer in a World of Science*, 35.

44. A. T. Pierson, "Proof of the Living God, as Found in the Prayer Life of George Muller, of Bristol" in *The Fundamentals*, vol. 1, ed. A. C. Dixon (Chicago: Testimony, 1909), 82.

45. Robert Bruce Mullin, *Miracles and the Modern Religious Imagination* (New Haven, CN: Yale University Press, 1996), 184.

46. Mita Giacomini, "Theory-based Medicine and the Role of Evidence: Why the Emperor Needs New Clothes, Again," *Perspectives in Biology and Medicine* 52, no. 2 (spring 2009): 234–51. ideas.repec.org/p/hpa/wpaper/200902.html.

47. I've written about this children's story before and it was publicized in an article in *The Toronto Star* in 2004, but hindsight has had such an impact on the development of my current perspective that I reiterate it here.

48. Erich Neumann, *The Great Mother*, trans. Ralph Manheim (Princeton, NJ: Princeton University Press, 1972), 115.

49. Jim Wallis, "Armed with the Truth about Nuclear Weapons" (lecture, Chautauqua Institution, Chautauqua, NY, July 2010).

Chapter 6: Hanging On to the Language

1. Steven Law, *Believing Bullshit: How Not to Get Sucked into an Intellectual Black Hole* (Amherst, NY: Prometheus, 2011), 115.

2. Unfortunately, Eck failed to note that the globalization of such commodities is happening predominantly within the "have" layers of society. Rather than bringing communities together, technology, until it is accessible to all, continues to fracture.

3. Diana Eck, "Honest to God: The Universe of Faith," in *God at 2000*, eds. Marcus Borg and Ross Mackenzie (Harrisburg, PA: Morehouse, 2000), 22.

4. Ibid., 26–27.

5. Joan D. Chittister, "God Become Infinitely Larger," in ibid., 62.

6. Ibid.

7. Ibid., 64.

8. Ibid., 69.

9. Ibid.

10. The campaign was designed by Randy Varcho, graphic designer for the UCC's Proclamation, Identity and Communication Ministry. I'm sure he'll be amused when he sees the cover of the late Christopher Hitchens' recent book, *The Quotable Hitchens: From Alcohol to Zionism,* published by DaCapo Press in 2011.

11. J. Bennett Guess, "Buford, Architect of Still Speaking Campaign, to Assume New Role," *United Church News,* August/September 2006, A3. www.uccfiles.com/ucnews/sep06.pdf.

12. Richard Holloway, *Between the Monster and the Saint* (Edinburgh: Canongate, 2008), 125.

13. Ibid., 127

14. Law, *Believing Bullshit,* 115, 116.

15. Progressive thinkers might also make a bunch of other objections to this campaign. If God is still revealing stuff, then either he is developing right alongside human reason and understanding or he is even more despicable than might have been the case had he stopped talking a long time ago. If slavery was wrong, why wait so long to speak to us about it? If killing homosexuals is wrong, same question. We can't possibly think of bowing down to a deity that, for undisclosed reasons, doesn't get around to telling us the life-changing, life-preserving details of his laws. To do so is to worship the God and not the love he is purported to represent.

16. Zaleski and Zaleski, *Prayer: A History,* 3.

17. Barbara Bradley Hagerty, *Fingerprints of God: What Science Is Learning About the Brain and Spiritual Experience* (New York: Riverhead, 2009), 47–48.

18. Ibid., 2–3.

19. Ibid., 5.

20. Richard Tarnas, *Cosmos and Psyche: Intimations of a New World View* (New York: Viking, 2006).

21. Raymond Pelly and Peter Stuart, eds., *A Religious Atheist? Critical Essays on the Work of Lloyd Geering* (Dunedin, NZ: Otago University Press, 2006).

22. John Bishop, "Revisionary Theology: Realism and Non-realism," in ibid., 99.

23. Ibid., 103.

Chapter 7: Moving On with the Values

1. Tony Windross, *The Thoughtful Guide to Faith* (Abingdon, UK: O Books, 2004), 16.

2. A colleague recently suggested our real problem was that we don't actual live out what the Bible says to do. I asked what that would look like. As though the first to ever suggest it, she

emphatically announced that if we were living up to the Bible, we'd feed the poor. Really feed the poor. Interesting. I said I didn't need the Bible to tell me to do that. What would have happened if we'd never had the Bible? Would we have never figured out that we should feed the poor?

3. Nigel Leaves, *Religion Under Attack: Getting Theology Right* (Salem, OR: Polebridge Press, 2011), 211.

4. Ibid., 207.

5. Crossan, *The Greatest Prayer,* 154.

6. Letter to John A. T. Robinson, quoted in John A. T. Robinson and David L. Edwards, *The Honest to God Debate* (London: SCM Press, 1963), 53.

7. "A New Century, A New Calling," Report of the Strategic Vision Committee of the Washington National Cathedral (January 18, 2007), 5.

8. John Burroughs, "Dr. Munger on *Robert Elsmere,*" *Christian Union* 39 (January 3, 1889), 9, cited in Mullin, *Modern Religious Imagination,* 81–82.

9. In my years at Queen's Theological College, the books I studied would have been considered heretical by some. William Countryman's *Dirt, Greed, and Sex* was one of the texts for my Hebrew Scriptures class; Elaine Pagels's *Gnostic Gospels* introduced me to early church history. My New Testament professor, Dr. Robert Bater, was a member of the Jesus Seminar. We read Phyllis Trible's *Tests of Terror* and Rosemary Radford Ruether's *Fratricide.* I studied with gay and lesbian classmates with no expectation that their contributions were of less value than anyone else's.

10. Sam Harris, *The Moral Landscape: How Science Can Determine Human Values* (Toronto: Simon and Schuster, 2010).

11. The conversation about what categories of life are considered sacred—that is, not divinely approved but nevertheless worthy of our respect and protection—is an important one. Recently, we have become sensitive to the experiences of sentient life beyond human beings. Movements in Great Britain have sought to extend the same protection rights to invertebrates such as octopuses and cuttlefish as are currently extended to dogs and cats. Some might argue that if we extend rights to sentient life, we should at least acknowledge the value of all life and refrain from the destruction or consumption of (through the use of the life form as a commodity, not necessarily for food) or experimentation upon non-sentient life as well. Certainly those engaged in the debates

around the genetic modification of food or the harvesting of old-growth forests would be aware of these issues. But in these conversations, it is not the well-being of the grain or the trees that is considered; it is the well-being of humans, even when enfolded in a discussion on the health of ecosystems and the planet. I have chosen to identify only sentient life at this time but reserve the right to expand my reference as awareness of our impact on other life forms increases.

Chapter 8: (Prayer) Naturally

1. Heiler, *Prayer*, 353.

2. Elizabeth Roberts and Elias Amidon, eds., *Life Prayers: 365 Prayers, Blessings, and Affirmations from Around the World to Celebrate the Human Journey* (New York: HarperCollins, 1996), xx.

3. Kathleen Norris, *Amazing Grace: A Vocabulary of Faith* (New York: Riverhead, 1998).

4. John Shelby Spong, *A New Christianity for a New World: Why Traditional Faith Is Dying and Why a New Faith Is Being Born* (New York: HarperCollins, 2001), 197, 198.

5. Frederick Buechner, *Beyond Words: Daily Readings in the ABC's of Faith* (New York: HarperCollins, 2004), 320–21.

6. The phrase "break our hearts with truth" was offered up by Ryan Croken's article "No Garden to Get Back To: Understanding Post-*Avatar* Ecological Depressive Disorder," *Religion Dispatches* (January 28, 2010). www.religiondispatches.org/archive/culture/2226/no_garden_to_get_back_to%3A_understanding_post-avatar_ecological_depressive_disorder__/.

7. Oriah Mountain Dreamer, *The Invitation* (New York: HarperSanFrancisco, 1999), 2. "The Invitation," the poem, is also available on her website, www.oriahmountaindreamer.com.

8. I'm speaking figuratively here. I don't believe in demon possession and I don't believe that individuals are ordained to cast out demons. But I do know that there are many who are unable to wrestle with the truths that torment them, and that any who are strong enough to offer these fragile ones shelter, to take on the struggle on their behalf, or to ease their journeys must offer themselves, wherever possible, to those tasks. It is the only humane response to suffering.

9. Tim LaHaye and Jerry Jenkins created the apocalyptic series *Left Behind*, which has sold millions of copies around the world. The video game, *Left Behind: Eternal Forces*, features Tribulation Forces contending with the Global Community and seeking to convert as many as possible to Christianity before the end of the tribulation period. The game was criticized for promoting religious warfare, the killing of those who do not believe in Jesus, and racial and

sexual stereotyping. It has been followed by two further versions, with a third due for release in time for 2011 Christmas giving.

10. Potential, *adjective*. The Free Online Dictionary. www.thefreedictionary.com/potential.

11. Lionel Tiger and Michael McGuire, *God's Brain* (Amherst, NY: Prometheus Books, 2010), 12.

12. Ibid., 155.

13. Ibid., 156.

14. Ibid., 146.

15. Ibid., 147.

16. Ibid., 145.

17. Ibid., 158.

18. Ibid., 159.

19. Chaeyoon Lim and Robert Putnam, "Religion, Social Networks and Life Satisfaction," *American Sociological Review* 75, no. 6 (December, 2010): 914–33.

20. Ibid., 928.

21. Ibid.

22. Tiger and McGuire, *God's Brain*. It is interesting to watch the dynamics that happen in groups when new dominant males enter them. Those who once held leadership positions and are displaced often become disruptive, attention-seeking, or even abusive toward those from whom they had previously received affirmative responses. My experience in such groups is that the displaced men will often leave and seek affirmation elsewhere.

23. The Charter for Compassion (charterforcompassion.org) was made possible through a TED prize. The TED organization brings together the brightest minds in technology, entertainment, and design to spark creative energy for building a better world. See www.ted.com.

24. Jill Bolte Taylor, "Stroke of Insight," TED lecture delivered February 2008. www.ted.com/talks/lang/eng/jill_bolte_taylor_s_powerful_stroke_of_insight.html.

Chapter 9: Natural ACTS

1. The prayers (now referred to as "Focused Moments") that appear in these ACTS sections were written by me for use at West Hill United. You'll note the absence of any lingering theistic agency, a considerable shift from the prayers I wrote just a few years earlier.

2. Marjorie Harris, *Seasons of My Garden* (Toronto: HarperCollins Canada, 2001).

3. Andrew Newberg and Mark Robert Waldman, *How God Changes Your Brain: Breakthrough Findings from a Leading Neuroscientist* (New York, Ballantine, 2009), 75.

4. Ibid., 102.

5. R. Scott Kearns, "Our Thoughts We Now Centre," in *The Wonder of Life: Songs for the Spirit* (Toronto: File 14 Resources, 2009), 9.

6. R. Paul Olson, *The Reconciled Life: A Critical Theory of Counseling* (Westport, CT: Praeger Publishers, 1997), 98.

7. For further reading on Buber's theology, see Maurice S. Friedman, *Martin Buber: The Life of Dialogue* (Chicago: University of Chicago Press, 1955).

8. Douglas Adams, *The Ultimate Hitchhiker's Guide: Six Stories* (Toronto: Random House, 1996), 198.

9. Newberg and Waldman, *How God Changes Your Brain*, 13.

10. Douglas Wood, *Grandad's Prayers of the Earth* (Somerville, MA: Candlewick, 1999).

11. Jerome A. Stone, *The Minimalist Vision of Transcendence: A Naturalist Philosophy of Religion* (Albany, NY: SUNY, 1992), 13–16.

12. Krista Vernoff, "Grandma Got Run Over by a Reindeer," *Grey's Anatomy*, season 2, episode 12, aired December 11, 2005.

13. Lance Sectretan, *Inspire!* (Mississauga: Wiley, 2004).

14. Robin Dunbar and Susanne Shultz, "Evolution in the Social Brain," *Science* 7, vol. 317, no. 5843 (September 2007): 1344–47.

15. Owen Lovejoy, quoted in John Allman, *Evolving Brains* (New York: Scientific American Library/W. H. Freeman, 2000), 259.

16. Jeremy Rifkin, *The Empathic Civilization: The Race to Global Consciousness in a World in Crisis* (New York: Penguin, 2010), 39.

17. John M. Allman, Atiya Hakeem, Joseph M. Erwin, Esther Nimchinsky, and Patrick Hof, "The Anterior Cingulate Cortex: The Evolution of an Interface between Emotion and Cognition," *Annals of the New York Academy of Science* 935 (May 2001): 107. www.allmanlab.caltech.edu/PDFs/AllmanHakeemHofetal2001.pdf.

18. John M. Allman, Nicole A. Tetreault, Atiyz Y. Hakeem, Kebreten F. Manaye, Katerina Semenderferi, Joseph M. Erwin, Soyoung Park, Virginie Boubert and Patrick R. Hof, "The Von Economo Neurons in Frontoinsular and Anterior Cingulate Cortex in Great Apes and Humans," *Brain Structure and Function* 214, nos. 5–6 (June 2010): 495.

19. Allman et al, "The Anterior Cingulate Cortex," 107.

20. Two options for further study interest me here. The effect drill sergeants have on the VENs in the brains of military recruits would be an interesting study. Would we find that the VENs were starved through a consistently abusive training program? Also, were we able to get the early histories of the incredibly high number of Alzheimer's and dementia patients, would we find that the environments of their infancy were insufficiently nurturing to provide a good number of VENs? Since VENs are the first to deteriorate during dementia, it would seem likely that weakened anterior cingulates would be highly vulnerable to the effects of dementia and Alzheimer's.

21. Newberg and Waldman, *How God Changes Your Brain*, 22–40.

Chapter 10: Empact

1. VisionWorks 2009, West Hill United Church, Toronto. westhillunited.squarespace.com/visionworks-2009/.

2. Of course, that's the good Day of the Lord theology. The other Day of the Lord theology is quite dreadful. We pick and choose.

3. Keith Olbermann interviews Dorli Rainey, who was pepper-sprayed at Occupy Seattle in November 2011. www.youtube.com/watch?v=Xwo5eumXxyA.

4. Pulitzer Prize–winning journalist Laura Sessions Stepp argues against the "all-is-well-in-evangelical-land" in her review of the decline in the participation of youth and young adults. www.cnn.com/2011/12/16/opinion/stepp-millenials-church/index.html.

5. Lillian Daniel, "Spiritual But Not Religious? Stop Boring Me," *The Huffington Post*, September 13, 2011. www.huffingtonpost.com/lillian-daniel/spiritual-but-not-religio_b_959216.html.

6. Diana Butler Bass Blog, "Spiritual But Not Religious: Listening to Their Absence," blog entry by Diana Butler Bass, September 20, 2011. www.patheos.com/blogs/dianabutlerbass/.

7. www.parade.com/news/2009/10/04-how-spiritual-are-we.html?index=3.

8. Timothy Avery, "One in Four Don't Believe in God," *Toronto Star*, May 31, 2008. www.thestar.com/News/Canada/article/434725.

9. Newberg and Waldman, *How God Changes Your Brain*, 69.

10. Ibid., 72. The survey, located at www.neurotheology.net, was created in 2005 and conducted entirely online. Participants self-selected, registered, and completed the survey. There are at least two problems with this kind of survey: 1) self-selection immediately excludes a significant portion of the population, and so results can be legitimate only for the demographic, if there

is an identifiable one, that responds; and 2) an online survey, while perhaps allowing for more open disclosure, targets a particular demographic, and so again, results can be applied only to the demographic that responded. In terms of religious and spiritual topics, many older, traditional believers who do not use the Internet would not be included. It is assumed that these people might more regularly use a word like "god" in their descriptions of spiritual experience.

11. Jeremy Rifkin, *The Empathic Civilization*, 292–300.

12. No, Adam and Eve never hooked up. Mitochondrial Eve lived around 140,000 years ago. Y-chromosomal Adam was 50,000 to 80,000 years younger. For more information on this interesting work on our genetic family history, visit genographic.nationalgeographic.com/genographic/index.html or spend a fascinating few weeks with Richard Dawkins' *The Ancestor's Tale* (Boston: Houghton Mifflin, 2004).

13. A brilliant animation of Rifkin's argument by RSAnimation is available at www.youtube.com/watch?v=l7AWnfFRc7g. Further information is available through the National Geographic's Genographic program. See James Shreeve's "The Greatest Journey," *National Geographic*, March 2006. ngm.nationalgeographic.com/2006/03/human-journey/shreeve-text/1.

14. For further reading on corporatism, see Naomi Klein, *Shock Doctrine* (Toronto: Vintage, 2008).

15. Madame Justice Rosalie Abella, quoted by Michael Enright, *The Sunday Edition*, Canadian Broadcasting Corporation, aired February 13, 2011. www.cbc.ca/video/news/audioplayer.html?clipid=1793497969.

16. On the same segment of *The Sunday Edition*, Michael Enright explored the use and abuse of the folk-Christian song "Kumbaya." www.cbc.ca/video/news/audioplayer.html?clipid=1793509807.

17. Daniel Dennett, *Breaking the Spell: Religion as a Natural Phenomenon* (Toronto: Viking Penguin, 2006), 10.


Epilogue

1. Loyal Rue, *By the Grace of Guile: The Role of Deception in Natural History and Human Affairs* (New York: Oxford University Press, 1994), 279, 306.

2. Ryan Cleary, "Calgary Artist Drops 'Watchers' at Flatrock," *The Telegram* (St. John's), June 26, 2001. www.tiesenhausen.net/press3.htm.

3. Mitzi Budde, email correspondence with author, January 10, 2012. Joseph Packard, *Recollections of a Long Life* (New York: Byron S. Adams, 1902), 169.

4. Dean Koontz, *Watchers*, in "A New Collection" (New York: Wings, 1992), 655.

# INDEX